urban crayon

DELHI

urban crayon

DELHI

Kim Barrington Narisetti

RANDOM BUSINESS
An imprint of Penguin Random House

Published by Random House India in 2009
Second impression in 2015

Published by Penguin Random House India Pvt. Ltd
No: 04-010 to 04-012, 4th Floor, Capital Tower -1,
M G Road, Gurugram -122002, Haryana, India

Random House Group Limited
20 Vauxhall Bridge Road
London SW1V 2SA
United Kingdom

978 81 8400 080 1

Typeset in PMN Caecilia by SwaRadha Typesetting, New Delhi

Printed at Repro India Limited

A PENGUIN RANDOM HOUSE COMPANY

www.penguin.co.in

CONTENTS

INTRODUCTION

Namaste!

Built on the banks of the Yamuna River, New Delhi, the second largest city in India, beautifully intertwines the country's historical past and a bustling, vibrant present. The city, which dates back to at least the sixth century BC, has survived numerous invasions over the centuries and many ancient monuments depicting the style of the invaders survive in Delhi to this day. The seventh city, the walled city of Old Delhi was constructed by Emperor Shah Jahan beginning in 1639 when he moved the Mughal capital from Agra and it served as the capital from 1639–1857. New Delhi is actually the eighth city of Delhi, having been established by the British, who gained control of much of India in the eighteenth and nineteenth centuries. The British built up most of what we see today in Delhi beginning in the 1920s. New Delhi became the capital and seat of government when India became independent of British rule in 1947.

One of the fastest growing cities in all of India, Delhi is comprised of two architecturally and historically contrasting, yet symbiotic parts, the Old Delhi and New Delhi, making it an ideal place to get the feel for northern India. New Delhi has come a long way from its beginnings as a city with maze-like streets that were once the domains of forts with markets and bazaars at the centre, to one that is now dominated by trendy restaurants, high-end shopping malls, art galleries and well-manicured parks. With a population of nearly 18 million people who have come to Delhi from neighbouring states to put down roots, the city is truly cosmopolitan.

For families looking for adventure or to get a bit of culture, New Delhi is full of ways to have great outings every day of the week. The city is full of historic and architectural sights. Although the city is spread out, it is quite easy to get around, that is, if a strong gust of wind doesn't blow the streets signs in the opposite direction. This is one of the reasons that I felt the need to write *Urban Crayon Delhi*.

As a parent of two young daughters, ages four and seven, who prefer a picnic in Lodhi Garden instead of making it to the next level of the latest Wii game, I found that parent-friendly information on how to navigate Delhi easily isn't readily available. So we three set out to discover Delhi—the real Delhi—and make it easy for other parents who are likely wrestling a stroller, children, juice boxes and Kleenex packs all at the same time. From the beauty of Lodhi Gardens, to the petals of the Lotus Temple, the brilliant chaos of Chandni Chowk and the calm of Gandhi Smriti, we walked, drove, took cycle rickshaws and auto rickshaws. We went on guided tours in air-conditioned buses and took the metro from the first stop to the last. We had camel rides, splashed in swimming pools and water parks and watched the sun set at India Gate. We did arts and crafts and ate delicious Sunday brunches at Yum Yum Tree, took in the brilliance of modern art at the National Gallery and were in awe at the sound and light show at the Red Fort.

There were days filled with bowling and 3D movies and other days when we all learned about the bird species that are drawn to Delhi's lakes year after year. An ostrich got friendly with us at the Delhi Zoo, and the camel wouldn't budge at the Garden of Five Senses. And Janpath and Connaught Place offered a wide selection of gifts for friends and family.

I took notes, the kids drew pictures to chronicle our Delhi adventures that quickly moved from just weekend activities to mid-week afternoons when school was out of session and the temperature was cool. We discovered things that are definitely for those who live in Delhi, and a great deal more for visitors who are here for three days or three weeks. There's something for every member of the family. There are girly-girl activities and manly-man adventures. But at the end of the day, what will prove to be particularly helpful if this guide is used properly is that parents will feel that the family had the vacation it wanted, with plenty of 'us' time *and* enough 'kid' time so there's no whining at the end of the trip.

Restaurants that offer many selections at great value with food that isn't served in paper bags made the cut as well as those that do. This guide book moves away from backpackers' picks to picks only parents will appreciate—a balance of fun and education. Kids will enjoy boating on lakes and following nature trails at wildlife sanctuaries; and they will learn about how Delhi came to be Delhi through visits to memorials, museums, Parliament House, India Gate, the Red Fort and much much more. There are plenty of festivals that are brimming with colour and delicacies seeped in masala. Walk around the architecture designed by Lutyens or feast on dripping paranthas at Paranthe Wali Gali. Whether you're looking for a shopper's paradise or to try Patanjali yoga, Delhi is the place for it.

Chalo!

When to Visit

Delhi weather is one of extremes. The summer can be unbearably hot and humid with nary a breeze, unless you count the sometime frequent dust storms. And winter is cold enough to require thick sweaters, coats, hats and scarves. Delhi's peak tourist season is when the weather in the city is quite pleasant. Spring is the best time to visit. While Delhi has a very brief period of spring in February and March (20–25°C), September to November also enjoy spring-like weather (20–30°C). There is an abundance of festivals and cultural events during these months.

Although the temperature stays in the 30s during the day, it can get cold at night in December and January, with temperatures sometimes dropping to as low as 4°C. On average though, winter temperatures range from 15 to 25°C. By the end of April, it's hot. During the unbearable summer months of April to July, the temperature of 46° plus will require hats, buckets of sun block and an elaborate dance down the roads in an effort to hug every shady spot. Summer in north India is harsh, dry and dusty with frequent power cuts. The thought of the monsoon is appealing, but the humidity intensifies the heat, making travel uncomfortable. Try to avoid the rainy season, which lasts from July to September (30–35°C) and can result in flooded roads.

Get Your Bearings

The National Capital Territory of Delhi is divided into nine districts. They are the Central, North, South, East, West, Northeast, Southeast, Northwest, and Southwest districts.

Central Delhi

Central Delhi is the hub of many tourist attractions, commerce and politics. Many historical monuments and attractions can be found here, such as Jantar Mantar (see *If You Have to be a Tourist*, pp.102–3), Janpath Market (see *Shopping*, p.166) and St James Church.

North Delhi
North Delhi comprises the area between Delhi Gate and Kashmere Gate, Shah Jahanabad, is a spider web crowded with winding lanes bulging with big wholesale markets, such as the one in Khari Baoli. It also has middle-class residential areas with the chaotic markets of Paharganj and is home to Delhi University.

South Delhi/Southeast Delhi
Considered to be one of the most posh areas of the city, it has some of the best stores, restaurants, hotels, tourist attractions, markets and monuments. Despite Delhi's congestion, south Delhi has the greenest space in the entire city. Many monuments are found here including Humayun's Tomb, Qutab Minar, and Tughlaqabad. Newer attractions like the Lotus Temple (see *If You Have to be a Tourist*, p.104) and the Sports Complex at Siri Fort (see *Playground Paradise*, p.75) can also be found here.

West Delhi/Northwest Delhi
The western areas mainly consist of residential areas. Numerous trendy restaurants have come up in recent years.

East Delhi/Northeast Delhi
This consists of the residential districts of Preet Vihar, Gandhi Nagar, Vivek Vihar and Shahdara.

Some Health Precautions

The term 'Delhi belly' isn't part of the gastronomic landscape for nothing. While Delhi boasts of a variety of delicious cuisines from five-star hotel restaurants to roadside chaat stands, one should always take precautions before trying anything. Buy bottled water or request filtered water at restaurants. Don't buy that slice of coconut being sold by the hawker at traffic lights. You will be eating the fumes from the cars, and you don't know the source of the water that is being used to keep the coconut from drying out. The most annoying thing is to fall ill and spend more time in the bathroom than at the Red Fort. Diseases from food and water are the chief cause of illness among travellers.

Some invaluable tips on hygiene:

- Wash your hands often with soap and water, especially before eating.

If soap and water are not available, use an alcohol-based hand gel.

- Avoid dairy products, unless you know they have been pasteurized.
- Unless you have spent every waking moment of your life in India and have spent the vast majority of your time eating from the roadside vendors, avoid roadside food like the plague or you may end up with what feels like the plague when your stomach starts cramping. But having said that, if that parantha for Rs 10 is calling your name, at least survey the surrounding area to make sure it is clean and hygienic and that all food is fully cooked.
- Never ever drink water from the roadside stalls. Insist on bottled water from well-known brands such as Catch, Kingfisher, Evian, Aquafina, Bisleri etc. Also, make sure that the seal of the bottle is intact when you are given the bottle. Do not accept a bottle that was not opened in front of you. Water is not safe to drink directly from the tap. Boiled or filtered water is a good alternative to bottled water. Avoid tap water and ice cubes unless you are being served in a reputable restaurant.
- Do not eat cut fruits and vegetables or drink fresh juice from roadside stalls.
- Always carry mosquito repellent, especially during the summer. Make a habit of wearing light-cotton long-sleeved shirts and pants. Not only will they protect you from the sun, but also from the mosquito bites. The most popular local mosquito repellent which comes in a lotion and cream is Odomos. It can be found at most chemist and corner shops. The latest mosquito fighting tool is a patch that can be worn on clothing. This will be handy for parents who are wary of lathering their children in creams that need to be applied frequently.
- Drink lots of fluids during the summer months; again be mindful of the source of the water.
- Also, to prevent sunburn and heat stroke in the summer, apply sunscreen lotion and wear caps or hats, respectively.

Some Safety Precautions

In any big city, especially one the size of New Delhi, it is important to consider personal safety, especially when you're a tourist or new to the city.

- Moms and dads had best be mindful of the luggage. Unless you need help with heavy suitcases, don't let your luggage cart be commandeered by strangers like luggage porters or agents once you leave the airport or railway station and head to the taxi stand.
- Only use official taxi stands because you pre-pay based on your destination and will not be at the mercy of the driver who may take you for a tour of the city.
- Always keep your belongings in sight, especially in open areas like restaurants, snack bars, parks, and even in the event's venue. Don't leave backpacks, purses, bags, photo or video cameras hanging on chairs or on the floor. Carry sturdy bags with zip closings and keep them zipped. Flimsy bags are targeted, especially at markets, where they can easily be slashed in order for the contents to fall to the ground. It's important to choose a leather bag with a lining.
- Moms are well advised to keep the fancy jewellery in the hotel safe when the family's out shopping or touring.
- Try not to carry large amounts of cash. If you do carry cash, carry small bills as you don't have to make change and can bargain harder holding a Rs 50 note instead of a Rs 1,000 note. Avoid ATMs on streets or dark places.
- Do not share your personal data including hotel information to people you do not know. Carry a photo copy of passports or driver's licenses. In case of loss or theft, report the incident to the police and your hotel's front desk. Both will be able to assist you.

Emergency contacts

Police	100
Fire	101
Ambulance	102
Accident and Trauma	1099
Children	1098
Women	1091
	011 2412 1234
Seniors	1091
	1291
Traffic	011 2301 0101
Vigilance cell	011 2321 3355
Delhi Police website	www.delhipolice.nic.in

Directory Assistance

Just dial	011 2222 2222
Directory enquiry	197
Local assistance	199
Talking Yellow Pages	011 2601 4444

Publications and Websites

To find out what's going on in Delhi, check out *TimeOut Delhi*, a twice monthly publication that is likely the definitive guide for what's happening right now. It is found at most newspaper stands. You could also look at *Delhi Diary*, a small weekly publication; and *First City*, a monthly magazine with restaurants reviews, important numbers and listings on a calendar.

Although guidebooks, including this one, are super helpful and convenient for getting around the city, websites usually provide the most up-to-date information. It's always helpful to log on to certain websites before heading out for the day, to find out the most current information of what's happening in and around Delhi. You'll find loads of restaurant reviews, films, children's events etc. They are by no means comprehensive, but they give you tastier opinions and the address and phone numbers of places. For useful services you might want to look up asklaila.com or d4delhi.com, and for a comprehensive list of what's going in Delhi (and seven other cities) log on to buzzintown.com. The following websites will certainly give the family a few excellent ideas how to make its day out a truly enjoyable one.

- www.burrp.com: Restaurant reviews. Listings can be sent to your mobile phone.
- www.delhievents.com: Has section devoted to events and workshops for kids.
- www.bookmyshow.com: Online booking site for movies and sometimes has events listed for children.
- www.afindia.org/delhi/calendar.htm: The Alliance Francaise screens movies with English subtitles and hosts melas, wine tastings, barbecues etc.
- India Habitat Centre (http://www.indiahabitat.org/main.htm): There's always a lot happening at the India Habitat Centre by way of cultural events, film screenings, exhibitions etc. Just click on the calendar. For children's events and activities, visit Habitat World (www.habitatworld.com/events-kids.asp).
- www.nationalbalbhavan.nic.in: The National Bal Bhavan lists many, many children's activities that can be attended on a drop-in basis.

No. 1: Delhi National Zoological Park. With its abundant wildlife, water bodies, and picnic spots, the zoo is the perfect place to visit.

Keep your little angels and mini-monsters entertained with fabulous outdoor fun in the city. From animal gazing at the Delhi National Zoological Park, picnicking in Lodhi Gardens, birdwatching in Asola Bhatti Wildlife Sanctuary and conquering Shanti Niketan's rock climbing wall, Delhi has it all. On cool winter nights and warm summer days, discovering Delhi's beautiful gardens and shady tree-lined parks will keep the family entertained and the kids can burn off excess energy. Delhi may seem daunting for parents travelling with young people, but its many green spaces keep both local and touring parents sane. Most parks are free and all you will really need is a blanket, snacks and free time.

Nature, Birds and Wildlife

Asola Bhatti Wildlife Sanctuary

Home to hundreds of species of wildlife, the Asola Bhatti Wildlife Sanctuary provides a great view of nature, up close and personal. The Conservation Education Centre conducts daily guided walks through the forest, year round. Wildlife that can be spotted include nilgai (deer), porcupines, black bucks (a protected species), jackals and many smaller animals. The walk is about 90 minutes and for Rs 50 a person, the price really can't be beat. The walk winds its way through a small area of the 6,874 acres of forest land that comprise the sanctuary. Kids not only learn about the animals that roam the sanctuary, but also get insights on why ant hills are formed, learn about good moss and bad moss on trees and different kinds of plants and shrubs. And the giggle fits will start when the conversation turns to what kind of animal poo is on the path. An environmentalist conducts the walks. There's a film on vultures afterwards that is quite interesting. Pack a few sandwiches and juice boxes as there's nothing on sale for eating. Clean toilet facilities can be found close to the centre. Call ahead to book a guided tour.

>Conservation Education Centre, Asola Bhatti Wildlife Sanctuary
Near Karni Singh Shooting Range, Tughlaqabad
Tel: 011 2604 2010
Timings: Daily 9:30 am to sunset
Entry: Rs 50 for adults, Rs 35 for children

Delhi National Zoological Park

Established in 1959, Delhi National Zoological Park lies near the famous Old Fort. The zoo also has some historical monuments including the Kos Minar, built by Sher Shah Suri. The Delhi Zoo occupies land that once formed part of the Mughal road to Agra. One of the best zoos in Asia, it provides an almost natural habitat for the flora and fauna that is housed there. It is an ideal picnic spot, especially in winters, and is spread over an area of 214 acres. The National Zoological Gardens of New Delhi house more than 2,000 species of animals and birds, including the royal Bengal tiger and the white tiger.

In addition to the wildlife, the zoo also houses a library (on whose stairs the Mughal Emperor Humayun fell to his death) that provides a bounty of information on animals, birds, plants and rare zoological species in India. Animals of note include chimpanzees, hippopotami, spider monkeys, elephants and African wild buffalo. The various water bodies inside the zoo are home to a number of migratory birds. There's also an underground reptile complex for nocturnal animals like king cobras, pythons and a number of other species.

The walk around the zoo will be quite a trek for little ones so it's probably best to rent a trolley to go between the sights or bring a push chair. There are concession stands throughout for buying water, juices and ice cream. Eatables are forbidden as they don't want you to feed the animals. The sign boards are in Hindi but there are photos of the animals to guide you along. Beware of stray monkeys. If you have anything in your hand that remotely looks like food, they will try to take it from you. Toilets are located at the entrance and throughout the park. The toilets are Indian style, not Western style and not very clean, even if you're the first ones in there in the early morning. Within the park, toilets can be found near the black bear enclosure; canteen; white tiger enclosure; near the swamp deer enclosure; close to the giraffe area; and near the Indian hornbill enclosure. They are free to use. Outside the park, concession stands sell freshly prepared chaat, chips, water, soda and juices. There's a picnic area with tables and chairs and lots of benches for sitting.

>Mathura Road
Tel: 011 2388 1585
Timings: Daily 8:30 am to 5:30 pm (April to Oct); 9:30 am to 4:30 pm (Oct to March); closed Fri
Nearest railway station: Nizamuddin Railway Station
Nearest Metro: Central Secretariat
Entry: Adults Rs 10, foreigners Rs 50 (includes guide map); children (5–12 years) Rs 5, children below 5 years free
Trolley: Rs 35 per adult; Rs 20 per child ages 5–12; children under 5 free; school groups get a Rs 50 discount on the trolley and can pay a flat rate of Rs 450 for a 14-seater and Rs 400 for a 12-seater
Photography charges: Video camera: Self Rs 50; Commercial Rs 500
Nearby sights: Walking distance: Purana Qila, Humayun's Tomb; Within 3 km: India Gate, Ashokan Rock Edict, Nizamuddin's Shrine, Khairul Manzil Masjid
Nearby places to eat: Sweet Corner, Nathu's (both in Sunder Nagar Market), Hotel Oberoi, Flavors of Defence Colony, India Habitat Centre in Lodhi Road, Karim's at Nizamuddin and many roadside food stalls

Delhi Ridge

The Delhi Ridge is an extension of the Aravalli Range, located southeast of Tughlaqabad near the Bhatti mines. It is made up of quartzite rocks that cover almost 35 kilometres until it narrows where it meets the Yamuna river. The ridge attracts many birds.

>Tughlaqabad
Nearest Metro: Rajiv Chowk Station
Timings: Daily 10 am to 4 pm

Eco-farming camp

It's not enough to tell children to turn off running taps to conserve water and protect the environment by not wasting energy and littering. The Energy and Resources Institute's (TERI's) Deragreen Ecotourism camp at Mukteshwar (near Nainital, Uttarakhand) offers a 4-day camp that lets children experience nature by exposing them to farming techniques, bio-diversity, understanding herbs, the problems farmers face with climate changes and generally, about life in a small farming village. The children share a 3-camper (separated by sex) solar-powered tent, work with scientists and alongside farmers. The group size is of about 60, with 20 children, experts, and support staff. All meals are provided. Parents cannot accompany the child as the scientists want children to get the maximum exposure to nature through their own instincts and the guidance of the teachers. For children ages 10 to 18.

>India Habitat Centre, Lodhi Road
Tel: Amit Kumar Thakur at 011 4150 4900; 98119 90879
Timings: Year round except July through Sept and Dec through Jan
Entry: Rs 5,000 per child all inclusive

Okhla Bird Sanctuary
The Okhla Bird Sanctuary is located on the Yamuna River between New Delhi and Uttar Pradesh, at the southeastern end of New Delhi. It came into existence in the 1950s with the construction of the Okhla Barrage in the late 1950s and 1960s. Each year, hundreds of birds, including endangered ducks, waders and raptors migrate from as far away as Siberia and China and make the sanctuary their winter home. More than 330 species have been at the sanctuary. A large lake in the sanctuary was created by damming the river, which lies sandwiched between Okhla village toward the west and Gautambudh Nagar toward the east.

>Between Delhi and Uttar Pradesh
Timings: Daily sunrise to sunset

Boating

Delhi Tourism has provided pedal boats on various bodies of water in the heart of the city. These include the lakes near India Gate, Purana Qila Prasad Nagar Lake and Naini Lake in Model Town. A variety of fibreglass boats have been acquired by the corporation and can be hired at reasonable rates. Special training programmes in kayaking and canoeing can be organized, too.

Badhkal Lake
Located 32 km from Delhi, the man-made lake is set in the middle of the Aravalli Hills and is bordered by scenic gardens. Badhkal Lake is very famous for its water sports like boating, canoeing, kayaking, etc. The lake is also a good place to watch migratory birds during the winters. Situated near Faridabad, this place is also a favourite picnic spot. Although the lake dries up in summer, the mid monsoon season is the best

time to visit. Camel rides and horse-back riding is also available and there is a children's park the kids will really enjoy. The state government-run rest house is the most logical choice for an overnight stay, but with such a short distance from Delhi, a day trip is quite doable. It also has facilities for boating and fishing which is certainly worth a try. Lakeside tents are available on request, though not a great idea if the kids are squeamish about bugs. Numerous other facilities offered near the lake include a deluxe bath complex complete with swimming pool and sauna. Snacks can be bought from kiosks and a sit-down meal can be had at an onsite restaurant. Excursions can be booked through the Indian tourism office. (See *Day Trippin'*, p.120)

>Haryana Government Tourist Bureau
36, Janpath, Chanderlok Building
Tel: 011 2332 4910/11
Web: http://haryanatourism.com/destinations/r_badkhal.asp

Bhalswa Lake

Bhalswa Lake located in northeast Delhi is also home to a multi-sport and leisure complex. There are facilities for boating in pedal boats, kayaks, canoes and speed boats. It is located about 20 km from India Gate and will take nearly an hour by car. (See *Dudes*, pp.38–9.)

>Adventure Tourism Division
10th Flr, Mayur Bhavan, Connaught Place
Tel: 011 2341 4011; 011 2341 3256

India Gate

(See *If You Have to be a Tourist*, pp.100–101.)

>**Timings:** From 9 am
Entry: Rs 30 for 15 minutes

Purana Qila Prasad Nagar Lake

Located on the eastern side of India Gate and north of Humayun's tomb, the Purana Qila occupies the ancient mound, which perhaps conceals the ruins of the city of Indraprastha from the Indian epic the *Mahabharata*. Purana Qila offers a spectacular view of the Red Fort in the background. Boating/shikara rides/water scooter rides are available at the Prasad Nagar Lake adjacent to the Qila. It has a separate entry just before the main entrance of Purana Qila if you are coming from the Pragati Maidan exhibition grounds. (See *If You Have to be a Tourist*, pp.106–7.)

>**Timings:** Noon to 7 pm during summer; 11 am to 6 pm in winter

Entry: Rs 40 for 30 minutes; Rs 100 for 2 rounds

Tilyar Lake

Situated 70 km from New Delhi in Rohtak district, the Tilyar Lake is a favourite excursion for tourists in New Delhi. The lake offers facilities for boating, accommodation, restaurants, bar, a children's park and a mini zoo.

>Delhi Tourism and Transportation Development Corporation Ltd.
Coffee Home, 1, Baba Kharak Singh Marg
Tel: 011 2336 3607; 011 2336 5358

Gardens

Mughal Gardens

Sprawled across 15 acres of Rashtrapati Bhavan, the home of the presidential palace, the famous Mughal Gardens designed by Sir Edwin Lutyens for Lady Harding are open to visitors every year for a little over a month. These gardens combine the formal Mughal style with British garden designs. There is a musical garden, spiritual garden, herb garden and a bio-diversity park within the complex. Boasting more than 250 varieties of roses, the gardens hold the distinction of having the best and largest collection of Indian marigolds. The grounds include a butterfly garden, Moulsari trees and a bonsai. A fleet of over 150 gardeners is said to maintain the garden daily. Note, you are not allowed to take ANYTHING inside. Everything, including mobiles and bags has to be left at the entry at your own risk. However, when inside, there are several sitting areas labelled 'lounges' where you can take a rest and water stations where free water is handed out in Styrofoam cups. The walk at a steady pace will take about 45 minutes, so bear that in mind if you have small kids. Push chairs are allowed and the paths are paved. There are no toilets in the garden so do the needful before the walk. There are lots of roaming vendors hawking sandwiches, chaat and other snacks in the parking lot directly outside. There is no admission fee.

>Enter from Gate No. 35, North Avenue, Church Road
Timings: Tue to Sun 10 am to 5 pm, Feb to March
Tel: 011 2301 2960 ext 4229 for school and group visits

National Rose Garden

The National Rose Garden at Chanakyapuri in Delhi is a garden exclusively for roses, famous for the large variety of roses from all over the world. At the Delhi Rose Garden you can see some of the rarest of rare and imported varieties of roses. The best season to visit the rose garden is between December and January when the flowers are in full bloom. (Lodhi Garden also has a rose garden that boasts to have at least 200 varieties of roses.)

>Chanakyapuri
At the intersection of Satya Marg and Shanti Path
Timings: Sunrise to sunset

Roshanara Garden
Once one of the most beautiful Mughal gardens in the city, Roshanara Garden still attracts tourists to the tomb of Roshanara which is located in the middle of the garden. Built in 1650, the garden is named for the youngest daughter of Shah Jahan Roshanara. Roshanara helped dethrone Shah Jahan and helped her brother Aurangzeb rise to power. She was later poisoned on the order of her brother. In 1923, a club was built in the garden, and it is still one of the most prestigious clubs in the city that requires membership for entry. It is a nice place to picnic or just take a walk around admiring the grounds.

>North Delhi, near Northern Ridge
Nearest Metro: Delhi University Metro Station
Timings: Sunrise to sunset

Horse Riding

Beeya's Riding Facility
Beeya's Riding Facility has 25 horses, both big and small on site. It's open to the public so kids who haven't experienced horse riding before, can get a start here.

>Munirka Farms, off Green Avenue
Vasant Kunj
Tel: 98100 62736
Timings: Mon to Sat
Cost: Rs 250 for 30 minutes

The Children's Riding Club
The Children's Riding Club which is part of the Delhi Riding Club usually holds classes in the afternoon, for kids 4 and above while evenings are mainly reserved for adults. At a membership charge of Rs 1,700 (including other miscellaneous payments), you can look forward to classes twice a week, of one hour each. Getting membership is worth it if you're a frequent visitor to Delhi or staying for a while. The price is quite reasonable.

>Safdarjung Road, Safdarjung Enclave
Tel: 011 2301 1891; 98106 79090

The Delhi Horse Show
The Delhi Horse Show, one of India's premier horse riding events, is held annually in February or March. The 2-day sporting event draws competitors from all over India to take part in show jumping, dressage events and tent-pegging. Competitors who participate in the show include civilian riders, teams and participants from the services, the police, the paramilitary forces, colleges and schools. The Delhi Horse Show is the only show in the country which is conducted under bright artificial lights. Over 500 horses and riders, including children, compete in the meet. The best of equestrian talent from across the country can be seen in action. For dates of the event, contact the Army Polo and Riding Club.

>B Squadron 61 Cavalry, Cariappa Marg (Cantonment)
Tel: 011 2569 9444; 2569 9555; 2569 9666,
Web: www.armypoloclub.com/index.html

DDA Saket Sports Complex
The DDA Saket Sports Complex stables horses for children and adults. Membership is required but one can get a temporary membership in under 20 minutes if all you're after is one afternoon of riding.

>J Block, Saket
Tel: 011 2956 1742
Timings: Tue to Sun
Entry: Temporary membership at Rs 120 per hour

Picnic Spots

There's nothing better than people watching when you've got a picnic basket stocked with goodies and a blanket big enough to sprawl out on when you want to really enjoy a nice Delhi day. Many parks around the city fill the need.

Ajmal Khan Park
Located near Karol Bagh, Ajmal Khan Park is spread over an area of 5 acres and has musical fountains. The musical fountain operates for 2 hours every day after sunset except on Tuesdays. For this reason, the park is very popular with children who delight in the music and lights.

>Karol Bagh
Timings: Sunrise to sunset

Buddha Jayanti Park
Buddha Jayanti Park was founded on the 2500th anniversary of Lord Gautam Buddha's attainment of nirvana. The park covers the major portion of the Southern Ridge and can be reached either through the Ridge Road or Sardar Patel

Marg, opposite Assam House. This park is special because a sapling of the Bodhi Tree was brought from Sri Lanka and was planted here. In the third century BC, Emperor Ashoka's daughter took a sapling from the original Bodhi Tree under which Buddha meditated and obtained enlightenment at Bodhgaya in Bihar, to Sri Lanka. The park is full of flowers, greenery and paved walkways. It has a forest-like atmosphere and is ideal for a picnic. Buddhist organizations host programmes in the park frequently. Indeed, another great picnic spot.

>Ridge Road, Dhaula Kuan (Central Delhi)
Timings: Daily 5 am to 7 pm
Nearest Metro: Rajiv Chowk
Nearby sights: Talkatora Gardens, Cathedral of the Sacred Heart, Rashtrapati Bhavan, India Gate, Jantar Mantar, Gurudwara Bangla Sahib and Hanuman Mandir

Central Park

One of the busiest shopping centres in the city also sports one of the most beautiful and serene parks. Central Park is situated above the Rajiv Chowk Metro station. Spread over 39,000 square metres, the park has a green area of 27,000 square metres, including 10,000 square metres of paved walkways for morning joggers. Central Park also has four water bodies and 21 fountains, besides a water cascade. However, the main attraction, just above the Metro station, is a quarter-arc shaped amphitheatre that can seat about 500 people. Numerous cultural events are held there, so it's likely the family can enjoy concerts and other entertainment. Check out *Time Out Delhi* for listings. The parking nearest to the park is the Palika parking across the road. The main entrance to the park is opposite Palika Gate No. 2.

>Inner Circle, Connaught Place
Timings: Sunrise to sunset
Nearest Metro: Rajiv Chowk
Nearby sights: Connaught Place, Janpath, India Gate

Children's Park

The Children's Park near India Gate is a little slice of heaven. Replete with swings, slides and an aquarium, the park has large well maintained lawns that provide good sitting grounds. At night, the lights come on and various snacks and toys (likely to break before you even make it to the car) can be purchased from the many vendors. Adults are not allowed if not accompanied with a child.

Deer Park

The Deer Park, located in Hauz Khas, is home to hundreds of birds, spotted deer, guinea pigs, peacocks and rabbits that the kids can feed. Situated in the Chanakyapuri area, it is easily accessible from Hauz Khas Village and Safdarjung Enclave. The ideal place to go for a picnic or take a walk, the Deer Park was intended to serve as a break from the hectic and stressful life of the city. The Deer Park has been beautifully landscaped with shady trees along a peaceful lake. The Deer Park is also a birdwatcher's paradise as its lake attracts a variety of birds. It also has a special play area for children, making it the perfect place to take children on an outing and also to bring them closer to nature. Park Baluchi restaurant is located inside the park. Hauz Khas Village also has many restaurants to choose from.

>Hauz Khas Village
Timings: Sunrise to sunset
Nearest Metro: Central Secretariat
Nearby sights: Hauz Khas Enclave, Kalkaji Temple, Lotus Temple, Nizamuddin's Shrine and Chirag Dehlvi's Dargah
Nearby places to eat: Many restaurants in Hauz Khas Village and Connaught Place

Dhaula Kuan Complex

The park has an artificial lake, hanging bridge, playground and waterfalls which can provide hours of fun.
>Near Dhaula Kuan
Timings: Sunrise to sunset

Garden of Five Senses

Located on the outskirts of the city, the Garden of Five Senses is a spectacular park which was designed to stimulate our five senses with its sights. It's definitely a great place to picnic since the foot traffic is cut down exponentially. At the entrance of the park is a brass tree fountain, and the prime sights of the 20-acre park are the Khas Bagh (a beautiful garden), food and shopping court, Neel Bagh, Colour Gardens, the Courts of Specimen Plants, amazing sculptures and the Solar Energy Park. The garden houses art works by established as well as up and coming artists. Over 200 varieties of plants, numerous species of butterflies, pools of water lilies, many murals and sculptures (25 of which are unique to Indian art), wind chimes and an amphitheatre together make this a garden like no other.

> Said-Ul-Azaib village, situated near Mahavirsthal on the Mehrauli–Badarpur Road
Timings: Daily 6 am to 9 pm
Nearby sights: Khirki Masjid, Kalkaji Temple, Lotus Temple, Nizamuddin's Shrine and Chirag Dehlvi's Dargah
Nearby places to eat: Food Court at the garden; McDonald's; Nirula's and many popular eateries in PVR Saket Complex and Malviya Nagar Market

India Gate

Built as a monument in memory of the Indian soldiers who died in World War I, India Gate's lawns are bustling with locals and tourists from sunrise to sunset. In order to honour the numerous unknown gallant soldiers who died fighting for the country, an eternal flame or Amar Jawan Jyoti was lit under the arch of India Gate in 1971. Beautiful lawns encircle the monument, providing visitors with a lush clean and green place to take in the view of Lutyen's Delhi. It is more popular in the evening when the sun is dipping in the sky. Ice cream, cold drinks and many kinds of small snacks are available from mobile vendors. (See *If You Have to be a Tourist*, pp.100–101.)

>Eastern end of Rajpath
Timings: Daily, sunrise to sunset
Nearest Metro: Kendriya Terminal
Nearby sights: Rashtrapati Bhavan, Parliament House where Indian leaders meet, the National Museum, and the National Gallery of Modern Art

Jahanapanah city forest

Bird lovers will find Jahanapanah an ideal place to bird watch. Frequented by nature enthusiasts and morning walkers alike, the city forest, which is spread over 20 colonies, is also a favourite picnic spot during winter months. The place occupies a magnificent 800 acres, has lots of trees, and is hence called a forest.
It is located between Tughlaqabad and Chiragh Delhi and passes through Alaknanda and Greater Kailash Part II.
The entrance is opposite Don Bosco School. A free toilet is right at the entrance and about 100 metres down the path to the left is a covered area with stone benches and a stone floor. It is great for relaxing with a book when the sun is too hot.

>Enter from GK II (opposite Don Bosco School)
Timings: Daily 4 am to 10 am; 4 pm to 6 pm

Japanese Garden

Developed and maintained by

the DDA (Delhi Development Authority) the Japanese Garden in Rohini in Delhi is located at Sector 11. With a lake, woods, boating facilities and nature walks, the Japanese Garden is great for family outings. It is best to go during the week as there are long lines on the weekends. Pack a picnic or buy tikkis, samosas, kebabs or Chinese food from the various stalls. There are several drinks and ice cream vendors, too.

>Rohini, near the Rajiv Gandhi Cancer Institute, Sector 11
Timings: Sunrise to sunset
Nearest Metro: Rohini

Kalindi Kunj
Near the Haryana border, close to the Apollo hospital is a pretty park with fountains, lit in the evenings with colourful lights. Kalindi Kunj park is situated right on the banks of the Yamuna river. It has extensive manicured lawns and is another great spot for birdwatching. A large number of tourists come in the evening to enjoy the fountains. During September, thousands of migratory birds including shovellers, pintail, common teal, gadwall and blue winged teal visit the area.

>Delhi–Noida border, Near Sarita Vihar and Apollo Hospital
Timings: Sunrise to sunset; fountain is lit after sunset

Leisure Valley Park
The Leisure Valley Park spans an area of over 25 acres and is one of the best gardens located at the Sector 29 main road in Gurgaon. The park has a musical fountain which is lit at night. The Haryana Urban Development Authority has constructed a shopping complex and restaurant with a big parking space around the gardens. The kids will enjoy the variety of amusement park type rides within the park. One can also picnic here on the huge green lawn, walk or run on the jogging paths and see a variety of roses within the garden. A flower festival is held every spring within the park. There are lots of vendors outside the park selling balloons, chaat and ice cream.

>DLF City, Sector 29, Gurgaon
Timings: Daily 11am to 8 pm

Lodhi Garden
An impressive landscape with lots of shady trees, benches, flowers, fauna and jogging and walking trails, Lodhi Garden is probably the perfect place for a picnic every day of the year with the exception of the monsoon season. Numerous beautiful ancient tombs of the Sayyid and Lodhi sultans

(who ruled north India in the 15th and 16th centuries) are dispersed all over the park. The designs of the tombs speak of the genius of Mughal architecture. The tombs are great for exploring. The structures within Lodhi Garden are:

- Muhammad Shah's Tomb (the third ruler of the Sayyid dynasty is located in the south-western part of the garden).
- Bara Gumbad and Masjid, a square tomb surmounted by a large dome, situated 300 metres northeast of Muhammad Shah's tomb. The person buried inside is unidentified. It is assumed that he is a high-ranking officer because of the magnificent structure constructed for him.
- Bara Gumbad Masjid is situated on the western side of the tomb just next to it. It was built in 1494 AD.
- Sheesh Gumbad Tomb, also known as the 'glazed dome' because of the beautiful blue tile decoration, is a few metres north of Bara Gumbad.

Lodhi Garden is 2 kilometres away from Humayun's Tomb and is adjacent to India International Centre. The garden is sprawling with lush, green, manicured bushes and huge trees. They are extremely well-maintained and are particularly breathtaking in the evenings as the monuments are lit with halogen lights. There's a relatively clean toilet near Gate 1 that charges Rs 2 per use. Ideal for a day out with the kids in the sun or the shade, whichever is preferred.

>On the main Lodhi Road, about a kilometre east of Safdarjung's Tomb
Timings: Daily; sunrise to sunset
Nearest Metro: Central Secretariat
Nearby sights: India Gate, Rashtrapati Bhavan, Ugrasen-ki-Baoli, Moth-ki-Masjid, Lotus Temple, Nizamuddin's Shrine and Chirag Dehlvi's Dargah
Nearby places to eat: Eatopia at India Habitat Centre; Khan Market; Lodhi, the Garden Restaurant; Basil and Thyme at Santushti Shopping Complex; Race Course Road

Mahavir Gardens

Located on the Ridge it is named after the founder of Jainism, Lord Mahavir.

Timings: Daily; sunrise to sunset

Millennium Indraprastha Park

Spread over 34 hectares, the

Millennium Indraprastha Park is the largest landscaped garden in the city, and is popular among school kids, retirees and those looking to become one with nature. It houses a food court, Japanese rock garden, amphitheatre and lots of trees for shade from the summer sun. Humayun's Tomb is a perfect backdrop and the Vishwa Shanti Stupa, a monument dedicated to peace and brotherhood, draws the requisite crowds.

>Ring Road, near the Sarai Kale Khan bus terminal
Timings: Daily sunrise to 10:30 pm
Nearby sights: India Gate, Jantar Mantar, Lodhi Garden and Nehru Park

NDMC Lake Park
Has a musical fountain and is located near the Safdarjung Flyover in Lakshmibai Nagar.

Timings: Daily sunrise to sunset

Nehru Park
Spread over 85 acres in what is considered diplomat's row, Nehru Park has everything, including a swimming pool, snack park, an abundance of trees and open space to spread a blanket and bring out the picnic lunch. Rocks throughout are inscribed with the sayings of Jawaharlal Nehru, the first prime minister of India. Free open-air concerts and art events are held at the park regularly, mainly on Sunday mornings. There's a toilet with just urinals near the entrance that is closest to the Australian Embassy.

>Chanakyapuri Diplomatic Enclave, Panchsheel Road
Timings: Daily sunrise to sunset
Entry: Free, but car parking is Rs 10
Nearest Metro: Central Secretariat
Nearby sights: National Rail Museum, Nehru Planetarium and Memorial Museum, Indira Gandhi Memorial Museum, Safdarjung's Tomb and Dilli Haat
Nearby places to eat: Hotel Ashok, Taj Palace, Maurya Sheraton, Hotel Le Meridien, Imperial Hotel, Hotel Inter-Continental, Parikrama Revolving Restaurant, Gaylord, El Rodeo, Bercos, Zen Restaurant, Delhi Darbar, Nizam's Kathi Kebabs and Standard Restaurant. For snacks and fast foods: Connaught Place.

Qudsia Bagh
This garden was built by Qudsia Begum, the first mistress and then wife of Emperor Mohammad Shah (1719–1748). A huge part of the garden was destroyed to make way for the Inter

State Bus Terminal and the adjacent tourist camp site. Many of the structures are now used by the Masonic Lodge. The gateway and the mosque were recently restored and efforts have been made to bring the garden back to its original beauty. Qudsia Bagh is still a wonderful spot in which to picnic, and more sightseeing can be done as it is close to the historic Kashmere Gate.

>Shamnath Road, East Delhi
Timings: Daily sunrise to sunset

Rose Gardens

The Rose Gardens are located opposite Safdarjang's Tomb in Hauz Khas. The roses there seem to bloom all year round. There's a nice fountain inside the park, toilets near the entrance by the parking lot and lots of paths and grassy areas for having a picnic.

>Hauz Khas
Timings: Sunrise to sunset
Entry: Free, but there's a car park in front that charges from Rs 10

Shalimar Garden

Enjoying a special place in history, Shalimar Garden was where Aurangzeb the Mughal king was crowned emperor in 1658. The pavilion in the centre, called Shish Mahal, was built by Shah Jahan and some of the original painting is still visible. It has also been said that this garden was the summer retreat of Sir David Ochterlony, the British Resident Commissioner of Delhi. The garden was used by Emperor Aurangzeb as his country house and is considered one of the most significant Mughal gardens of Delhi. It used to serve as the first-night staging post for the Mughals on their way to Kashmir and Lahore. The best time to visit the garden, situated near the northern ridge behind Delhi University, is in the spring, when the greenery is at its best. Even though most of the monuments are ruins, tourists still spend time exploring them. One of the best and possibly worst thing about Delhi is that most of these monuments are not roped off so kids can literally grab history by the crumbling bricks.

>Near Badli Sarai; 10 km northwest of Old Delhi
Timings: Sunrise to sunset
Nearest Metro: Kashmere Gate
Nearby places to eat: Good Indian restaurants in Shalimar Bagh Market and Pitampura Market; McDonald's in Kamla Nagar and Model Town; Nirula's; Grant Plaza in Model Town and many roadside dhabas.

Talkatora Gardens
A perfect picnic spot, these gardens provide all the beauty and serenity that help a person to relax. The Talkatora Gardens are built on what was once the venue of a battle in which the Mughals defeated the Marathas. Roller skating can be done at the Talkatora Skating Rink.

>Main Willingdon Crescent Road
Timings: Open all day. Preferred timings 3 pm to 6 pm
Nearest Metro: Rajiv Chowk
Nearby sights: Cathedral of Sacred Heart, Rashtrapati Bhavan, India Gate, Jantar Mantar, Gurudwara Bangla Sahib and Hanuman Mandir
Nearby places to eat: Many restaurants in Connaught Place

Other Parks

The following are worth a visit, but leave the blanket in the car.

Mahatma Gandhi Park
The Mahatma Gandhi Park is located behind the Town Hall building on the main Church Mission Road, near the Old Delhi Railway Station. The park is popular for its historical significance, not for of its great picnic spots which in fact are sorely lacking. Mahatma Gandhi Park was set up during the British period and was officially known as 'Queen's Park'. However, in later years, it came to be known as the 'Company Bagh'. In the early part of the 19th century, Company Bagh was the outdoor club for Delhi's posh set. The park took on its current name after India gained independence in 1947. It boasts of a number of big shady trees and a statue of Gandhi. It is one of the few green spaces left in the congested Chandni Chowk area.

>Church Mission Road, near the Old Delhi Railway Station
Nearest Metro: Delhi Main Station
Nearby sights: Rajghat, Jama Masjid, St James Church, Chandni Chowk, Dara Shikoh Library, Salimgarh Fort, Lothian Cemetery, Kashmere Gate and Old Town Hall
Nearby eats: Karim Hotel, Ghantewala Sweet Shop, food stalls near Jama Masjid, Paranthe Wali Gali, Moti Mahal Restaurant; many roadside food stalls

Netaji Subhash Park
Named after Netaji Subhash Chandra Bose, a great leader who formed the Indian National Army (INA) to fight the British forces, Netaji Subhash Park is a small, but beautiful

park that abuts Urdu Park. Situated on Netaji Subhash Marg, opposite Sunehri Masjid in the Old Delhi, the park is quite famous for *malishwallahs* (body masseurs) and most people go there to get a body massage from some highly skilled masseurs. The park also has a regal statue of Netaji Subhash Chandra Bose.

>Netaji Subhash Marg, opposite Sunehri Masjid, Old Delhi
Timings: 6 am to 7 pm
Nearby sights: Red Fort, Jama Masjid, Chandni Chowk, Salimgarh Fort, St James Church and Rajghat
Nearby places to eat: Karim Hotel, Ghantewala Sweet Shop, food stalls near Jama Masjid, Paranthe Wali Gali, Moti Mahal Restaurant; many roadside food stalls

Parasailing

Delhi Tourism Adventure division

You can go parasailing at Kanwarshikha near Sohna in Haryana, about 60 kms from Delhi. Professional instructors are on hand to make sure you land in one piece. Make bookings through the Delhi Tourism Development Corporation. Gather relatives or friends as a minimum of 10 people is required. This is best for somewhat adventurous parents and slightly older children.

>Central Reservation Office Baba Kharak Singh Marg
Tel: 011 2336 3607
Entry: Depend on group size and activity
Web: www.delhitourism.nic.in/publicpage/adventurelist.aspx

Rock Climbing

Adventure Club

The Adventure Club is run by the Delhi government and offers climbing between October and March. Don't let that scare you off. In this case, it's actually a good thing. The natural rocks are located among lush, sprawling lawns and are adjacent to the Qutab Golf Course. They are 10 metres high and offer interesting routes for both experts and beginners.

>Natural Rocks, Lado Sarai
Tel: 011 2332 1238, 011 2332 1242

Camp Wild at Dhauj

Children 10 years and older can get an introduction to adventure sports through rock climbing. Camp Wild at Dhauj, 7 kilometres from the Chattarpur border, has day-long courses that teach kids how to tie knots, rapelling, river-crossing and different techniques of climbing. The younger kids aren't left out, however. They can participate in their own adventure course which includes nature walks and other outdoor activities.

>Holiday Moods
3/6 DB Gupta Road,
Paharganj
Tel: 011 4300 0800
Timings: Oct to April
Entry: Starts from Rs 850 per child

Indian Mountaineering Foundation
The Indian Mountaineering Foundation (IMF) has several artificial walls including a vertical wall with varying degrees of difficulty. More experienced climbers can choose a natural boulder wall or do some rapelling. Best for children ages 6 and older. The IMF also offers climbing for those who feel they are so good they should be teaching the teachers. The Tenzing Norgay Museum at the IMF exhibits pictures, panoramas and dioramas of various facets of the Himalayas and the history of Himalyan exploration.

>6 Benito Jaurez Marg, Anand Niketan,
Near Delhi University South Campus
Tel: 011 2411 1211
Entry: Rs 50 for 4 hours; group climbing workshops Rs 150 per person (minimum 10 people)
Timings: Tue to Sat 9 am to 1 pm and 3 pm to 7 pm in winter; Tue to Sat 8 am to noon and 4 pm to 8 pm in summer; closed on national holidays

KSHITIJ Adventure League
KSHITIJ Adventure League conducts adventure type activities on weekend mornings throughout the year. Activities include rock-climbing, rapelling, trail biking and trekking through parks and to heritage sites around the city. Venues change so call in advance.

>**Tel:** 95 1124 408 1500
Timings: Sat and Sun10 am to 6 pm

Walks

The Indian National Trust for Art and Cultural Heritage holds a variety of walks around Delhi for visitors to better appreciate the city.

Chandni Chowk
Chandni Chowk is one of the busiest of roads in the city; it links the Red Fort with the Fatehpuri Masjid. Chandni Chowk is a colourful bazaar, very popular with traders and locals. It is considered as the best place to shop for fabrics in wholesale prices. It gets so crowded that vehicles are not allowed in its bylanes. Chandni Chowk has retained its old magic

and is a bustling shopping area, with historic alleys and hotels, mosques and temples that will take multiple visits to truly explore fully. Some food stalls in the area are 100 years old. It is a favourite hangout for cuisine buffs. You'll have to try your luck at various restaurants if you need a bathroom break.

>Red Fort area

Hauz Khas

The highlight of the walk includes a 13th century reservoir. The water and the lush green areas attract lots of birds. The walk covers the reservoir, tombs, mosques and pavilions.

>Hauz Khas
Tel: 011 2464 1304; 011 2469 2774
Timings: From 8:30 am
Cost: Rs 50 per person
Details: Register by Friday for the Intach walks (held mainly on the weekend) by sending an email to intachdelhi@rediffmail.com or calling the numbers above.

Lodhi Garden

Lodhi Garden's beauty is held under the spotlight through this walk which takes visitors to some of the Syed and Lodhi tombs and mosques, the Mughal garden and other structures. The walk lasts about one and a half hours. You'll build up quite an appetite that will be satiated at Lodhi, The Garden Restaurant. (*See Eats*, pp.139–40.) The walk is stroller and kid friendly. Toilet facilities for Rs 2 near Gate 1.

>Lodhi Road
Tel: 011 2464 1304
Timings: From 8:30 am
Cost: Rs 50 per person

Mehrauli Archaeological Park

The guided walk at Mehrauli Archaeological Park, which is spread over hundreds of acres of land near the Qutab Minar, takes visits to Balban's tomb, Jamili Kamali mosque and tomb, Metcalfe's bridge, Quli Khan's tomb, a mosque, a sarai and other tombs. It lasts about 2 hours. Call ahead for reservations and meeting point for all walks. It is best to carry very young kids in a back carrier. Be prepared for lots of walking so you might hear some whining by the time the walk is over.

>Near Qutab Minar
Tel: 011 2464 1304
Timings: From 8:30 am
Cost: Rs 50 per person

Nature walk

The India Habitat Centre also organizes a walk, conducted by an environmentalist, which explores forests from Malcha Marg to Dhaula Kuan.

>**Tel:** 011 2468 2222
Timings: From 7:30 am
Cost: Rs 50 per person
Details: You can register for the walk (mainly on weekends) by sending an email to habitatprogrammes@gmail.com or phoning the number above. Registration closes at 20 people per group.

Rashtrapati Bhavan
Up in the sky, it's a plane, it's a bird, it's Superman. Actually, it's more likely to be a bird you see soaring through the sky during a very enjoyable nature walk at Rashtrapati Bhavan, the official residence of the President of India. The nature trail is open for visitors on Saturdays who come to see the weekly 40-minute changing of the guard ceremony, akin to the one at Buckingham Palace in London. There's a butterfly garden and horticulture, citrus grove, guava grove and a parakeet grove too (also see *If You Have to be a Tourist*, pp.109–10).

>Near Connaught Place, at the western end of Rajpath.
Nearest Metro: Central Secretariat
Changing of the guard ceremony: Every Saturday between 10:35 am to 11 am in winter and 8:30 am to 9:15 am in summer.

Shahjahanabad
Delhi, more accurately Old Delhi, is famous for its monuments, bazaars and abundance of street vendors hawking everything under the hot Delhi sun. What is considered Old Delhi today was the Mughal city of Shahjahanabad, built by Emperor Shah Jahan, builder of the Taj Mahal, when he moved his imperial capital from Agra to Delhi. A wall with 14 gates encloses the area. However, only 3 survive—Delhi, Turkman and Ajmeri Gate. The walk through time begins from Shri Digambara Jain Lal Mandir and ends at the north gate of Jama Masjid. Sights include a plethora of religious houses including the Gauri Shankar Temple, the Central Baptist Church, the Sis Ganj Gurudwara and the Jama Masjid. Make pit stops at Sunehri Masjid, Kinari Bazaar and Gali Guliyan. The municipal corporation of Delhi (MCD) has decided to make an extensive map of the Walled City which will be helpful for tourists and researchers. The map will include an extensive listing of the major heritage monuments, guest houses, eateries and the all important maze of roads which can be terribly confusing. The maps will be on signage inside and outside the Walled City, and should

soon be available for sale in bookshops.

>Duration: 2 to 3 hours
Best time: Mid-morning or evening
Tel: 011 2464 1304; 011 2469 2774; 011 2463 2269

Around Delhi

Badhkal Lake

A popular picnic spot, Badhkal Lake has facilities for water sports. The lake however has been fast drying up due to rain shortage, and it might just disappear one of these days. (See pp.12–13 above; see *Day Trippin'*, p.120.)

Surajkund

Surajkund is the site of the annual Surajkund Mela, there is a golf course, an exotic hotel and one can fish and also go boating. (*See Day Trippin'*, pp.121–2.)

Sultanpur Bird Sanctuary

The Sultanpur Bird Sanctuary, located just 46 km from Delhi in Gurgaon, is the closest bird reserve to the city. This birder's paradise, at 359 acres, is the most ideal destination for environmentalists and bird watchers. It was established as a bird sanctuary in 1971 and was upgraded to a National Park by the Haryana government in 1991. There is a calm that cannot be found elsewhere in the region. The winter months of December and January are the ideal time to visit, when several birds from distant places such as Siberia, Europe and Afghanistan visit the park. There are about 250 species of birds in the Sultanpur Bird Sanctuary, some stay year round and others are migratory. Be sure to pack a pair of binoculars to spot the birds from the top of the 4 towers located in the park. Sultanpur also boasts of a wide variety of wild animals including antelopes like neelgai (blue bull), black bucks, porcupines, wild cats, hedgehogs, pigs, mongoose, leopards and deer roaming the park. A guide can be hired for the visit and there is an onsite educational centre. A tourist lodge is located inside the park with AC rooms for an overnight stay. There is also a restaurant on the premises.

>Sultanpur National Park
Gurgaon–Farukh Nagar Road, Haryana
Tel: 95124 237 5242 for Sultanpur; 011 2332 4910/11 for Haryana Tourism
Entry: Rs 5
Web: www.haryana-online.com

Roller Skating

Roller Skating can be done at the Talkatora Skating Rink and several other parks in the city. (Also see *Playground Paradise*, pp.74–5.)

>Talkatora Skating Rink
Main Willingdon Crescent Road
Timings: Open all day. Preferred timings 3 pm to 6 pm
Nearest Metro: Rajiv Chowk

No. 1: Shankar's International Doll Museum. What better place to see a collection of thousands of dolls from around the world?

Hit the hot spots for girls out on the town. Turn favourite pastimes into a cultural event and then some. Your little diva can build a teddy bear exactly how she likes it; envision how any of the more than 6,000 dolls from around the world in the doll museum spent their time back home before coming to India; appreciate various forms of Indian dances and unwind with scones and tea at the Imperial or in a beautician's chair for a few hours of pampering.

Get Creative

Build-a-Bear Workshop
Why buy a teddy bear for your little angel when she can build one exactly to her liking? The US-based Build-a-Bear Workshop operates more than 300 stores in 15 countries and has an outlet at the Shopper's Stop in Rajouri Garden. The showroom has nearly 40 kinds of animals to choose from, not just teddy bears. There are monkeys, leopards and puppies that are also waiting to find a new home. Of course, the customization is the best part as kids can choose the animal, colour, clothing, stuffing and voice. Yes, they can speak. Kids can even use their own voices. Special considerations are made for young children, with toys that have no removable parts. Even the eyes are embroidered. Those with dust allergies can rest assured because there are some bears without fur. Many shop assistants are available to help with the stuffing, sewing and fluffing. There's a wide selection of outfits and shoes to choose from as no bear would be complete without those perfect to-die-for threads.

>Shopper's Stop, Eros Mall, Rajouri Garden
Tel: 011 3243 8692
Prices: From Rs 395 to Rs 1,195 for the bear; clothing and shoes range from Rs 195 to Rs 800

The Colour Factory
Take extra pleasure at tea time knowing you've painted

your own tea set. The Colour Factory bills itself as India's first 'paint your own pottery' store. There's a wide range of colours and mugs, cups, vases, platters and photo frames to choose from that can all be personalized. The finished pieces will be glazed and finished and returned in a week. If you're not going to hang around Delhi long enough to retrieve the finished pieces, you can purchase ceramics a la carte along with paints and brushes and get the firing done at home. Ready-made pieces can be purchased, but what's the fun in that? It can get crowded on weekends and school holidays so reservations are advised.

>2nd Flr, Select Citywalk Mall, Press Enclave Road, Saket
Tel: 011 4059 7515
Timings: Daily 11 am to 8 pm
Entry: From Rs 225
Web: www.thecolourfactory.in/contact.htm

>120, 1st Flr, DT Mega Mall, DLF
Tel: 0124 437 0958
Timings: Daily 11 am to 8 pm; 11 am to 9 pm on weekends

Other Activities

Bindis, bangles and butterflies
An array of fashionable accessories is piled high in markets across the city. Change bindis, bangles and hairclips that come in a countless range from butterflies, dragon flies, bows and ladybugs to match outfits or moods. Check out the markets in *Shopping*, pp.163–88.

Dances of India
For little ladies who fashion themselves as the next Sonal Mansingh or Birju Maharaj, this will make for an unforgettable evening. The show—around for 29 years—has internationally renowned artists performing 6 folk, tribal and classical dances of India. Although geared towards tourists, the dance forms represented include traditional dance forms such as Kathak and Bharatanatyam. The footwork, hand gestures, expressive eye movements, and sheer variety and energy of the performances make the show a memorable experience.

>Parsi Anjuman Hall, Bahadur Shah Zafar Marg, next to Maulana Azad Medical College
Tel: 011 2323 1228 or Laljah at 98102 31644
Timings: Daily 6:45 pm. Come 15 minutes early if you want to buy tickets at the door
Entry: Rs 200 per person

Getting dolled up

Spend a few hours being pampered with a pedicure and manicure and maybe even a glamorous hair cut. Looks salon is used to clients who don't yet have credit cards and treat them with the same care and professionalism.

>10 Khan Market
Tel: 011 4175 7233, 4175 7244
Timings: 10 am to 8 pm
Web: www.lookssalon.in for more locations

>D-1 Defence Colony
Tel: 011 4155 2800; 011 4155 2801

High teas

With pinkies extended and tea cups raised, gals will surely enjoy the tradition of English high tea. A selection of sandwiches, cakes, scones, cakes and juices, tea and coffee make the experience enjoyable for everyone. The lawns at both hotels are magnificent for a walk or a romp, after the tea.

The Claridges—The Senate
>12 Aurangzeb Road
Tel: 011 4133 5264
Timings: Daily 3 pm to 6 pm
Entry: Rs 650 per person plus tax

The Atrium at the Imperial Hotel
>1 Janpath, Connaught Place (Opposite Cottage Emporium)
Tel: 011 2334 1234, 011 4150 1234
Timings: Daily 3 pm to 6 pm
Entry: Rs 650 per person plus tax

Mehendi

Although Mehendi is generally associated with Hindu festivals, celebrations and the wedding ceremony, most girls love to have the beautiful henna patterns on their feet and hands on any given day. Mehendi is a small tropical shrub, whose leaves when dried and ground into a paste emit a rusty-red pigment, suitable for making intricate designs on the hands and feet. There are no side effects on the skin. Mehendi is a painless alternative to permanent tattoos. The Mughals brought mehendi to India in the 12th century and the intricacy of the patterns has evolved over the years. One doesn't have to look very far in most markets to find a mehendiwali. They are ever present at Dilli Haat, Janpath, Khan Market, Sarojini Nagar and Hanuman Mandir on Tuesdays. Prices vary greatly with Hanuman Mandir charging as little as Rs 10 per hand and Khan Market charging as much as Rs 275 per hand.

>Dilli Haat, Sri Aurobindo Marg, opposite INA Market

Timings: Daily 10:30 am to 10 pm
Entry: Rs 15 adults; Rs 5 children

>Janpath, near Connaught Place
Timings: Daily 11 am to 8 pm

>Khan Market, close to India Gate, near Lodhi Road
Timings: Daily 11 am to 8 pm

>Sarojini Nagar, near Dilli Haat
Timings: Tue to Sun 11 am to 8:30 pm

>Hanuman Mandir, Baba Kharak Singh Marg
Timings: Tue market from 10 am; closed Sun

Shankar's International Doll Museum

A collection of dolls brought together by cartoonist K Shankar Pillai during his world travels. Housed in the building of the Children's Book Trust, the Shankar International Doll Museum occupies over 5,000 square feet on the first floor of the building. There are special displays of over 150 Indian dolls in various costumes made at the doll's workshop attached to the museum. But the entire display houses more than 6,000 dolls. Dolls from China, Russia, England, Japan, Spain and Africa are among the selection from more than 80 countries. Doll-size tea sets, sofas, toys and, of course, houses are also preserved.

>Bahadur Shah Zafar Marg, Near ITO
Tel: 011 2331 6970/74 (5 lines)
Timings: Tue to Sun 10 am to 6 pm
Entry: Rs 10 Adults; Rs 5 children. Ticket counter closes at 5:30 pm
Web: www.childrenbooktrust.com

Sugar & Spice and everything nice

Choko la offers chocolate, cookie and cupcake classes during the summer, usually beginning in May. Children learn everything about the sweeter things in life from decorating, preparing dough from scratch, melting, mixing flavours and of course, lots and lots of tasting. The business of making sweets begins with a film on the history of chocolates, which Choko la makes by hand. Kids are properly attired with a chef's hat and apron. They get to take home what they have made in the class, if they haven't already eaten it. Kids need to be able to follow directions. Ideal for children ages 4 and older.

>36 Khan Market, Middle Lane

Tel: 011 4175 7570
Timings: Early May
Entry: Rs 1,800 for a 2-day course; Rs 2,100 for 3 days. Class lasts about 3 hours.

>Choko la Vasant Vihar, Priya Cinema Complex,
Basant Lok, Vasant Vihar
Tel: 011 4166 9595

No. 1: The whole of India is bowled over by cricket, so do not be a couch potato. Experience the thrill from the seats at Ferozshah Kotla Stadium.

Boys will be boys and they certainly love their toys. They can meander through the Car Parts Bazaar and even spy a complete engine ready to be bought. Car, plane and train enthusiasts can spend an afternoon zipping around a go-karting track; learning about India's history with railway travel at the Metro Museum or the Rail Museum; and see fighter jets up close at the Air Force Museum. 20/20 has nothing to do with having perfect eyesight, though fervent cricket fans have a tendency to question the eyesight of the field referee when a player on their favourite team is called out. Check out IPL and test matches at Ferozshah Kotla Stadium. Go team! Need some down time? There's always fishing in Okhla dam. And for those who like spy games, paintballing is just the ticket.

Buyer's Guide

Modelart

Although your son may be years away from a driver's license, yet alone owning wheels of his own, it's never too early to start. Check out the scale models of little red Corvettes, Porsches, BMWs, Harley Davidsons, Hummers and vintage WWII planes, tanks and helicopters at Modelart. Forget about Tata's one lakh Nano. With these cars, you don't have to hire a driver.

>F-27 Select Citywalk Mall, Saket, 1st flr
Tel: 011 4056 6966
Timings: Daily 10:30 am to 9:30 pm
Prices: From Rs 1,500

Gift Palace

If toy ambassadors, CNG taxis and auto rickshaws are more to his liking, pop in to the Gift Palace at Khan market.

>B-52 Khan Market
Tel: 011 2461 8613
Timings: Mon to Sat 11 am to 8:30 pm
Prices: From Rs 86

Car Parts Bazaar

One of the largest secondhand spare parts markets in the world can be found in Chandni Chowk. South of the Jama Masjid, the stalls that make up this bazaar pile seemingly impossibly high new and secondhand automobile parts from all models, ranging from speedometers and the all-important horn for Delhi traffic. One can even find complete engines waiting to be purchased. Big and little boys who are good with their hands, and even those who aren't, can find all the things they need to trick out any car.

>Khari Baoli Road after crossing the Fatehpuri Masjid on the western end of the main Chandni Chowk Road
Nearest Metro: Chawri Bazaar
Timings: Mon to Sat 11:30 am to 6 pm
Entry: Free

Cricket

You cannot say India without saying cricket. King Khan reigns supreme in Bollywood and cricket reigns supreme, well, everywhere else in India. The game is played anywhere there is grass or a street or a small wedge of space. Test matches are played at Ferozshah Kotla Stadium. You can also catch the Delhi Daredevils of the Indian Premier League (20/20) matches here.

>Ferozshah Kotla Stadium
Bahadur Shah Zafar Marg
Test matches: Sept to March
IPL matches: April to June
Tel for tickets: Tejpal Cricket Club 011 205 1994; Sunrise Cricket Club 011 248 4611.
Web: Go to www.kyazoonga.com for tickets to the Delhi Daredevils matches and for handy directions to the stadium. Cheap seats cost Rs 500. The more expensive ones go for Rs 4,000.

Fishing

Fishing is a wonderfully relaxing pastime and if you enjoy this sport or want to try it for the first time, try the Badhkal Lake, Surajkund Lake, Okhla Dam located on Mathura Road (closed on Mondays).

Badhkal Lake
Located 32 km from Delhi, the man-made lake is set in the middle of the Aravalli Hills in Haryana and is bordered by scenic gardens. Badhkal Lake is very famous for its water sports like boating, canoeing, kayaking, etc. (See *Beauty and the Beast*, pp.12–13.)

Bhalswa Lake
Bhalswa Lake located in

northeast Delhi is also home to a multi-sport and leisure complex. (See *Beauty and the Beast*, p.13.)

Okhla Dam
This dam is situated near the Yamuna river canal and has good facilities for fishing. It is a popular picnic spot surrounded with lush lawns. Friday is a good day to go and it is buzzing with visitors and local vendors.

>Okhla, Delhi–Mathura Road, near Holy Family Hospital
Timings: Sunrise to sunset
Tel: 011 2462 9365

Surajkund Lake
The site of the annual Surajkund Mela, there is a golf course, an exotic hotel and one can fish and also go boating on Surajkund Lake in Haryana. (See *Beauty and the Beast*, p.29.)

Go-Karting

Go-karting is a craze that has really caught fire in India, especially in and around Delhi in the last couple of years. It was launched in Faridabad in 1997 by JK Tyre. It provides quite an adrenaline rush to race around the track at high speeds. Formula 1 Champion Michael Schumacher learned the art and science of motor-racing on a go-karting track. Go-karting is suited for kids 10 and older.

Chandigarh (15 Scorpion cars)
>Albert Ross Racing, 41/8 Milestone, Ambala–Chandigarh highway, Zikrakpur. On the Delhi–Chandigarh GT Road at the union territory border just 20 minutes from Delhi. The track is 350 m and the facility offers 3 twin-engine karts, the rest as usual are with single engines.
Timings: Daily 3 pm to 10 pm
Entry: Rs 50 for 3 laps; Rs 100 for 8 laps; Rs 150 for 15 laps.
Length of track: 350 metres

Destination Point (10 Scorpion cars)
>12/2 Main Mathura Road, Faridabad
Tel: 0129 227 5139
Timings: Daily 11 am to 9 pm
Cost: Rs 100 for 6 laps; Rs 120 for 8 laps; Rs 180 for 15 laps.
Length of track: 320 metres

Fun and Fair (10 Scorpion cars)
>A-38 Mohan Cooperative Industrial Area
Main Mathura Road
Tel: 011 2695 9563
Timings: Daily 10 am to 9 pm
Cost: Rs 100 for 8 laps

Length of track: Less than 1 km

Planet Bowling (5 go-karts)
>A-38 Mohan Cooperative Industrial Estate
Mathura Road, Badarpur
Tel: 011 2695 9665
Timings: 10 am to 9:30 pm
Cost: Rs 100 per go-kart; Rs 50 per bumper car

Thirty Second Milestone (8 Mobile go-karts)
>Chander Nagar Gurgaon (Near Signature Tower)
Tel: 0124 233 2571
Timings: 11 am to 11 pm
Cost: Rs 100 for 6 laps
Web: www.32ndmilestone.com

Horse Play

Polo matches are fun to watch and even more fun to participate in. The Haryana Polo Club provides horses and trainers to whet the appetite of budding polo players. Managed by one of India's families that have almost become synonymous with polo, the Kalaans, boys will get a rush out on the field. Mornings are the best time to learn and games are usually played in the afternoons.

>Haryana Polo Club
Village Garhi—Harsaru, Gurgaon–Pataudi Road, Haryana
Tel: 011 2619 2407
Entry: Rs 4,500 for 90 minutes
Timings: Call for timings

Paintballing

We all like to paint the town red. But sometimes, we get to paint...each other...a rainbow of colours. Paintballing is some of the best fun that can be had in under an hour. It's action packed and takes some strategy to dodge the 'enemy' without being tagged. But half of the fun for kids would be to get tagged. Players get extra lives, after getting shot, they step off the field for 1 minute and join the game again. The paint is non-toxic and washable, though it's not advised kids wear their fancy clothes for the event. The intensity of the pellets from the guns is downgraded for children. Prices include rental of all equipment and gear: markers, C02 gas tanks, paintball pellets, overalls, chest guards, masks, gloves and field rental. All games are conducted under the supervision of trained instructors. For ages 10 and older.

>Best Westin Resort Country Club Resort, Gurgaon,
About 40 km from Delhi
Tel: 91 9971 200 530; 98187 38378 for information or for reservations

Timings: 10 am to 6:30 pm; closed Tue
Cost: Rs 500 per person plus taxes. Includes equipment rental and 50 paintballs. Reload packets of 50 paintballs are Rs 250. Food and drinks along with paintballing starts at Rs 850 per person.
Duration: About one hour, but the time depends on the kids
Web: paintballdelhi@gmail.com

Shooting

If you want to practice skeet, double trap, trap, air pistol shooting, the best place to go is the Dr Karni Singh shooting range close to Tughlaqabad Fort. Maharaja Karni Singh won the National Championship in Clay Pigeon Trap and Skeet for 17 years from 1960 to 1977. He led the Indian team in various international competitions and participated in 5 Olympic Games—Rome, Tokyo, Mexico, Munich and Moscow. Abhinav Bindra won a Gold medal for India in the 2008 Olympics in Beijing. The stadium is considered one of the best shooting ranges in Asia and is the location for shooting events of the Commonwealth Games of 2010. Equipment can be rented, so parents and kids can try out an afternoon of fun and won't have to commit to the sport.

>Tughlaqabad
Tel: 011 2698 6802
Timings: Daily 9 am to 5 pm
Entry: Imported air pistol rifles on rent and 50 pellets from Rs 100
Nearby sights: Qutab Minar, Humayun's Tomb, Akshardham Temple

Siri Fort Complex
>August Kranti Marg, near Siri Fort Auditorium
Tel: 011 2649 7482
Timings: Daily 6 am to 9 pm

Other Attractions

Indian Air Force Museum
Boys who love toys would really enjoy a visit to the Indian Air Force Museum. From pictures to uniforms and of course, a collection of different types of military aircraft, visitors get a true history of the Indian Air Force. The collection even houses some model aircraft that were donated from other countries. 'Heroes' walls, (please explain to your son it is not the sci-fi TV series) are dedicated to the men who died in various conflicts. The hangar is the very best part of the exhibition because it is more visual than reading intensive. About 15 aircraft are on display including the Westland, the first

plane to fly through Khyber Pass in 1929. There's the Night Fighter variant of the Vampire, 2-hunter fighter-bomber, the first generation Dassault Ouragan, the Sikorsky Whirlwind, MiG-21 and the Sukhoi-7. Also on display are a MiG-25 and troop and freight carrier. Just outside the main hangar lie the other fascinating displays of captured vehicles and aircraft wreckages. Perhaps the most intriguing of all the equipment is a missile guidance radar. Every year on October 8, which is celebrated as Air Force Day, visitors can view the larger transport aircrafts kept in the flight apron of Palam Air Base and a special parade of Indian Air Force. The museum has a cafeteria. (Also see *Make the Most of Museums*, p.83)

>Palam Air Force Station
Timings: Wed to Sun 10 am to 5 pm, closed on national holidays
Metro: Dwarka Morh
Tel: 011 2568 7194
Web site: http://indianairforce.nic.in
Nearby sights: Sulabh International Museum of Toilets, Buddha Jayanti Park and Sanskriti Museum of Indian Terracotta and Everyday Art
Nearby places to eat: Radisson, Centaur Hotel; Wimpy's in Janakpuri, McDonald's, Pizza Hut, Barista, Ruby Tuesday

Indian War Memorial
There are 3 museums at the Red Fort. The Indian Archaeological Museum, Indian War Memorial, Swatantra Sanghralaya and Senani Smarak contain artifacts from the Mughal period to India's freedom movement. Boys will probably be most fascinated with the Indian War Memorial which was once called the 'Red Fort Museum of Arms and Weapons'. It has a nice collection of weapons, including some from the Mughal era, signal lamps, telescopes and other instruments used during war. (See *Make the Most of Museums*, p.90.) Why settle for playing with the plastic variety when one can get a first-hand look at the real things that helped shape the India of today.

>Red Fort
Chandni Chowk, opposite Dariba Kalan
Tel: 011 2327 3703
Nearest Metro: Chandni Chowk
Timings: Tue to Sun 10 am to 5 pm
Entry: Rs 11 for Indians; Rs 100 for foreigners (includes tickets for all 3 museums)
Parking: Rs 10 for 4 hours
Nearby sights: Jama Masjid,

Chandni Chowk, Khari Baoli, Daryaganj, Gates of Old Delhi, St James Church, Car Parts Bazaar
Nearby places to eat: Food stalls in Chandni Chowk, Paranthe Wali Gali, Moti Mahal Restaurant, Karim's

Metro Museum
The Delhi Metro Rail Corporation (DMRC) has opened a Metro Museum, the first in the country, to catalogue its achievements. Located at the Patel Chowk station, the museum houses artifacts from various stages as the metro expanded across India. There are uniforms, grilling machines and other tools used to build the metro. A souvenir shop sells books, tokens, ties and other knick-knacks. For those kids who really enjoy taking the metro, this is definitely a must-see stop. The Museum has 2 touch screen computers that play a movie about the DMRC, mannequins wearing the different uniforms worn by staff, a model of the Metro train, models of stations and close-circuit television camera which visitors can also operate. This is a temporary location for the museum as plans are afoot to open a more comprehensive museum at the Qutab Minar station. (See *Make the Most of Museums*, pp.84–5.)

>Patel Chowk metro station
Timings: Tue to Sun 10 am to 4 pm
Entry: Visitors will need a journey token or smart card to enter.
Web: www.delhimetrorail.com/commuters for a nice slideshow (click on the bottom right corner of the metro museum page)
Nearby sights: India Gate, Safdarjung Tomb, Indira Gandhi Memorial Museum, Gandhi Smriti, Dilli Haat, India Gate, Jantar Mantar
Nearby places to eat: Hotel Le Meridien, Imperial Hotel, Hotel Inter-Continental, Parikrama, Delhi Darbar, Nizam's Kathi Kebabs, McDonald's, Pizza Hut, Domino's Pizza, Nirula's, Ruby Tuesday, Barista, Café Coffee Day and the food stalls at Dilli Haat

National Police Museum
A great place for aspiring Agent Cody Bankses to learn facts about the police force is the National Police Museum. Items on display include confiscated goods, records of forgery, and fascinating articles, of national as well as international importance. Visitors also get an insight into forensic techniques used to solve crimes.

>Central Bureau of Investigation HQ, CGO Complex, Lodhi Road
Timings: Mon to Fri 10:30 am

to 4:30 pm; closed weekends
Nearest Metro: Central Secretariat
Entry: Free
Nearby sights: India Gate, Rashtrapati Bhavan, Lotus Temple, Nizamuddin's Shrine
Nearby places to eat: Eatopia at India Habitat Centre, restaurants at Khan Market, Basil and Thyme. If you're thinking you want to do some shopping too, head over to Ansal Plaza or South Ex Part II.

National Science Centre
Dinosaurs reign supreme at the National Science Centre (see *Make the Most of Museums*, pp.88–9). What's great about the Dinosaur Gallery is that it recreates how the world probably looked millions of years ago. Visitors are lead through a dark chamber full of models of strange-looking creatures akin to Jurassic Park.
Some of the creatures are mechanized and move their heads, including being wired for sound, so it does add a realistic dimension to the experience. Little children may get scared when the big dinosaurs start to move and roar, but the older ones are likely to want to go through the display again. The interactive displays also give information on how the earth was populated and the evolution of mankind.
>Just before Gate No.1, Bhairon Road, Pragati Maidan
Tel: 011 2337 1893/2337 1945
Metro: Pragati Maidan
Timings: Daily 10 am to 5:30 pm
Entry: Rs 20
Nearby sights: Crafts Museum, Purana Qila, National Zoo, India Gate, Nizamuddin's Shrine
Nearby places to eat: Nathu's and Baci (see *Eats*, pp.132–3) in Sunder Nagar market; Oberoi Hotel (check out the café in the basement); Flavors (see *Eats*, p.136) in Defence Colony, All American Diner (see *Eats*, p.128) at the India Habitat Centre on Lodhi Road

Pro Bono Publico Museum for Vintage and Classic Cars
Gentlemen, start your engines. Pro Bono Publico, the Titus & Co. Museum for Vintage and Classic Cars, has a 6,000 square foot space that has nearly 70 vintage cars, including old American cars like a 1947 Chrysler Windsor and Buicks dating back from 1938. Some more modern offerings include the likes of a 4.2 turbo charged diesel Toyota Land Cruiser, Land Rover and Prado.
About 90% of the cars in the collection once belonged to the country's royals. The name of the museum, which means for the public good, showcases the private cars

owned by collector Diljeet Titus.

>Titus farm, Jaunpur village, near Bishan Singh Bedi farms, Mehrauli
Tel: 011 2665 8635 (call for directions and an appointment)
Timings: Mon to Sat 10 am to 6 pm

Sulabh International Museum of Toilets
Boys can't resist bathroom humour. The Sulabh International Museum of Toilets fits the bill. It goes without saying that this museum is one of a kind. The museum's artifacts trace the evolution of the toilet or 'loo', dating from 2,500 BC to the present. Keen visitors will get all they need to know about toilet-based technology, toilet etiquette, various laws and social customs through photos and even odes written to the toilet. Kids will learn how the first flushable indoor toilet came to be known as the crapper. Complete the visit by checking out the bounty of jokes to share with friends on the school yard.

>At Mahavir Enclave, on the main Palam Dabri Marg
Nearest Metro: Dwarka Morh
Tel: 011 2503 1518
Timings: Mon to Sat 10 am to 5 pm
Nearby places to eat: Nirula's in Dwarka; Wimpy's in Janakpuri; McDonald's, Pizza Hut, Barista, Ruby Tuesday and many popular restaurants serving all types of cuisines can be found in Janakpuri District Centre.

No. 1: Bal Bhavan National Children's Museum and Aquarium. It's like having 10 different activities rolled into one.

It can be rather difficult choosing activities that are somewhat more 'indoor' that both guys and dolls will enjoy, and that will equally stimulate their interests. One can never go wrong when the activities involve other kids, adventure, creativity and just plain fun. Whether they enjoy working with their hands, singing, dancing or exercising, the menu of things for kids to enjoy is vast. Let your child bring out the artist in herself at The Colour Factory; scale a wall or just be free at Weekend clubs. Or if the kids are restless to step out, and still be treated as kids, they could take the special guided walks for children to learn a bit about the city's monuments.

Lots to See and Do

Bal Bhavan National Children's Museum and Aquarium

Imagine throwing the National Zoo, Nehru Planetarium and Children's Park near India Gate into a bowl and adding a little water and stirring. It is likely you would end up with the Bal Bhavan National Children's Museum and Aquarium. The Aviary has over 20 breeds of birds. Children learn about their food habits and how they survive in the wild. As the sessions are quite interactive, kids even learn how to maintain the pH balance of an aquarium if they decide to have one at home. A gallery displays art by children. Additionally, kids will find toys from India and other countries, workshops on traditional jewellery making, and creative and performing arts including puppet making, theatre, music and dance. Kids can even enjoy a ride on a mini train in the Science Park. Summer camps are also organized. The fees are unbelievably low. Ideal for children ages 5 to 16.

>1 Kotla Road, near ITO
Tel: 011 2326 7961
Nearest Metro: Central Secretariat

Timings: Mon to Fri 9 am to 5:30 pm
Entry: Membership Rs 7; annual fee of Rs 50 for children ages 5 to 12; Rs 100 for ages 12 to 16
Web: www.nationalbalbhavan.nic.in

Children's Heritage Museum

The Archaeological Survey of India has set up a Heritage Museum for children, the first of its kind, in a building next to the fifteenth century Siri Fort wall in South Delhi. The museum caters to children aged 6 to 18 years, bringing the history of India alive through displays and artifacts. The Past–Present hall has photos of many monuments showing how they have evolved over time. The photos emphasize how important it is to preserve the monuments as some have fallen into disrepair, and to not deface them as some monuments have been photographed with graffiti and posters glued to them. The museum also houses artifacts and antiquities recovered from historical sites all over the country and have on display rare findings by the ASI during their many excavation projects. A guide quizzes children about how well they know their history after the tour.

>Siri Fort complex
Timings: Daily 10 am to 6 pm

The Colour Factory

The plates and cups at Good Earth will have nothing like the ceramics the kids will produce at The Colour Factory. A range of items from cups, soap dishes, motorcycles, plates and figurines can be painted. The more adventurous can try their hands on the potter's wheel and create their own knick-knacks. Everything is provided and art work can be left for glazing and picked up in 4 to 5 days. Birthday parties can be held for Rs 300 per person which includes a snack.

>2nd Flr, Select Citywalk Mall, Press Enclave Road, Saket
Tel: 011 4059 7515
Timings: Daily 11 am to 8 pm
Cost: From Rs 225
Web: www.thecolourfactory.in/contact.htm

>120, 1st Flr, DT Mega Mall, DLF
Tel: 0124 437 0958
Timings: Mon to Fri 11 am to 8 pm; weekends 11 am to 9 pm

Crafts Museum

Crafts Museum, opened in 1956, showcases materials, techniques, designs and traditional crafts from across India. Some of the best artisans from around the country demonstrate their wares in stalls, giving the feel of a typical day in the life of the extraordinarily skilled village people who make their living this way. The museum honours artisans who have kept traditional art alive. The museum has a collection of 20,000 items in all media from across India. Children can assist the artisans if they are so inclined. Great for all ages. The museum shop sells crafts, books and other knick-knacks.

>Gate No. 2, Bhairon Road, Pragati Maidan
Tel: 011 2337 1641/1370/1887
Timings: Tue to Sun 10 am to 5:30 pm; closed on government holidays

CribRocka Weekend Club
The name is a bit of a tongue-twister. However, it is quite appropriate as the CribRocka Weekend Club will get kids twisting, shaking, jamming, rockin' and rollin' and painting and crafting. Can one club fit so much into a weekend? The answer is a resounding yes. The two-and-a-half-hour activity sessions include various forms of dance including ballet and hip-hop. Kids can also channel their inner Kareena Kapoors or Akshay Kumars by acting in front of a camera. The arts and crafts, bamboo works and math and science activities breed stimulation and creativity. Parents can make this a 2-day affair as on Sundays, the kids can look forward to animal yoga, where they can derive the benefits of yoga through various animal poses. Crouching tiger, hidden dragon anyone? There are also lavish doses of story-telling, puppet making and charades. The activities are appropriate for children ages 3 to 9. Class sizes are kept to 12 to 15 kids.

>F-40 South Extension Part I, Ground Flr (next to Wills Lifestyle)
Tel: 99582 01185; 98105 27828
Timings: Sat and Sun 3 pm to 5:30 pm; during the summer months (May to July) 3 pm to 5 pm. The weekend club may extend into the weekdays. Call for details.
Entry: Rs 2,800 for a month of activities or a drop-in fee of Rs 700

Diksha Weekend Classical Workshop
Forget about hip-hop and bhangra. The Diksha Weekend Classical Workshop offers theatre, music, classical dance, Sanskrit chanting, drawings and paintings for children ages 4 to 14. Children learn from professional artistes.

>11-B Baba Kharak Singh Marg,
Next to RML Hospital Emergency
Tel: 011 2374 2083
Timings: Fri and Sat 4 pm to 7:30 pm
Nearest Metro: Patel Chowk, Rajiv Chowk
Email: aksharatheatre@rediffmail.com

Flight to nowhere

Bahadur Chand Gupta, a retired Indian Airlines engineer, helps kids soar without actually taking off. The 'virtual journeys' are on a discontinued Airbus 300 he purchased on a whim. It allows passengers to experience sitting on a plane, listening to announcements and receiving in-flight food service. For about Rs 150, 'passengers' are shown how to buckle up, served snacks, allowed into the cockpit, given the chance to try on an oxygen mask, and even exit via the emergency slide. The aircraft, located in Dwarka, near the domestic airport, is missing some sections, but still accommodates 170 people.

>Centre for Civil Aviation Training
Sector 8, A Block, opposite CRPF camp, Dwarka
Tel: 011 55 772 2466
Metro: Dwarka Sector 9
Timings: Daily 9 am to 2 pm
Entry: Rs 150
Web: www.ccat.in/aeroplanet.htm

Get the Scoop

One museum that you'll be begging the kids to leave is Nirula's Ice Cream Museum. Part of the Noida ice cream factory was converted to celebrate one of the joys of hot summer days. Visitors are greeted by posters of ice cream cones and melted chocolate is painted on the stairs. The wall facing the entrance is a colourful world map with dotted lines and ice cream cones that trace the journey of the frozen dessert through various countries. The museum provides visitors an entertaining mix of ice cream-related facts, trivia and ice cream making action in the mixing room. Children will learn about manufacturing and packaging processes of the more than 15,000 litres of fresh ice cream which Nirula's produces daily. All of the flavours that are sold in the stores are also displayed on stickers which are framed on various walls. The visit takes about 30 minutes and kids are treated to snacks at the adjacent restaurant afterward. The museum is open twice a week for children between ages 7 and 11. Entry is free but batches of 30 to 40 kids only. Individuals can't take a tour.

>C-135 Sector 2, Noida (near the Delhi–Noida border just beyond the DND tollgates)
Tel: 95 120 244 52607; to confirm time and date call Tulsi Walia at 93133 73 819
Timings: By appointment only; Tue to Fri

Habitat Children's Book Forum

The Habitat Children's Book Forum at the India Habitat Centre holds creative writing classes, readings and meet-the-author sessions once a month. Set up by a group of children's writers, the forum highlights books by Indian authors. Call for details.

>Habitat World, India Habitat Centre, Lodhi Estate
Tel: 011 2468 2222

House of Puppets

From the Mumbai slums featured in Oscar-winning movie *Slumdog Millionaire* to the slums near Shadipur depot on the Dwarka–Indraprastha metro line, absolute gems can be found within these walls. For over 50 years, puppeteers, magicians, acrobats, drummers and dancers have been coming to Kathputli Colony to showcase their art. The colony is named for the Hindi word for wooden puppet. The House of Puppets hosts a puppet show twice a month. From dancing Rajasthani puppets to children on stilts, the show also includes fire eaters and a man who swallows a sword. After seeing the spectacle of the dancers and the magicians, kids definitely won't mind *slumming* it.

>Kathputli Colony, near Shadipur depot
Tel: Kailash Bhatt 99683 84447
Timings: 4 pm every second and fourth Saturday
Entry: Rs 400 per person

Katkatha Puppet Arts Trust

Katkatha Puppet Arts Trust offers workshops on how to create and work with puppets, an art form that has been around in India for more than 3,000 years. Children are taught how to make puppets, create stories around the puppets and sometimes put it all together in a show. The trust also holds performances including staging of Shakespeare's *Twelfth Night* and the *Little Blue Planet*.

>India Habitat Centre, Lodhi Road; Cambridge School in New Friends Colony among the venues around the city
Tel: Anurupa Roy 98105 11360
Timings: Workshops vary, call Ms Roy for details
Web: www.katkatha.org

Kite Market

For those who want to

indulge in flights of fancy or become fleet-footed kite runners, go to Lal Kuan kite market to find kites of all shapes, sizes, colours and motifs. Fancy a Spiderman kite? No problem. How about Shah Rukh Khan? It can be had for Rs 100. There are kites that fit every pocketbook with prices ranging from Rs 50 for basic kites to Rs 250 for the more elaborate, aerodynamic varieties. About 15 to 20 stalls sell kites year round, but in 'kite season'—yes, there's a kite season that runs from about 1 to 15 August—at least 150 to 200 stalls spring up selling kites of all shapes and sizes. It is a tradition to fly the kites on 15 August, which is Independence day. The most popular kites are the tricolour, which range in price from Rs 15 to Rs 100. Check out Jawahar Kite House or Bishen Chand and Sons, the latter around since the 1930s.

>Lal Kuan Market, Old Delhi
Timings: Closed on Sun

Leap Years School and Activity Centre
There's no better way to discover Delhi than by foot. Leap Years School and Activity Centre organizes walks for children ages 4 to 14 through the city's historical past. Areas covered include Old Delhi, Purana Qila, Tughlaqabad and Sanjay Van. Kids are dropped off and picked up from the school.

>23 Green Avenue, Vasant Kunj
Tel: 011 2689 1223
Timings: Call for timings as activities vary
Entry: Rs 300 including a small snack

Mast Monkeys Hobby Classes
Mast Monkeys Fun and Learning Hobby Classes has a full menu of activities for children from ages 18 months to 18 years old. Activities are geared for specific ages and skill levels. From creating beautiful rangolis, creative writing, arts and crafts, theatre, puppetry, gardening, Bollywood dance and kathak, music and sing-alongs, yoga, tae-kwan-do and magic workshops taught by actual magicians, there are limitless possibilities for the kids. Parents can pay a monthly membership or a drop-in fee.

>B-518 New Friends Colony
Tel: Malavida Kaura at 98100 15723
Timings: Varies, call and mention the activities you are interested in
Entry: Rs 300 for an activity or Rs 2,000 per month

National Philatelic Museum
For laypersons, the National Philatelic Museum, also known as the stamp museum, has an extensive collection of rare stamps. A real treat for stamp enthusiasts is the first stamp issued in India by the Sindh Dak in 1854. There is a lot of information about India's postal history and all of the stamps issued thus far by the government are on display. There is also a large collection of foreign stamps, first day covers and special cancelations. A sales counter which sells stamps from around the globe can help budding collectors get started.

>Department of Post, In Dak Bhavan, Sardar Patel Chowk on Parliament Street or Sansad Marg
Tel: 011 2303 6447
Timings: Mon to Fri 10 am to 5 pm
Nearest Metro: Patel Chowk
Nearby places to eat: Hotel The Park, Hotel Le Meridien, Imperial Hotel, Hotel Inter-Continental, Parikrama Revolving Restaurant, Gaylord, El Rodeo, Bercos, Zen Restaurant, Delhi Darbar, Nizam's Kathi Kebabs and Standard Restaurant. For snacks and fast foods: Bengali Market (sweets and chat), Kake da hotel (Indian food), Wenger's, McDonald's, Pizza Hut, Domino's Pizza, Nirula's, Ruby Tuesday, Sona Rupa, Starbeans, Barista, Café Coffee Day and innumerable roadside food stalls.

National Rail Museum
Fun for everyone who has ever ridden a train and those who have not, the National Rail Museum has long retired locomotives from the mid-19th and 20th centuries from all over India. Take a ride on a working train for Rs 10 to see all the trains, and then decide what you want to revisit on foot later. The indoor gallery has models of trains from the Raj era to more recent times, life-like models of English railway officials, crockery, maps and a section for the blind. The Joy Express is also a favourite. The model station sells chips and juice. Green lawns to run on and a bookshop round out the experience.

>Chanakyapuri
Tel: 011 2688 0804
Timings: Tue to Sun 9:30 am to 7:30 pm (April to Sept); Closed on national holidays.
Entry: Rs 10 for adults; Rs 3 for children. Admission is free on Tue for children under 12.

Sangeet Natak Akademi
Do, Re, Mi, Fa, Sol, La, Ti, Do. Sangeet Natak Akademi is a music lover's delight. India's

first National Academy for music, dance and drama also has a fabulous musical instruments collection. The main gallery of the museum has over 200 musical instruments and an extensive audio-visual archive where kids can listen to various music styles.

>Rabindra Bhavan, Feroze Shah Road
Tel: 011 2338 7246
Metro: Central Secretariat
Timings: Tue to Sun 9:30 am to 6 pm
Web: www.sangeetnatak.org

Yoga

Om. Om. Om. Yoga isn't just for adults as one can tell from looking at kids who have now actively taken up the exercise regime. Yoga classes for children emphasize breathing and channeling energy to attain calmness. Children should wear comfortable clothing, carry a water bottle and go to the class on an empty stomach.

Laughter Yoga
Regulars are mainly the retired set and stay-at-home wives, but that doesn't mean young people won't enjoy an early morning laughing session. The sessions begin around 6 to 6:30 am every day in various parks around the city. Kids will get a kick out of the 'mobile laugh' and the politically incorrect 'Chinese laugh'. Lots of self-appreciation with calls of 'very good' after each phase. Soon pretend laughter will turn into real belly-jiggling giggles. Check the Web for a club nearest to your location.

>Laughter Club of Delhi
Tel: 011 2721 7164; call for timings and locations
Web: www.laughteryoga.org

Mother and Child Yoga
Keep fit together in a fun interactive hour of movement, stretching and breathing.

>Mast Monkeys Fun and Learning Hobby Classes
B-518 New Friends Colony
Tel: Malavika Kaura 98100 15723
Timings: 9 am to 10 am
Entry: Rs 650 per month, call for drop-in rates

Sivananda
What a great way for kids to spend a Sunday morning before heading to a fabulous brunch. Children learn the 5 pillars of Sivananda Yoga—asana (proper exercise); pranayam (proper breathing); shavasan (proper relaxation); diet and meditation.

> Sector 6, behind DAV School, Dwarka
Tel: 011 4556 6015

Timings: Sun 10 am to 11:30 am
Nearest Metro: Dwarka Sector 11
Entry: Rs 50 per class

>A-41, Kailash Colony
Tel: 011 2924 086; 011 2923 0962
Entry: Rs 50 per class for kids ages 6 to 10
Timings: Sun 10 am to noon
Web: www.sivananda.org/delhi

Weekend Club

The weekend might actually end up being a proper weekend after all. Sure the kids will still get up at 6 am, though you have to drag them out of bed on school days. Kids can be dropped off at the Weekend Club at Select Citywalk Mall to participate in activities from pottery and T-shirt making, body art, jewellery designing to bouncy castles and a toy train. Live music, though a bit on the LOUD side, plays throughout. Food stalls are in the area selling the typical fare. The activities are appropriate for kids ages 2 and older, though tweens and teens will probably turn their noses up at this sort of thing.

>Kids Fountain Terrace, Level 2, Select Citywalk Mall
Press Enclave Road, Saket
Tel: 99991 19414 (Harpeet Suri)
Timings: Sat and Sun noon to 10 pm
Entry: Activities are priced between Rs 50 and Rs 150

Yoga Studio

Parents and children alike who have never tried yoga, have become converts due to the excellent instruction by teacher Seema Sondhi at Yoga Studio. Children as young as 18 months are encouraged to improve flexibility and breathing. Some activities involve parent and child or sometimes just the child. Yoga mats are provided. Ideal for children from 18 months old.

>D-43 Hauz Khas
Tel: Seema Sondhi 98111 31368
Timings: Sat 10 am onwards
Entry: Rs 500 per session; price includes ice cream or another treat for the child.
Web: www.theyogastudio.info

Yogalife Studio

The aim of the classes is to increase energy levels in children and instill calmness through meditation and breathing exercises. The asanas will improve flexibility, and laughter yoga, which is also part of the class, is a fun way to boost immunity and just put the kids in a good mood. Ideal for children ages 6 to 13.

>C-366 Defence Colony
Tel: Manoj 98118 63332
Timings: Conducted per demand, call for timings
Entry: Rs 250 per class
Web: www.yogalifestudio.org
Email: info@yogalife.org

No. 1: All the entertainment fit for kings, queens, princes and princesses at Ambience Mall in Gurgaon.

When the weather is great in Delhi and a nice breeze is kissing the air, it's time to get out and get moving to discover the gems in the city that will put a smile on your face and a skip in your step. From well-maintained sports complexes that offer everything from swimming to tennis to teeing off at internationally renowned golf courses; catching the latest flick at movie theatres; enjoying the 3 big Bs of bowling, bungee jumping and ballooning; horse-back riding; going to swimming pools and water parks and getting the thrill of your life at various amusement parks, give museums a rest for the day and rediscover your inner child with your children.

Adventure Sports / Operators

Aero Club of India

You don't need wings when the Aero Club of India can provide them for you in the form of paragliders, bungee cords, micro light flying, skydiving and hang gliding. The club is recognized by the Ministry of Youth Affairs and Sports by the Government of India and is a member of the international aviation organization, Federation Aeronautique Internationale (FAI). This is ideal for children 12 and older.

>Safdarjung Airport, Aurobindo Marg
Tel: 011 2461 8931
Web: www.aeroclubofindia.org

The Ballooning Club of India

Before security became an issue, hot air balloons from The Ballooning Club of India used to soar above Delhi's monuments, forts and parks, allowing a breathtaking aerial view of the city. Now, the balloon takes off from Damdama Lake. Instead of spying monuments, one is likely to see wild rabbits and foxes, and is a wonderful way to view nature from above. The balloons hold up to 10 people and rise to heights of over 800 feet. The basket has no seats, so you will have to stand. The ride is best suited for children 5 and older. They will have to be accompanied by an adult. Kids love the thrill of taking off and landing and regular rides last one hour. It costs Rs 10,000 for 10 people, but a 15% discount is given for groups of 10. There are no toilets on board the balloon so do the needful before the ascent. It can get windy so pack a sweater or pull-over. Winter months are best for the balloon ride. The club also organizes the International Balloon Mela every year (see also *Day Trippin'*, p.116).

>Office: 8-B Bahadur Shah Zafar Marg
Tel: 011 2371 6665; Mr Gupta (chairman) 98100 11382
Departure point: Damdama Lake, Haryana
Entry: Rs 300 per child, Rs 500 for adults with a minimum of 10 people.
Timings: Sept to March 6:30 am. It's usually too hot from April to May, but it really depends on the weather. You can call and make a booking if the weather is fine.

Delhi Tourism Adventure division
From day picnics, water sports, rock climbing, parasailing, rafting and other activities that will have you gliding, sliding, flying and swimming, Delhi Tourism organizes it all. You can go parasailing at Kanwarshikha near Sohna in Haryana, about 60 km from Delhi. Professional instructors on hand make sure you land in one piece. Make bookings through the Delhi Tourism Development Corporation. Gather relatives or friends as a minimum of 10 people is required. Larger group sizes are required for the trekking trips, but smaller groups can pay slightly more per person and tailor their own trips.

>Central Reservation Office Baba Kharak Singh Marg
Tel: 011 2336 3607
Entry: Depend on group size and activity
Web: www.delhitourism.nic.in/publicpage/adventurelist.aspx

Indian Mountaineering Foundation
The Indian Mountaineering Foundation offers rock climbing and rappelling (also see *Beauty and the Beast*, p.26).

>Indian Mountaineering Federation
6 Benito Jaurez Marg, opposite Anand Niketan
Tel: 011 2411 1211
Entry: Rs 50 per 4 hours
Timings: 3 pm to 7 pm daily, except national holidays

Isan Sky Explorers
Isan Sky Explorers provides all kinds of adventure sports

including hot air ballooning, parasailing, rappelling and camping. Rates include breakfast and lunch or all meals for overnight stays. The activities are organized all year round in Gurgaon and Damdama Lake.

>C-123 Defence Colony
Tel: Ms Singh 98103 72327
Entry: From 650 without meals depending on the activity; minimum group of 20 for trekking; smaller groups are OK for camping and other activities

Peak Adventure Travel
Specializes in trekking, camping, climbing and river expeditions.

Corporate Office
>C-114, Sector 2, Noida
Tel: 0120 405 2615 to 99; 9811636814/9810352536
Web: www.peakadventuretour.com

Operational Office
>A/2A-2, 1st Flr Shiv Arcade
Acharya Niketan, Mayur Vihar Phase I

Wanderlust
Other than the Ballooning Club, balloon rides are also offered by Wanderlust.

>G-18, 2nd Flr, Masjid Moth, GK Part II
Tel: 011 4163 6757
Timings: 10 am to 10 pm

mainly in the month of July. According to a representative, it really depends on permissions from the Indian government.

Amusement / Water Parks

Aapno Ghar
Aapno Ghar gives entertainment a whole new meaning and for an entry fee of Rs 200 that gives you access to all the rides all day long. You just cannot beat the price on what you get. There are rides of every shape, speed, for every age group so even the little kids won't feel left out; coin-operated, flying saucers, trains and merry-go-rounds too. Large green open spaces means you don't have to buy the food from the concession stands and can pitch a blanket and have a picnic as you recover from the activities. Aapno Ghar would make a wonderful venue for a kids' birthday party.

>43rd Mile Stone Village Shikhopur
Delhi–Jaipur Road, NH-8
Gurgaon
Tel: 0124 237 1281
Timings: Daily 11 am to 7 pm
Entry: Rs 200
Web: www.aapnoghar.com

Adventure Island
Taking up a massive 62 acres in northwest Delhi,

Adventure Island is chock full of rides and a water park. The park is adjacent to Metro Walk Mall. The 26 rides cater to kids from age 2 and up. Teens will especially like the cyclone and the Derby Devil bumper cars are perfect for the 4 and under set. There are lots of food options, rides, shows and parking spaces. The water park is nice to look at but perilous to be in. We would advise against it unless you can guarantee that you and your kids will not laugh with your mouths open and ingest any water!

>Metro Walk, Sector 10, Rohini, opposite Rithala Metro Station
Metro: Rithala
Phone information centre: 120 465 0000
Timings: Mon to Fri noon to 9 pm; Sat and Sun 2 pm to 11 pm
Entry: Mon to Fri Rs 300 for adults, Rs 250 for children; Weekends and holidays Rs 375 for adults, Rs 300 for children

Ansal Plaza

Funkie Orbits (See below, pp.67–8.)

> CG-5/A, (near South Extension)
Tel: 011 2626 1365
Timings: 11 am to 10:30 pm

Drizzling Land

Drizzling Land is more amusement park than water park but the water rides are a nice way to cool off during the summer.

>Delhi–Rohtak Road Asauda More, Bahadurgarh
Tel: 011 4234 0980
Timings: Daily 10 am to 7 pm
Entry: Rs 250

>Ghaziabad Duhai, NH-58, near NRIMR College, Ghaziabad
Tel: 95120 323 4130
Timings: Daily 11 am to 9 pm
Entry: Rs 100

Fun 'n' Food Village

Spread over an area of 10 acres, the Fun 'n' Food Village has the largest wave pool in Delhi, longest water slide in the country and the largest indoor snow park which includes ice skating in the winter. The water park has a wide range of water rides, pools and other rides. The seemingly never-ending water slides are the biggest draw. It also showcases culture and traditional arts and crafts of India. There are many performances by the local artists and crafts displays inside the park. There are more than 20 rides in the amusement park, of which the most popular are the Mono Rail and the Flying Carpet. There's also a play area with balls, a ferris wheel and mini-train.

>Old Delhi–Gurgaon Road, Kapashera
Metro: From Rohini and get off at the Kapashera station
Tel: 011 2506 4503
Timings: Daily 10 am to 10 pm in summer; 10 am to 8 pm in winter; closed Diwali
Entry: Rs 350 adults, Rs 300 children; Rs 50 extra on weekends and holidays
Web: www.funfood.com

Fun Town

Fun Town is an amusement park and water park with lots of big slides; resort facilities, swimming pool and restaurant.

>Delhi–Rohtak Highway, Asauda Mod, Bahadurgarh
Tel: 951276 280180
Timings: Daily 10 am to 8 pm
Entry: Rs 250 adults, Rs 200 children; free for kids less than 33 inches

Splash Water Park

Go splash about in a wave pool, kiddie pool, curving slides, family slide, cyclone slide, straight slide or get jiggy and do the electric slide under the sprinklers at Splash Water Park. You can even glide down the lazy river in a tube. Essentially, water, water everywhere but please don't have a drink. Amusement park rides such as bumper cars, a sky train and tea cup rides are also on offer after you've put on dry clothes.

>Main GT Karnal Road near Alipur
Tel: 011 6515 0989, 011 2770 8503, 011 2770 8504
Timings: Daily 10 am to 8 pm
Entry: Rs 250 adults (above 4 ft 6 in); Rs 200 children (below 4 ft 6 in); Weekends adults Rs 300, children Rs 250
Web: www.splashwaterpark.co.in

Wet 'n' Wild Resort

Wet 'n' Wild Resort lives up to the name. Located at about 30 km from Daula Kuan near Gurgaon, the water rides and bowling alley attract hordes of visitors. There is an amusement park within the amusement park where children have regular playground equipment including swings. Huge green lawns almost beg to be played on.

>45 Milestone, National Highway 8
Village Naurangpur, Gurgaon
Tel: 0124 237 2931
Timings: Daily 10 am to 8 pm
Entry: Adults Rs 200; Children Rs 150 ages 10 and younger

Worlds of Wonder @ Entertainment City
Ideal for kids 10 and older as there is a strict height requirement of at least 5 feet at Worlds of Wonder. The rides are for those who possess a lot of courage, certainly not for the faint-hearted, and can rival rides at international amusement parks. The park has more than 30 rides and is divided into entertainment zones for kids, teenagers and for families. Each zone has a specific set of entertainment and food courts geared toward that segment. If there's any energy left, go next door to The Great India Place and catch a flick at the 6-screen cinema.

> The Great India Place, Plot No. A-2, Sector 38, Noida
Tel: 0120 465 0000
Timings: Daily noon to 8 pm
Entry: Rs 275 adults, Rs 225 children

Bowling

Amoeba (4 lanes)
>Shop No. 4A, Metropolitan Mall (MGF), MG Road Gurgaon
Tel: 0124 320 8288
Timings: Daily 11 am to 11 pm
Entry: Rs 100 to Rs 125 per game

Blu-O (24 lanes)
Spread over 42,500 square feet in Ambi Mall in Gurgaon, it is a complete gaming experience with karaoke rooms, a tattoo bar, gaming stations, i.e., an X-box 360 room, and live music. Located on level 4, lanes can be booked for birthday parties also.

> NH-8 Road, Ambience Mall, Level 4, Gurgaon
Tel: 0124 466 5611
Timings: 11 am to 11:30 pm
Entry: Rs 100 per game before 5 pm; Rs 175 after 5 pm; Rs 35 for shoe rental

City Bowl (4 lanes)
>Shopprix Mall, 2nd Flr, Sector 61, Noida
Tel: 0120 433 4477
Timings: Daily 11 am to 11 pm
Entry: Rs 125 per game

Destination Point (4 lanes)
Also offers a video game parlour, rock climbing and has a restaurant.

>12/2 Main Mathura Road, Faridabad
Tel: 95129 2275139
Timings: Daily 11 am to 9 pm
Entry: Rs 100 per game

First Bowl (4 lanes)
>32nd Milestone, NH-8 Gurgaon
Tel: 0124 233 2571
Timings: Daily 11:30 am to 11:30 pm
Entry: Rs 150 per game

Fun 'n' Fair (2 lanes)
>A-38 Mohan Cooperative Industrial Area, Main Mathura Road
Tel: 011 2695 9563
Timings: Daily 10 am to 9 pm
Entry: Rs 100 per game

Future Bowl (6 lanes)
Video game parlour and snack bar

>Essex Farms, Aurobindo Marg, under IIT Flyover
Tel: 011 2652 8080
Timings: Daily 11 am to 11:30 pm
Entry: Rs 200 per game

Galaxy Entertainment (6 lanes)
>The Great India Place, 3rd Flr, Entertainment City, Plot No. A-2, Noida
Tel: 93507 43866
Timings: Daily 11 am to 11 pm
Entry: Weekdays Rs 150 per game; weekends Rs 200 per game

Planet Bowling (4 lanes)
>A-38 Mohan Cooperative Industrial Estate Mathura Road, Badarpur (near Ford showroom)
Tel: 011 2695 9665
Timings: Daily 10 am to 9:30 pm
Entry: Rs 100 per game

Thirty Second Milestone (4 lanes)
>Chander Nagar Gurgaon (Near Signature Tower)
Tel: 0124 233 2571
Timings: Daily 11:30 am to 11:30 pm
Entry: Rs 150 per game
Web: www.32ndmilestone.com

Bungee Jumping

If braving Delhi traffic at rush hour doesn't produce enough of a high, then bungee jumping is the way to go. Landlocked city dwellers don't have to venture beyond Jawaharlal Nehru Stadium where a mobile crane has been set up. Wanderlust also has sites outside the city for those looking for adventure-themed outings.

Aero Club of India
Bungee jumping and other adventure sports. (See *Adventure Sports*, p.57.)

>Safdarjung Airport, Aurobindo Marg
Tel: 011 2462 1341

Wanderlust Travels
>G-18, 2nd Flr, Masjid Moth, GK Part II
Tel: 011 4163 6757
Timings: July 10 am to 10 pm. According to a representative, it really depends on permissions from the Indian government.
Specifications: From 90 to 330 feet.
Restrictions: For ages 14

to 50. Teens will need a parent signature and over 50s will need a doctor's note regarding their health.
Entry: From Rs 600 to Rs 1000 per person.
Web: www.wanderlustindia.com/bungee_jumping.htm

Cycling

DelhiByCycle

If you're looking for a pure street experience that will embrace the sights, sounds, smells and colours that make Delhi the dynamic place that it is, DelhiByCycle guided tours on bicycle will provide just that. The 3-hour tours that can take 2 routes in Old Delhi and one in New Delhi, cover the usual suspects like the Red Fort, Jama Masjid and the spice market. However, this tour takes a meandering ride through the many bazaars that are like no other place in the world. It is ideal for riders ages 12 and older. The only real criterion is that those interested already know how to ride a bike. The bikes, Atlas Sharp Shooters, are provided by the guide, Jack, a Dutch man who now calls New Delhi home. Water bottles are provided and helmets are available for those who request them. There are 2 rest stops along the way, one which includes a Mughal breakfast on the Old Delhi route. The average group size is 7 people, but there is a minimum of 4 for riding.

>**Meet:** New Delhi Railway Station Ajmeri Gate side
Tel: 98189 81194
Timings: Daily from 8:30 am in winter; 7:30 am in spring; 7 am in summer
Entry: Rs 950 per person for groups of 4 to 7. The cost includes bicycle usage, tour, breakfast and water; smaller groups can be customized but the price will have to be worked out with the guide.
Web: www.delhibycycle.com for bookings

Delhi Cycling Club

The Initiative for Transport and Development Programme organizes heritage bike tours, rallies and events to promote a cleaner city. It also runs the Delhi Cycling Club.

>11/1 Jangpura Road
Tel: 011 2437 3584
Web: www.itdp.org for more information

Go-Karting

Bowling and go-karting naturally go together and it is great when they can be found under one roof at some of the places below. Go-karting is suited for kids 10 and older so the little ones can enjoy bowling while the older siblings zoom around the track.

Chandigarh (15 Scorpion cars)
>Albert Ross Racing, 41/8 Milestone, Ambala–Chandigarh highway, Zikrakpur. On the Delhi–Chandigarh GT Road at the union territory border just 20 minutes from Delhi.
Timings: Daily 3 pm to 10 pm
Entry: Rs 50 for 3 laps; Rs 100 for 8 laps; Rs 150 for 15 laps.
Length of track: 350 metres

Destination Point (10 Scorpion cars)
>12/2 Main Mathura Road, Faridabad
Tel: 0129 227 5139
Timings: Daily 11 am to 9 pm
Entry: Rs 100 for 6 laps; Rs 120 for 8 laps; Rs 180 for 15 laps
Length of track: 320 metres

Fun and Fair (10 Scorpion cars)
>A-38 Mohan Cooperative Industrial Area
Main Mathura Road
Tel: 011 2695 9563
Timings: Daily 10 am to 9 pm
Entry: Rs 100 for 8 laps
Length of track: Less than 1 km

Planet Bowling (5 go-karts)
>A-38 Mohan Cooperative Industrial Estate
Mathura Road, Badarpur
Tel: 011 2695 9665
Timings: Daily 10 am to 9:30 pm
Entry: Rs 100 per go-kart; Rs 50 per bumper car

Thirty Second Milestone (8 Mobile go-karts)
>Chander Nagar Gurgaon (Near Signature Tower)
Tel: 0124 233 2571
Timings: 11 am to 11 pm
Entry: Rs 100 for 6 laps
Web: www.32ndmilestone.com

Golf

Aravalli Golf Club
A 9-hole course located about 30 km from the Delhi border.

>Near Nahar Singh Stadium, Faridabad
Tel: 0129 241 4810
Timings: 5:30 am until evening daily
Fees: Daily Indians Rs 100 / foreigners Rs 200

Classic Golf Resort
18-hole, par 72 course

>Delhi–Jaipur Highway, Naurangpur Tauru Road, Gurgaon
Tel: 0124 237 8841
Timings: Daily 9:30 am to 5:30 pm
Entry: Mon to Fri Rs 1,700,

Rs 2,900 weekends. Non-member fees are the same for Indians and foreigners.

DDA Lado Sarai Driving Range (Qutab Golf Course)
Driving range is open to members and non-members. For children 5 and older.

>Press Enclave Road
Tel: 011 2696 9086
Timings: Tue to Sun 5:45 am to 6 pm
Entry: Indians Rs 30 / foreigners Rs 150

DDA Siri Fort Sports Complex
There's a driving range that is open to members and non-members. There's a 9-hole course that takes a little over an hour to complete. Children 14 and younger must be accompanied by an adult. Only the putter and wedge are allowed on the course. For children 8 and older.

>Siri Fort
Tel: 011 2649 7482
Timings: Tue to Sun 6 am to 8:30 pm
Entry: Day memberships usually begin at Rs 40 for Indians, Rs 100 for foreigners

Delhi Golf Club
One of the finest, if not the finest 18-hole courses in town. For ages 5 and above.

>Dr Zakir Hussain Marg
Tel: 011 2436 0002; 011 2436 2235
Timings: Daily 5:30 am to 6 pm; 18-hole course closed Mon, but driving range is open
Entry: Mon to Fri Indians Rs 570 / foreigners Rs 2,000; Rs 850 / Rs 2,250 weekends

Noida Golf Club
The driving range is open to non-members.

>Sector 38, Noida
Tel: 0120 243 1467
Timings: Tue to Sun 5 am to 8 pm
Entry: Mon to Fri Rs 340, weekends and holidays Rs 560

Mall Play Areas

The mall crawl is easier when the kids have a place to bounce and jump and yell to their heart's content. Many malls have sections dedicated for kids ages 2 and up that have toy cars, slides and soft toys. But some malls, like Ambience Mall and The Great India Place up the fun quotient by 10,000 percent.

Ambience Mall
Fun city offers video games; bumping cars, a rocking boat, merry-go-round, table tennis, bike racing and other sports that help Ambience Mall outshine its competitors.

The gaming centre has everything and a card can be purchased to play games that can be returned once the games are over. There's plenty of food to give the sugar high to keep the adrenaline pumping for all the activities available. And of course there is the 24-lane bowling alley Blu-O. A visit to Ambience mall can definitely turn into a day-long trip.

>Ambience Mall, NH-8, Gurgaon
Timings: 10 am to 11 pm
Tel: 0124 466 5555
Web: www.ambiencemalls.com

Amoeba

Video games, trampoline and children's play area, electronics zone and bowling for Rs 125 a game. The best part about the Amoeba chain is the variety of video games that kids can enjoy.

>MGF Mall, Mehrauli–Gurgaon Road, Gurgaon
Tel: 0124 501 4606/07
Timings: Daily 9 am to midnight

>Pacific Mall, Plot No. 1, Site 4, Sahibabad Industrial Area, Ghaziabad
Tel: 0120 3012301
Timings: Daily 11 am to 8 pm

>Spice Mall, I-2, Sector 25A, Noida
4D movies are shown here for Rs 100 a ticket
Tel: 0120 436 6400
Timings: Mon to Sat 9:30 am to 11 pm; Sun noon to 11 pm

Ansal Plaza

The play station at Funkie Orbits in Ansal Plaza is a 2-storey area of big plastic pipes that a child can crawl through eventually sliding down into a pit filled with Styrofoam coloured balls. It is advertised as an area for children from 2–14 years of age. However, this play area could be dangerous for children below 6 years. To start with, a 2–3 year old cannot crawl up this structure on his own and if he gets stuck anywhere, he will not only be extremely scared, but may also tend to suffer from claustrophobia in later life. Further, though the station advertises the presence of 'park rangers' in case of difficulties, only 2 were present, both of whom were more concerned about whether we had paid the entry fee of Rs 150 rather than the safety of the children. Take your kids there only if they are 8 and above or if there are older children in the family to look after the younger ones.

>CG-5/A, Ansal Plaza (near South Extension)
Tel: 011 2626 1365

Timings: 11 am to 10:30 pm
Parking: Underground and outside parking; Rs 10 to Rs 30

Centrestage Mall
Play area in the basement, including an air hockey table

> L-1, Sector 18, Noida
Tel: 0120 251 2260
Timings: Mon to Sat 9:30 am to 11 pm; Sun noon to 11 pm

East Delhi Mall
The Entertainment Zone at the mall is huge. It is about 50,000 square feet and has a play area that includes video game stations, a bouncy castle and the multi-cuisine food court is nearby.

>1 Kaushambi, Ghaziabad
Tel: 0120 277 6649 / 277 6667

The Great India Place
There's a muzzle puzzle on the third floor where kids can explore and adults will be wishing they can too.

>Sector 38A, Near Atta Market, Opposite City Centre Mall, Noida
Tel: 91 120 465 0300
Timings: Daily 11 am to 11 pm

North Square Mall
>F-1, 2, 3 Netaji Subhash Place,
Tel: 011 4704 9061

Select Citywalk Mall, 3rd Flr
Small play area with Tyco toys and balls and blocks

>Saket
Tel: 011 4211 4211
Entry: Rs 150 an hour
Timings: Daily 11 am to 8 pm

Shipra Mall
U Kids is a family entertainment zone with activities aimed at children from ages to 2 to 16. The zone covers 17,000 square feet and includes 4D theatres.

>9 Vaibhav, Indirapuram, Ghaziabad
Tel: 0120 268 9650

Movie Theatres

Catch the latest flicks in both Hindi and English at these theatres around town. The big chains offer home delivery of the tickets.

Habitat World, India Habitat Centre
Though not a movie theatre in the traditional sense, international films are regularly showcased at the India Habitat Centre and movie buffs get to see a variety of movies that aren't shown elsewhere around town.

>Lodhi Road
Tel: 011 4366 3333

Web: www.habitatworld.com

IMAX (Adlabs 3D)
Online booking: www.
adlabscinemas.com

Central Delhi

Chanakya
>Vinay Marg, Chanakyapuri
Tel: 011 2467 4009

Delite
>4/1 Asaf Ali road, Daryaganj
Tel: 011 2327 2903; 011 2327
1067

PVR Plaza
>H Block, Connaught Place
Nearest Metro: Rajiv Chowk
Tel: 011 2794 4194
Online booking: www.
pvrcinemas.com

PVR Rivoli
>Baba Kharak Singh Marg,
Connaught Place
Nearest Metro: Rajiv Chowk
Tel: 011 2794 4194 / 011-
47604100

Regal
>Regal Building, Connaught
Place
Tel: 011 2336 1583; 011 2336
2245

Shakuntalam
>Gate No. 5, Pragati Maidan
Nearest Metro: Pragati
Maidan
Tel: 011 2337 1849

Sheila
>Deshbandhu Gupta Road,
Paharganj
Tel: 011 2367 2100

East Delhi

Fun Cinemas Shahadara
>Plot No. 9C, 9D CVD Ground,
CBD Shahdara,
Karkardooma District Centre,
near Karkardooma court
Metro: Shahdara
Tel: 0120 404 0404

Fun Cinemas Vikas Marg
>East Centre, Plot No. 10,
Main Vikas Marg,
Laxminagar District Centre
Nearest Metro: Shahdara
Tel: 95120 404 0404

Movie Palace
>Dilshad Garden, opposite
Delhi Transport Corp bus
depot
Nearest Metro: Shahdara
Tel: 0120 262 5502

North Delhi

Amba
>GT Karnal Road, Old Sabzi
Mandi, Kamal Nagar
Nearest Metro: Vishwa
Vidyalaya
Tel: 011 2382 6000/5000

Batra
>Mukherji Nagar
Nearest Metro: Vishwa
Vidyalaya
Tel: 011 2765 4202

Fun Cinemas
>North Square Mall, Netaji
Subhash Place,

District Centre, Wazirpur, Pitampura
Nearest Metro: Netaji Subhash Place
Tel: 95120 404 0404

Gagan
>Community Centre, Nandnagari, Shahdara
Nearest Metro: Shahdara
Tel: 011 2258 1989

M2K Pitampura
Road No. 44, Community Centre, Pitampura
Nearest Metro: Kohat
Tel: 011 2794 2944

M2K Rohini
>16 Mangalam Place, District Centre, Sector 3, Rohini
Nearest Metro: Pitampura
Tel: 011 2794 2944

Movietime Multiplex
North Pacific Mall, KP block Complex,
Near City Park Hotel, Pitampura
Nearest Metro: Pitampura
Tel: 011 4268 3160

South Delhi

Batra Glitz Cinemas
>1 Community Centre, New Friends Colony (near Surya Hotel)
Tel: 011 6613 3333

Paras
>1 Paras Cinema Building, Nehru Place (near Bank of India)
Tel: 011 2648 4401

PVR Anupam
>1 Community Centre, Saket Local Shopping Complex
Tel: 011 4167 1787

PVR Citywalk Gold Premiere
>Select Citywalk Mall
Tel: 011 4060 1710

PVR Premiere
>Select Citywalk Mall, 1st Flr
Tel: 9871113804

PVR Priya
>61 Basant Lok, Vasant Vihar
Tel: 011 4166 3787

PVR Saket
>1 Local Shopping Complex
Tel: 011 2794 4194

Sapna Cinema (near Amar Colony)
>54 Community Centre, Suraj Parbat, East of Kailash
Tel: 011 2643 1787

Satyam Cineplex Nehru Place
>Plot No. 45 Nehru Place, near Hotel InterContinental
Tel: 011 2589 3322
Web: www.satyamcineplexes.com

3 C's
>15 Feroze Gandhi Marg, Lajpat Nagar III (near central market)
Tel: 011 2984 7846

West Delhi

Fun Cinemas
>TDI Fun Republic,

Moti Nagar
Nearest Metro: Moti Nagar
Tel: 95120 404 0404

Janak Cinemas
>C Block, Janakpuri
Nearest Metro: Janakpuri East
Tel: 011 2555 1115

Liberty
>19B New Rohtak Road, Karol Bagh
Nearest Metro: Shastri Nagar
Tel: 011 2871 1800

PVR Naraina
>1 Community Centre, Naraina Industrial Area
Nearest Metro: Shadipur
Tel: 011 2794 4194

PVR Vikaspuri
>G-1 Community Centre, Vikaspuri
Nearest Metro: Janakpuri West
Tel: 011 4158 6143

Satyam Cineplex Janakpuri
>Plot No. 19, District Centre, Janakpuri
Nearest Metro: Janakpuri West
Tel: 011 2589 3322

Satyam Cineplex West Patel Nagar
>Patel Nagar, near metro station
Nearest Metro: Shadipur
Tel: 011 2589 3322
Online booking: www.satyamcineplexes.com

Old Delhi

Excelsior
>Cinema Sirkee Walan, Hauz Qazi
Nearest Metro: Hauz Qazi
Tel: 011 2321 3377

Golcha
>No. 3630 Netaji Subhash Marg, Daryaganj, near Dilli Gate
Nearest Metro: ITO
Tel: 011 2325 0945

Moti
>Chandni Chowk, near Red Fort
Nearest Metro: Chandni Chowk
Tel: 011 2386 0383

Ritz
>Kashmere Gate, near Inter State Bus Terminal
Nearest Metro: Kashmere Gate
Tel: 011 2386 4229

Faridabad

Cinemax Cinema
>Sector 20
Tel: 91 129 2220752/4

Inox Cinema
>Crown Interiorz Mall, Delhi Mathura Highway, Sector 35
Tel: 91 129 4161000/40

PVR Crown Plaza
>15/A Milestone Road, Crown Plaza, Sector A
Tel: 0129 428 0000

PVR SRS Faridabad
>SRS Mall, 2nd Flr, Sector 12, near Town Park
Tel: 0129 400 9898

Ghaziabad

Adlabs Kaushambi
>Pacific Mall, Kaushambi
Tel: 0129 3989 4040

Adlabs Vaishali
>Ansal Plaza, Vaishali
Tel: 0129 3989 4040

Big Cinemas Ansal Plaza
>Sahibabad
Tel: 91 120 3012222

Fun Cinemas
>TDI AEZ Carnival Country Mall,
Plot No. W1-W2, Sector 1, Vaishali
Tel: 0120 322 7274

Galaxie Multiplex
>Near Dabur Factory, Vaishali
Tel: 011 5166 2246

Jam Multiplex
>Shipra Mall, National Highway 24, Indirapuram
Tel: 0120 295 7610

Manohar
>Ghanta Ghar, GT Road
Tel: 95120 273 2780

Movie World
>Meerut Chungi, Ghaziabad–Meerut Road, near the police station
Tel: 92135 10290

PVR EDM
>East Delhi Mall, 3rd Flr, Plot No. 1, Kaushambi
Tel: 0120 301 2787

Silvercity
>South Side Industrial Area, near Lal Kuan
Tel: 0120 324 4720

Wave Cinemas
>East End Mall, Multiplex Plot
Tel: 0120 295 0796
Online booking: www.wavecinemas.com

Gurgaon

Big Cinemas Palam Vihar (in Ansal Plaza)
>4th Flr, G block, Palam Vihar, Gurgaon
Tel: 0124 398 9404
Web: www.bigcinemas.com

DT Cinemas City Centre
>DLF City Centre, Mehrauli Gurgaon Road (opposite MGF Mall)
Tel: 0124 401 4092
Web: http://dtcinemas.com/

DT Cinemas Mega Mall
>Mega Mall, Block A, DLF Phase I
Tel: 0124 401 4096/7
Web: http://dtcinemas.com/

Payal
>Sector 14, Old Delhi Road
Tel: 0124 232 3336

PVR Ambience Gold
>Ambience Mall,

Gurgaon Road
Tel: 011 4100 0462
Web: www.pvrcinemas.com

PVR MGF (Europa)
>Metropolitan Mall,
Mehrauli–Gurgaon Road
Tel: 0124 401 8880

Noida

Big Cinemas
>The Great India Place,
Sector 38A
Tel: 0120 3984 813

PVR Spice Noida
>I-2 Sector 25A
Tel: 0120 438 9000

Wave Cinemas
>Centrestage Mall, L-1 Sector
18, Noida
Tel: 0120 436 4666

Playgrounds / Play Areas

Children's Park
Located near India Gate, the Children's Park has a lot of well-maintained swings and other playground equipment that will allow kids to be just kids as you drag them from the museums to forts. Only adults with kids are allowed into the park and there is a guard at the gate, though it is not strictly enforced. It is best to go during the day as it gets very crowded in the evenings and on weekends.

>Children's Park
Near India Gate
Timings: Dawn till dusk

Garden of Five Senses
More than just a park, the Garden of Five Senses was set up to stimulate all senses. In addition to being a great picnic spot, kids can take a solar car/train and other interesting rides all powered by solar energy. Elephant and camel rides are also offered here. (Also see *Beauty and The Beast*, pp.18–19.)

>Garden of Five Senses
Said-ul-Ajaib (south of Saket)
Timings: From dawn till dusk

India Habitat Centre
There is a good free play area for little kids at the India Habitat Centre that has slides, swings, cars and a bridge to climb.

>Lodhi Road, located near the All American Diner.

Indira Gandhi International Airport
The children's play area in domestic terminal 1A of Indira Gandhi International Airport will help pass the time during a flight delay. With climbing structures, swings, a variety of games, balls and other play equipment, kids will be reluctant to get on the plane. Travel related themes are on the flooring and rugs. The

play area also has soft toys, baby cots and high chairs and even a diaper changing area.

>Terminal 1A
Palam

Roller Skating

Blade runners can do what they love at the many DDA complexes around town. There is no equipment rental so you have to bring your own skates.

Chilla Sports Complex
>Dallu Pura, near Vasundhara Enclave
Tel: 011 2262 3184
Timings: Tue to Sun 6 am to 9 pm in the summer; 6:30 am to 8:30 pm in the winter. Timings are listed for non-DDA complexes and DDA complexes with specific skating timings.
Entry: Rs 40 per day for Indians / Rs 100 per day for foreigners; school children pay Rs 10 from 10 am to 4 pm
Web: www.ddadelhi.com/sports

DDA Sports Complex
>Sector 12, Rohini
Tel: 011 2755 7314
Nearest Metro: Rohini
Timings: Tue to Sun 6 pm to 8:30 pm

DDA Sports Complex Vasant Kunj
>D-2 Vasant Kunj
Tel: 011 2613 6731
Timings: Daily 4:30 pm to 8 pm

Dwarka Sports Complex
>Sector 11, Dwarka
Nearest Metro: Dwarka Sector 11
Tel: 011 2508 9733
Timings: Daily 4 pm to 6:30 pm

Hari Nagar Sports Complex
>Hari Nagar,
Beri Wala Bagh,
Near Deen Dayal Upadhyah Hospital
Tel: 011 2513 6683

Major Dhyan Chand Sports Complex
>Ashok Vihar, behind Kanhaiya Nagar Metro Station
Nearest Metro: Kanhaiya Nagar
Tel: 011 2730 5338

Netaji Subhash Sports Complex
>Jasola Vihar, near Sarita Vihar
Tel: 011 2697 1301

Panjabi Bagh Club
>Ring Road
Tel: 011 2522 1082
Timings: Tue to Sat 4 pm to 8 pm

Paschim Vihar Sports Complex
>A-6 Paschim Vihar,
Near Shri Balaji Action Medical Institute
Tel: 011 2527 0959

Poorvi Delhi Khel Parisar
>Shahdara, near GTB Hospital
Tel: 011 2213 4167

Rashtriya Swabhiman Khel Parisar
>Pitam Pura, near Pitam Pura tower
Nearest Metro: Pitam Pura
Tel: 011 2744 6147

Rohini Sports Complex
>Sector 14, Rohini, near CRPF School
Nearest Metro: Rohini East
Tel: 011 2756 1986

Saket Sports Complex
>Saket, opposite Welcome Marriott Hotel
Tel: 011 2956 1742

Siri Fort Sports Complex
>August Kranti Marg, near Siri Fort Auditorium
Tel: 011 2649 7482
Timings: Tue to Sat 5 pm to 8 pm

Vasant Kunj Sports Complex
>Sector D-II, Vasant Kunj, near Surya Gardens
Tel: 011 2613 6731

Yamuna Sports Complex
>Sarajmal Vihar, near Vivekanand Mahila College
Tel: 011 2216 4726
Timings: Tue to Sat 4 pm to 7 pm

Sports Complexes

If you're staying at a guest house or with family and you don't have access to a gym, it may make financial sense to plunk down a monthly membership fee if you're in Delhi for a week or more instead of paying hundreds or even thousands of rupees for a few hours at a fancy spa/gym in a 5-star hotel. A few minutes of paperwork can save you a bundle.

DDA Sports Complexes
DDA Sports Complexes are located throughout the city and offer a variety of sporting activities including tennis, yoga, golf, swimming, gyms, aerobics, horse riding, yoga and skating.

>**Entry:** Day membership Rs 40 for Indians, Rs 100 for foreigners
Web: www.dda.org.in/sports_complex.htm

Pacific Sports Complex
Located in South Delhi, the Pacific Sports Complex offers a variety of fitness activities including a swimming pool.

>Andrews Ganj, next to Central School
Tel: 011 6452 0554
Timings: Daily 5 am to 9 am; 4 pm to 10 pm
Entry: From Rs 1,500 per month

Ryder Sports Academy
Facilities at the Ryder Sports Academy include tennis,

horse riding, roller skating and basketball. There are branches in Vasant Kunj and Gurgaon.

>D-1 Vasant Kunj (near Heritage School)
Tel: 011 5569 1920
Entry: From Rs 900 to Rs 1,600 per month
Web: www.rydersports.com/contactus

>Aardee City, Gate No. 2, B Block, Sector 52, Gurgaon
Tel: 92128 00 133; 98 101 41 889

Saket Sports Complex
The Saket Sports Complex offers riding, cricket pitches, a swimming pool, aerobics and chess among other activities.

>Saket, opposite Welcome Marriott Hotel
Tel: 011 2956 1742

Siri Fort Sports Complex
The Siri Fort Sports Complex set the gold standard in Delhi. It has everything including a golf course, Olympic size pool and skating rink.

>August Kranti Marg, near Siri Fort Auditorium
Tel: 011 2649 7482
Timings: Daily 6 am to 9 pm

DDA Sports Complex Rohini
>Sector 12, Rohini
Tel: 011 2756 1986
Nearest Metro: Rohini
Timings: Tue to Sun 6 am to 9 pm

DDA Sports Complex Vasant Kunj
>D-2 Vasant Kunj
Tel: 011 2613 6731
Timings: Daily 4:30 pm to 8 pm

Swimming Pools

If you're staying at a hotel or guest house without a pool or with relatives who aren't of the wealthy farm house variety, don't despair when the mercury hits 44°C and you're dying for a dip in some cool waters. Many hotels allow non-guests to use the pool, but keep in mind, this can be expensive.

Hotels

Aqua at the Park
The pool is small and located near the bar, so it's more for atmosphere than swimming laps.

>The Park Hotel
15 Parliament Street
Tel: 011 2374 3000
Nearest Metro: Rajiv Chowk
Timings: 7 am to 7 pm daily
Entry: Rs 700 per person per day

The Bristol
The rooftop pool is a decent size. The crowd tends to be more expat than local.

>Adjacent to DLF Phase I Gurgaon
Tel: 0124 4351111
Timings: 7 am to 9 pm daily
Entry: Rs 550 per person per day

Crowne Plaza Today
Hold on to your swimming caps. This 25-metre infinity pool is for deep pocketed non-guests.

>Sector 29 Gurgaon
Tel: 0124 4534000
Timings: Daily 7 am to 9 pm
Entry: Rs 1,600 per person per day

Gulmohar Club
>Gulmohar Park, opposite Kamla Nehru College, Balbir Saxena Marg
Tel: 011 2686 8139
Entry: Rs 120 per person per dip

Hotel Crown Plaza Surya
>New Friends Colony Community Centre
Tel: 011 2683 5070
Timings: Daily 7 am to 9 pm
Entry: Rs 750 adults;
Rs 500 children per person per day

The Metropolitan
Decent size pool and it's in the courtyard. It's pretty empty during the week.

>Bangla Sahib Road
Tel: 011 4250 0200
Timings: Daily 6:30 am to 7 pm
Entry: Rs 600 per person per day

Public Pools

Most public pools require monthly memberships. However, for a price starting at Rs 500, if you're in Delhi for more than a week or come to Delhi often, it sure beats the price of a one-off swimming session at a fancy hotel.

Indian Aquatic Academy
>Sector 24, Kendriya Vidyalaya, Noida
Tel: 0124 238 1544
Timings: Mon to Sat 5:30 am to 10:30 am; 4 pm to 10 pm
Entry: Rs 1,200 per month

Khazan Singh Academy
>Kendriya Vidyalaya, Old JNU Campus,
Baba Gangnath Marg
Tel: 011 3293 3828
Timings: Tue to Sun 5 am to 8 am; 8 pm to 9 pm
Entry: Rs 700 per month

NDMC Swimming Pool Mandir Marg
>NP Boys Senior Secondary School, Mandir Marg
Tel: 011 2336 3629
Entry: Adults Rs 400; children Rs 60 per month

NDMC Swimming Pool Sarojini Nagar
>Navyug School
Tel: 011 2334 7296
Timings: Daily 6:30 am to 10:20 am; 4 pm to 7:50 pm;

ladies 5 pm to 5:50 pm
Entry: Adults Rs 400; children Rs 60 per month

Pacific Sports Complex
>Kendriya Vidyalaya, Andrews Ganj
Tel: 011 6452 0554
Timings: Daily 5 am to 10 am; 2 pm to 10 pm
Entry: Adults Rs 1,400; children Rs 1,200 per month

Sports and Cultural Club
>Sector 15A, Noida
Tel: 95120 251 1586
Timings: Tue to Fri 4:30 pm to 5:15 pm
Entry: Rs 1,825 per month

YMCA
>Jai Singh Road
Tel: 011 2374 666
Timings: Mon to Sat 6:30 am to 10:30 am; 3 pm to 7:30 pm
Entry: Rs 900 per month

Tennis

DDA Sports Complexes
Siri Fort has the best tennis courts, but there are courts in DDA complexes throughout the city. Go to www.ddadelhi.com/sports for locations.

>Khel Gaon Marg
Tel: 011 2649 7482
Entry: Rs 40 Indian / Rs 100 foreigner for day membership; Rs 50 / Rs 100 court fees

Delhi Lawn Tennis Association
The Delhi Lawn Tennis Association is a great option for a game of tennis. The courts are well maintained and there are ball boys and lights for evening games. No matter where you're staying, the centrally located tennis courts will prove to be convenient. The entry fee is calculated by the court, not the number of players. Another great place to check out is the Jawaharlal Nehru Stadium. The tennis courts were built for the Asian games, so they are still in pretty good shape.

>1 Africa Avenue, opposite RK Puram and Safdarjung Enclave
Tel: 011 2649 7482
Timings: Mon to Fri 7 am to 10 pm
Entry: Rs 150/hr Mon to Fri; Rs 200/hr Sat to Sun; Rs 300/hr Mon to Sun evenings.

Jawaharlal Nehru Stadium
The courts in the old stadium of Rajpath are well maintained, but the registration process will have you screaming like John McEnroe. It's worth it to register and then take your frustrations out on the tennis ball.

>National Stadium, India Gate, near Patiala House
Tel: 011 2338 9740
Entry: Registration Rs 70, Rs 250 for an hour of play

MAKE THE MOST OF MUSEUMS

No. 1: National Rail Museum. Where else can you ride a toy train then take a trip through time as you explore other retired trains for so little money. All aboard!

There may be lots of whining when the museum itinerary is discussed before the family heads out for a day of sight-seeing, but if an outing to the Gandhi Museum is framed by a visit to the Crafts Museum where kids can make pottery alongside the artisans or indulge in some hands-on activities at the National Museum of Natural History, they'll actually thank you later. Delhi's multi-faceted history is displayed in a bounty of museum displays that span 5,000 years. History, however, isn't confined to walls full of art and glass displays. History can be seen everywhere through walking tours in Old Delhi or by catching the Delhi Parikrama Rail Sewa which winds its way past some historic monuments. Also included with the listings in this chapter, are nearby sights and nearby eats. It will help in planning visits and will save time by possibly fitting 2 museum visits in one day, especially if the museums are in close proximity. And after all that reading of note cards on the displays, you are bound to have built up an appetite. So, grab a water bottle, some comfortable walking shoes and get ready to discover Incredible India.

Chugging through History

One of the city's still undiscovered treasures, the **Delhi Parikrama Rail Sewa** will give passengers a different view of Delhi in just under 2 hours and 35 km. Built in 1975 as a single diesel haul, it was thrust into the spotlight for the 1982 Asian Games. The circular route of 12 passenger trains roughly follows the ring road. Starting from Hazrat Nizamuddin station, the 2-hour journey provides breathtaking views of Humayun's tomb and Gurudwara Damdama Sahib. You'll catch a glimpse of Connaught Place from the Shivaji (Minto) bridge. Lajpat Nagar is the final stop on the journey before the train returns to the Nizamuddin station. Tea and snacks will be provided, however, it is encouraged that you bring water and other snacks if so desired. Robinson guides you on the journey.

>Starting at the Hazrat Nizamuddin station
Timings: 8:45 am to 11:15 am
Entry: Rs 100

Museums and Monuments

Gandhi Smriti Museum

This museum is at the house where Mahatma Gandhi spent the last 144 days of his life before he was assassinated there on 30 January 1948. The memorial highlights many aspects of Gandhi's life including his ideas, principles and values. The room where he stayed has some of his things including a bed, mat on the floor, eye glasses, books and a spinning wheel. A film on Gandhi is shown daily.

>5 Tees January Marg
Nearest Metro: Central Secretariat
Tel: 011 2301 1480
Timings: Tue to Sat 9:30 am to 5:30 pm
Entry: Free
Nearby sights: Indira Gandhi Memorial, National Museum of Natural History
Nearby places to eat: Hotel Le Meridien, Imperial Hotel, Parikrama Revolving Restaurant, Nizam's Kathi Kebabs, Bengali Market, McDonald's, Pizza Hut, Domino's Pizza, Nirula's, Ruby Tuesday, Barista, Café Coffee Day and the food court at Dilli Haat.

Hauz Khas

Hauz Khas village once housed a large tank that provided a steady supply of water to Siri, the second city of Delhi. The village was founded by Sultan Ala-ud-din Khilji and the tank was excavated in 1300. The tank was known as Hauz-i-Alai, hence Hauz Khas meaning royal tank. The tank fell into disrepair and it wasn't until the reign of Firoz Shah Tughlaq, who ruled Delhi in the 14th century, that it was repaired. Additionally, several monuments were built by Firoz Shah including his tomb, a mosque and a madrassa (college). The monuments can be reached by taking a left turn just after the Aurobindo Palace on the main Aurobindo Marg. The entrance to the tomb of Firoz Shah is on the southern side. It has a big dome and decorated with Quranic inscriptions. To the west of the tomb is the madrassa which was built in 1352 for religious studies. Several staircases lead from the madrassa down to the tank which is encircled by paved pathways. Within the complex are several other monuments. The area is one of the most prestigious residential areas in the cities and it houses many chic restaurants, art galleries and boutiques. The Deer Park (see *Beauty and the Beast*, p.18) can also be found in the area.

>**Nearby sights:** Hauz Khas Enclave, Kalkaji Temple, Lotus Temple, Nizamuddin's Shrine
Nearby places to eat: Park Balluchi restaurant in the Deer Park, Naivedyam or the Village Bistro.

The Indian Air Force Museum
The entire family would really enjoy a visit to the Indian Air Force Museum. From pictures to uniforms and of course, a collection of different types of military aircraft, visitors get a true history of the Indian Air Force. Every year on 8 October, which is celebrated as Air Force Day, visitors can view the larger transport aircrafts kept in the flight apron of Palam Air Base and a special parade of the Indian Air Force. (See *Dudes*, pp.41–2.)

>Palam Air Force Station
Timings: Wed to Sun 10 am to 5 pm, closed Mon and Tue
Entry: Free
Tel: 011 2569 7551
Web: http://indianairforce.nic.in
Nearby places to eat: Radisson, Centaur Hotel, Wimpy's in Janakpuri, McDonald's, Pizza Hut, Barista, Ruby Tuesday.

Indira Gandhi Memorial
The house where Indira Gandhi lived when she was prime minister of India serves as the Indira Gandhi Memorial. It was here in her gardens that she was assassinated by her two bodyguards on 31 October 1984. The museum has limited items on display, but one can see the bloodstained sari she wore on the day she was killed. Also on display are the burned clothes and shoes of her son, Rajeev Gandhi, which he was wearing when he was assassinated by a bomb blast in May 1991. The whole stretch of the garden where she last walked is enclosed in glass, giving an eerie effect of time standing still. Children are certain to find a visit both enjoyable and educational, and the memorial is also very popular among domestic tourists who want to pay homage to their leaders and the sacrifices they made for the country.

>1 Safdarjung Road, near Safdarjung's Tomb and Airport

Nearest Metro: Central Secretariat
Tel: 011 2301 0094
Timings: Tue to Sun 9:30 am to 4:45 pm
Nearby sights: National Museum of Natural History, Gandhi Smriti Museum, National Gandhi Museum
Nearby places to eat: Hotel Le Meridien, Imperial Hotel, The Lalit, Parikrama, Wenger, McDonald's, Pizza Hut, Domino's Pizza, Nirula's, Ruby Tuesday, Delhi Darbar, Barista, Café Coffee Day and Nizam's Kathi Kebabs.

Mehrauli Archaeological Park

Famously known for the location of the Qutab Minar (see *If You Have to be a Tourist*, pp.107–8), tourists usually visit the minaret and then head back home missing out on one of the gems of the city. Mehrauli Archaeological Park, spread over 100 acres is a treasure trove for history lovers as it has more than 70 monuments on its grounds including the Zafar Mahal, Balban's tomb (he was the ruler of the Delhi Sultanate in the thirteenth century); and Jamali Kamali mosque and tomb. INTACH organizes tours with guides who have a background in architecture, art or history that take about 2 hours.

>For tours: INTACH, 71 Lodhi Estate
Tel: 011 2464 1304
Timings: Sat and Sun 8 am to 10 pm
Entry: Rs 30

Metro Museum

The Delhi Metro Rail Corporation (DMRC) has opened a Metro Museum along the lines of London's Transport Museum. Located at the Patel Chowk Metro station on the yellow line which runs from Delhi University to the Central Secretariat, the museum has 24 large panels cataloguing the Metro's history and how the Rail Corporation functions. A model of the Tunnel Boring Machine, soil samples collected from around the city and different coloured helmets used at construction sites and the prototype of the Metro train also are included in the exhibits. Two touch-screen computers play the DMRC corporate movie and an animated movie describes the way tunnel boring machines and launching girders are used in elevated construction work. A few souvenirs are on sale including a coffee book, *A Journey to Remember*, Metro ties and key chains. To round out the experience, mannequins wear the different uniforms worn by operations and construction staff; and there is a scale model of a Metro train, models of stations and ticket coupon booklets. It takes about 20 minutes to see everything. Souvenirs such as Metro ties, pens, keychains and books will be available for sale at the Metro Museum. Curator services at the Museum can be availed from 10 am to 4 pm on all days except Monday when the Museum is closed. Visitors who are not travelling by the Metro will have to buy entry tickets at the fare counters.

>Patel Chowk metro station
Timings: Tue to Sun 10 am to 4 pm
Entry: Visitors will need a journey token or smart card to enter.
Web: www.delhimetrorail.com/commuters for a nice slideshow (click on the bottom right corner of the metro museum page)
Nearby sights: India Gate, Safdarjung's Tomb, Indira Gandhi Memorial Museum, Gandhi Smriti, Dilli Haat, India Gate, Jantar Mantar
Nearby places to eat: Hotel Le Meridien, Imperial Hotel, Hotel Inter-Continental, Parikrama, Delhi Darbar, Nizam's Kathi Kebabs, McDonald's, Pizza Hut, Domino's Pizza, Nirula's, Ruby Tuesday, Barista, Café Coffee Day and the food stalls at Dilli Haat

Mutiny Memorial

Everyone has that sibling where comparisons are inevitable. The Mutiny Memorial is often compared to India Gate (see *If You Have to be a Tourist*, pp.100–101). Whereas India Gate has the distinction of being a memorial to honour soldiers who died in World War I, the Mutiny Memorial, built in 1863 by the British, commemorates the men who were fighting on the 'wrong side' (according to the plaque) in 1857, during the first War of Indian Independence. In 1972, on the 25th anniversary of India's independence, a second plaque was added to the memorial which mentions that the enemy mentioned by the British were the Indian freedom fighters who had fought against colonial rule. There's a great view of the city once you reach the top.

>Rani Jhansi Road, near Hindu Rao Hospital on the Northern Ridge.
Nearest Metro: Kashmere Gate
Timings: Sunrise to sunset

National Gallery of Modern Art

With approximately 15,000 paintings, sculptures and works of arts by Indian as well as international artists, the National Gallery of Modern Art collection is a reservoir of modern art from the mid nineteenth century to the present. The gallery also arranges exhibitions for up-and-coming artists. You may never own an MF Hussain, Souza or Raza, but you can get up close to them here. There are also paintings by prominent living artists such as Anjoli Ela Menon. Don't miss the sculpture garden. It is peaceful with lots of big trees. Pieces of sculpture are scattered amidst the regular sculpture. Take a breather in the shade. The museum sells prints, posters and monographs.

>Jaipur House near India Gate
Tel: 011 2338 4560/2338 2835
Metro: Central Secretariat
Timings: Daily 10 am to 5 pm; closed Monday and government holidays
Entry: Indians Rs 10, foreigners Rs 150
Web: www.ngmaindia.gov.in
Nearby sights: India Gate, Safdarjung's Tomb, Indira Gandhi Memorial Museum, Gandhi Smriti, Dilli Haat, India Gate, Jantar Mantar
Nearby places to eat: Hotel Le Meridien, Imperial Hotel, Hotel Inter-Continental, Parikrama, Delhi Darbar, Nizam's Kathi Kebabs, McDonald's, Pizza Hut, Domino's Pizza, Nirula's, Ruby Tuesday, Barista, Café Coffee Day and the food stalls at Dilli Haat

National Museum

The National Museum has reluctantly found a place in this guide. While it houses relics from India's glorious past dating back to 2,700 BC, it is frustratingly difficult to navigate. It houses over 200,000 works of art, ruins from the Indus Valley Civilization, Buddhist artifacts, manuscripts and jewellery. It would be best to get a guide or participate in one of the free tours. The third floor is worth a visit as it has a collection of more than 300 musical instruments dating from hundreds of years ago. Be sure to check out the National Museum Shop for souvenirs.

>Corner of Janpath and Maulana Azad Road
Tel: 011 2301 9272
Timings: Tue to Sun 10 am to 5 pm
Entry: Rs 10 Indians, Rs 300 foreigners
Web: www.nationalmueumindia.gov.in
Nearby sights: Connaught Place, Jantar Mantar
Nearby places to eat: Imperial Hotel, The Park Hotel, Hotel Le Meridien, The Lalit, Parikrama, Delhi Darbar, Nizam's Kathi Kebabs, Bengali Market, Wenger, McDonald's, Pizza

Hut, Domino's Pizza, Nirula's, Ruby Tuesday, Barista and Café Coffee Day

National Museum of Natural History

Dinosaurs reign supreme at the National Museum of Natural History. Divided into 4 galleries featuring the flora and fauna of India, the museum also has a large collection of fossils and stuffed animals and birds including films, discovery room, a bio-science computer room, an activity room and a mobile museum. Kids learn about evolution, life cycles, rain forests and some key environmental issues such as pollution, population crowding and man's encroachment on wildlife. A giant squid preserved in a tank is also worth a look.

>FICCI Building, Barakhamba Road, near Connaught Place
Nearest Metro: Mandi House
Tel: 011 2331 4849/4802/4932
Timings: Tue to Sat 10 am to 5 pm
Entry: Free
Web: http://nmnh.nic.in/
Nearby sights: Indira Gandhi Memorial, Gandhi Smriti Museum, National Gandhi Museum
Nearby places to eat: Imperial Hotel, The Park Hotel, Hotel Le Meridien, The Lalit, Parikrama, Delhi Darbar, Nizam's Kathi Kebabs, Bengali Market, Wenger's, McDonald's, Pizza Hut, Domino's Pizza, Nirula's, Ruby Tuesday, Barista and Café Coffee Day

National Police Museum

A great place for aspiring Agent Cody Bankses to learn facts about the police force is the National Police Museum. Items on display include confiscated goods, records of forgery, and fascinating articles, of national as well as international importance. Visitors also get an insight into forensic techniques used to solve crimes. (Also see *Dudes*, pp.43–4.)

>Central Bureau of Investigation HQ, CGO Complex, Lodhi Road
Timings: Mon to Friday 10:30 am to 4:30 pm; closed weekends
Nearest Metro: Central Secretariat
Entry: Free
Nearby sights: India Gate, Rashtrapati Bhavan, Lotus Temple, Nizamuddin's Shrine
Nearby eats: Eatopia at India Habitat Centre, restaurants at Khan Market, Basil and Thyme. If you're thinking you want to do some shopping too, head over to Ansal Plaza or South Extension Part II.

National Rail Museum

The National Rail Museum is a great place for kids. It houses a huge collection of rail engines and locomotives. It offers an exclusive exhibition of very uncommon examples of engines and carriages, such as the Patiala Monorail Teamway which was in service from 1907–1927. The indoor museum traces the history of Indian Railways. Covering a total area of about 10 acres, the best part of the visit is the toy train that takes a trip around the train yard. If a particular train catches your eye, you are free to wander the ground and pretend you're a conductor. In the collection is the first train, a steam engine, which started its journey from Mumbai to Thane for the first time in 1853. There's also a Viceregal Dining Car (1889) and the Prince of Wales Saloon (1875), Maharaja of Mysore's Saloon (1899), Maharaja of Baroda's Saloon (1886), etc. The museum also exhibits the famous Fairy Queen, the world's oldest operational steam locomotive which was built in the 1855 and certified by the Guinness Book of World Records. There's a central snack shop and outdoor toilet facilities. (Also see *Co-Ed*, p.53.)

>Chanakyapuri, behind Bhutan Embassy
Tel: 011 2688 1816; 011 2688 0939, ext 11
Timings: Tue to Sun 9:30 am to 5 pm during winter; closed on national holidays
Entry: Rs 10 for adults, Rs 3 for children; free entry for children on Tue
Web: www.railmuseum.org
Nearby sights: Lodhi Garden, Nehru Park
Nearby places to eat: The Ashok Hotel, Basil and Thyme, Khan Market

National Science Centre

Make the National Science Centre the first stop on your museum tour. The dinosaur gallery and the other interactive displays such as a hologram of one's head on a serving dish and disappearing hands and stretched bodies will lull them into thinking all the museums you want to visit on your Delhi tour will be like this.

>Just before Gate No.1, Bhairon Road, Pragati Maidan
Tel: 011 2337 1893/2337 1945
Nearest Metro: Pragati Maidan
Timings: Daily 10 am to 5:30 pm
Entry: Rs 20
Nearby sights: Pragati Maidan, Crafts Museum, Purana Qila, National Zoo, India Gate, Nizamuddin's Shrine
Nearby places to eat: Nathu's and Baci (see *Eats*, pp.132–3) in Sunder Nagar market; Oberoi Hotel (check out the café in the

basement); Flavors (see *Eats*, p.136) in Defence colony, All American Diner (see *Eats*, p.124) at the Indian Habitat Centre on Lodhi Road

Nehru Memorial

Originally the official home of the British commander-in-chief of the Indian army, the Nehru Memorial Museum and Library was the residence of India's first Prime Minister, Jawaharlal Nehru, who lived here for 16 years. The memorial collection features family photographs, personal letters and newspaper clippings of the political movement in India that led to its independence. Personal effects of Nehru, including clothing, awards and other mementos are on display throughout the house. There is a large rock on the front lawn that is inscribed with excerpts from his famous 'Tryst with destiny' speech. There are 3 perpetually burning flames for Nehru, Indira Gandhi and Rajiv Gandhi at the back of the building.

>Teen Murti Bhavan on Teen Murti Road (near Defence headquarters)
Tel: 011 2301 6734
Nearest Metro: Central Secretariat
Timings: Tue to Sun 10 am to 5 pm; closed on government holidays
Entry: Free
Nearby places to eat: Hotel Le Meridien, Imperial Hotel, The Lalit Hotel, Parikrama, Delhi Darbar, Nizam's Kathi Kebabs, Bengali Market, Wenger's, McDonald's, Pizza Hut, Domino's Pizza, Nirula's, Ruby Tuesday, Barista, Café Coffee Day and the food court at Dilli Haat. Venture out to South Extension Part II and enjoy some Mexican food at Sancho's.

Nehru Planetarium

Who would have ever thought that stargazing could be so much fun? The Nehru Planetarium, housed in a wing of the Nehru Memorial Museum and Library, has interesting programmes for serious enthusiasts and amateur astronomers. The air-conditioned theatre has a dome-shaped screen made up of 26 curved segments and one million hand-drilled holes to improve acoustics. The sky theatre, which screens taped and live public shows on various aspects of astronomy, can seat 270. There is a well in the centre of the theatre that houses the Carl Zeiss Spaceflight Master projector on a hydraulic lift which comes up during the shows. The Planetarium also has an exhibit area which displays many interactive models and pictures. Visitors can also view the space module Soyuz T-10 which carried India's first cosmonaut Rakesh Sharma, to space along with his space suit and mission journal. Throughout the year, there are a number of workshops or observing activities. There is also an Astronomy Quiz and Art Competitions in February and August.

>Teen Murti House on Teen Murti Road
Tel: 011 2301 6734
Timings: Tue to Sun 10 am to 5 pm
Show **timings:** Hindi 1:30 pm, 4 pm; English 11:30 am, 3:00 pm
Entry: Rs 15
Nearest Metro: Central Secretariat
Web: www.nehruplanetarium.org
Nearby sights: India Gate, Safdarjung's Tomb, Indira Gandhi Memorial Museum, Gandhi Smriti, Dilli Haat, India Gate, Jantar Mantar
Nearby eats: Hotel Le Meridien, Imperial Hotel, Hotel Inter-Continental, Parikrama, Delhi Darbar, Nizam's Kathi Kebabs, McDonald's, Pizza Hut, Domino's Pizza, Nirula's, Ruby Tuesday, Barista, Café Coffee Day and the food stalls at Dilli Haat

Museums at the Red Fort

There are 3 museums within the compound of the Red Fort. The Swatantrata Sangram Sangrahalay and Senani Smarak Museums cover the Indian freedom movement through newspaper clippings, books, exhibits and other memorabilia, including the origin of the Indian flag. The other museum inside the fort is the Indian Archaeological Museum, which has a collection of artifacts from the Mughal period. Also check out the Indian War Memorial which has a collection of weapons dating centuries.

>Red Fort
Chandni Chowk, opposite Dariba Kalan
Tel: 011 2327 3703
Nearest Metro: Chandi Chowk or Chawri Bazaar
Timings: Tue to Sun 10 am to 5 pm
Entry: Indians Rs 11, foreigners,Rs 100 (includes tickets for all 3 museums)
Parking: Rs 10 for 4 hours
Nearby sights: Jama Masjid, Chandni Chowk, Khari Baoli, Daryaganj, Gates of Old Delhi, St James Church, Car Parts Bazaar
Nearby places to eat: Food stalls in Chandni Chowk, Paranthe Wali Gali, Moti Mahal Restaurant, Karim's

Other Must Visits

Dances of India

Internationally renowned artists perform 6 folk,

tribal and classical dances of India. The show has been around for 29 years. Though it is mainly geared toward tourists, the show includes traditional dance forms such as Kathak and Bharatanatyam.
The footwork, hand gestures and expressive eye movements make the show most memorable. (See *Divas*, p.32.)

>Parsi Anjuman Hall, Bahadur Shah Zafar Marg, next to Maulana Azad Medical College
Tel: 011 2323 1228 or Laljah at 9810231644
Timings: Daily 6:45 pm
Come 15 minutes early if you want to buy tickets at the door.
Entry: Rs 200 per person

Jain Bird Hospital
Located just opposite the Red Fort, the Jain Bird Hospital is worth a visit. The hospital is located in the courtyard of the Digambara Jain Temple. The Jain principle goes against killing any living thing, and all of the 'patients' in the hospital are sick birds. The birds are cared for until they are well enough to be released, usually on a Saturday. Founded in 1956, the hospital has separate wards for various species of sparrows, pigeons, parrots and other domestic birds. The hospital admits about 60 birds a day. It also has a research laboratory and an intensive care unit to treat serious injuries. The patients are brought in by people who find them in parks, on the street or in their own homes. Part of the treatment at the hospital includes fixing the injury where possible, a bath and a nutritious diet. Those who visit the birds can learn about the species at the hospital and the birds in general that are found in the area.

>Digambar Jain Temple, opposite Red Fort, Chandni Chowk
Metro: Delhi Main
Timings: Daily
Entry: Free
Nearby sights: Red Fort, Jama Masjid, Chandni Chowk, Kashmere Gate, St James Church, Rajghat
Nearby places to eat: Karim's, Ghante Wala sweet shop, Paranthe Wali Gali, Chor Bizarre of Broadway Hotel, Moti Mahal

Kite Flying Festival
If you happen to be in Delhi in January, don't miss the Kite Flying Festival. It is celebrated on the Makar Sankranti Day (14 January) and has been an activity much anticipated by families and kite enthusiasts yearly. The skies all over the city are filled with colourful kites in countless shapes and

sizes. People gather on the lawns above Palika Bazaar and Connaught Place to participate in the festival. Go to the Lal Kuan (see *Co-ed*, pp.51–2) kite market to find a selection of thousands of kites. Two major events during the festival include the Fighter Kite Competition and display flying. Prizes can be won and trophies are awarded too.

>Palika Bazaar and Connaught Place
Timings: Every year on 14 January

Purana Qila
What better way to appreciate the history of Delhi than through music and lights? Various historical events in Delhi's history are told against the backdrop of Purana Qila (see *If You Have to be a Tourist* pp.106–7). The show is offered in Hindi and English.

>Old Delhi
Tel: 011 2462 9365; 011 2460 3178
Entry: Rs 25
Timings: Tue, Thu, Sat and Sun; Sept to Oct: 7 pm to 8 pm (Hindi), 8:30 pm to 9:30 pm (English); Nov to Jan: 6 pm to 7 pm (Hindi), 7:30 pm to 8:30 pm (English); Feb to April: 7 pm to 8 pm (Hindi), 8:30 pm to 9:30 pm (English); May to Aug: 7:30 pm to 8:30 pm (Hindi), 9 pm to 10 pm.

Walks

The Indian National Trust for Art and Cultural Heritage holds a variety of walks around Delhi for visitors to better appreciate the city.

Chandni Chowk
An amazingly overcrowded maze of narrow lanes, shops, houses and places of worship make up Chandni Chowk. The walk covers places of religious and historical importance. Of course you can take note of the shopping for after the nearly 2-hour walk. Unlike any other place in Delhi, Chandni Chowk is great because it truly does blend the old and the new. Kids can find toys, books, mehendi, bindi and bangles. Parents will find spices and teas and other household goods at great prices. But more than the shopping, it's the history that draws foreigners and locals to this place in throngs every day. Call INTACH for details.

>INTACH, 71 Lodhi Estate
Tel: 011 2464 1304
Timings: From 8:30 am
Entry: Rs 50 per person

City walk starting from the New Delhi Railway Staion
Developed by the Salaam Baalak Trust, a charity working with children, the walk is conducted by young people who really know

Delhi. Many, if not all, have grown up on the streets in and around the station and add authenticity to the talk. The walk meanders through the station and the neighbouring area to give the Nintendo-toting kids a realistic view of the kids who spend their lives on the street.

>New Delhi Railway Station
Tel: Brijesh at 99100 99348 to book
Timings: Mon to Sat 10 am to 12:30 pm
Entry: Rs 200 per person
Web: www.salaambaalaktrust.com/street_walk_delhi.asp

Nizamuddin
Visit the shrine of the Sufi saint Nizamuddin Aulia and explore the busy lanes of Nizamuddin. Other attractions include several Mughal tombs and the tomb of the famous Urdu poet Mirza Ghalib.

>**Tel:** 011 2464 1304; 011 2463 1818; 011 2463 2267
Timings: From 7:45 am on Sundays
Entry: Rs 50 per person
Details: Register the previous Friday by sending an email to intachdelhi@rediffmail.com or call one of the telephone numbers listed above.

IF YOU HAVE TO BE A TOURIST

No. 1: India Gate. It marks the bravery of soldiers, it is free to visit, parking is convenient, the lawns are great for running or picnicking on and ice cream is sold from vendors.

Discover the wonderment of all the sight-seeing must-sees New Delhi has to offer the family. It's all about adventure and education, but more importantly, fun. Nowhere else in the world can one find a fort the size of the Red Fort, with such a rich history. India Gate, which commemorates the soldiers who have given their lives for India's freedom is definitely worth a visit and the lawns are great for a picnic. If you can't make it to Agra, soak up the magnificence of Mughal architecture at Humayun's Tomb. The Jantar Mantar will amaze the kids with its layout and function. Who knew one could tell time without a Mickey Mouse watch? All of these places and more provide great opportunities to take fabulous family photos at some of the most photographed historic sites in Delhi. Get ready to point and shoot. And, to better understand the historical significance of the monuments, the Archaeological Survey of India (ASI) has placed kiosks around the monuments for tourists to rent audio guides for Rs 100. Languages offered include English, French, German, Spanish, Japanese and Chinese.

Akshardham Temple

Calling the Akshardham Temple a religious place would be a misnomer if you only consider the fantastic lawns, boat rides, musical fountains and the animatronics show. But all of this is built around prayer and reflection at the Mandir. The Akshardham experience traces India's history, values, art and humanity. Akshardham means the eternal, divine abode of the supreme God, the abode of eternal values and virtues of Akshar as defined in the Vedas and Upanishads where divine bhakti, purity and peace forever pervades. Cameras, video cameras, mobile phones or any electronic items are not allowed inside the complex. Forget about the crackers and juice boxes too, as no outside food is allowed inside. Hot and cold vegetarian snacks are sold at the food court though, so the kids certainly won't go hungry.

>NH-24, near Noida Morh
Tel: 011 2201 6688
Timings: Tue to Sat 9 am to 6 pm
Entry: Free; Exhibitions
Entry: Rs 125 for adults; Rs 75 for children 4 to 12; free for children 4 and under
Web: www.akshardham.com

Begumpur Masjid

The Begumpur Masjid is sure to appeal to children who like the majesty of big structures. Preceding Shah Jahan's wondrous Jama Masjid (see pp.101–2), it is a massive 14th century stone mosque built during the Tughlaq era. Located in the middle of Begumpur and Kalu Sarai, the area was once the centre of the Tughlaq city of Jahanapanah. There's a staircase that still leads to the roof. The huge mosque, built almost entirely of gray Delhi quartzite and mortar, is covered with lime plaster. The courtyard is surrounded on 3 sides by arched colonnades known as riwwaqs, each topped by low, hemispherical domes. The size of the mosque came in handy during the British rule of India. An entire village moved into the mosque for a period.

>Take a left toward Sarvodaya Enclave from Aurobindo Marg. Proceed to Begumpur village. Park in front of the Sarvpriya Vihar Club, and then take the straight lane that leads past Bijai Mandal. The masjid takes 2 minutes on foot. Entry is free, and since the mosque isn't in use any more, visitors do not have to remove their shoes. It is best to go before sunset.

Birla Mandir

No kids are probably keen to go to any religious place be it a church, mosque or temple. But if parents had to pick one place, this would be it because of the sheer size which is magnificent and the wall carvings. The Laxmi Narayan Temple, also known as Birla Mandir, is one of Delhi's major temples and draws lots of devotees. The temple, built in 1938 by industrialist GD Birla, is located in the west of Connaught Place. Dedicated to Laxmi, the goddess of prosperity and Narayan, the preserver, the temple has the distinction of being inaugurated by Mahatma Gandhi. He had one condition: all castes should be allowed to enter the temple. The walls of the temple are decorated with various Hindu symbols including many swastikas. The original swastika, separate from the modern-day association with Hitler, is an ancient Aryan symbol for perfection. That is explained on one of the walls. A Buddha temple in the complex has paintings that describe his life and work. It can get crowded, but the morning is best.

>Mandir Marg (Central Delhi)
Nearest Metro: Ramakrishna Ashram Marg
Timings: Sunrise to sunset
Entry: Free
Nearby sights: Rashtrapati Bhavan, India Gate, Jantar Mantar, Gurudwara Bangla Sahib and Hanuman Mandir
Nearby places to eat: Restaurants at Connaught Place
Time required: 20 minutes

Gates of Old Delhi
The gates of the seventh city of Delhi, Shahjahanabad, played an integral part in its survival. The city, which was completed in 1649, was surrounded by 14 imposing gates used for people and the royal procession to exit and enter. During Emperor Shah Jahan's reign, all these gates were well guarded and were closed at night. Five gates survive today. Visitors will most appreciate the magnificence of the high arches and the heavy structures. One cannot walk from gate to gate with kids given the distance and traffic. Have the driver of the car on speed dial. A look and photo at all of the gates will take about 45 minutes. Lots of food and bathroom break options at Kashmere and Ajmeri gates. What the family should take away from the visit is how many thousands of soldiers it took to guard the gates to keep the citizens within safe at a time when numerous people were angling for power. The fact that they are battled scarred from cannon balls, swords and other crude weapons and are still standing is an architectural feat.

- **Kashmere Gate**
  The royal processions of emperors and other royalty used to pass through this gate on their trips to Kashmir or northern India. The gate was the scene of intense fighting in the 1857 War of Independence against the British. It is located near the Inter State Bus Terminal. The damage caused by the battle is still visible.
- **Ajmeri Gate**
  The thoroughfare of Ajmeri Gate led to the city of Ajmer. It is located on the southwest of the walled city, near

the New Delhi Railway Station. The gate has been restored and is surrounded by a nice park.

- **Delhi Gate**
  Delhi Gate is found opposite the Daryaganj Police Station and Ambedkar Ground. It was the southeast gate. This gate got its name because the road from this gate led to the previous cities of Delhi. Made of red sandstone, it used to be an imposing gateway and had a wooden locking system. The popular Sunday book market in Daryaganj starts at this point.
- **Turkman Gate**
  Built in the late 1650s, Turkman Gate was the southern gate of the old walled city. It is named after the Muslim saint, Hazrat Shah Turkman Bayabani whose tomb predates Shahjahanabad. Turkman Gate, located near the Ramlila Ground can be reached by taking the Jawahar Lal Nehru Marg, a densely populated area in the city.
- **Nigambodh Gate**
  Located on the northeastern edge of the city on the Ring Road near the Yamuna Bazaar, Nigambodh Gate gets its name from the Nigambodh Ghat. According to the legend, it was on this ghat that Lord Brahma is said to have bathed and recovered his lost memory and sacred books. The name Nigambodh Ghat means realization of knowledge.

Gurudwara Sisganj
We do not usually visit places of worship other than our own religions, but the Gurudwara Sisganj offers an opportunity for both parents and kids to do so. Given that India has dozens of sub-sects, it is wonderful to find places like this which also offer a tour. The gurudwara commemorates the site where Guru Tegh Bahadur, the ninth guru of the Sikhs was beheaded under a banyan tree on the orders of Mughal Emperor Aurangzeb, when he objected to the emperor's use of force against the Hindus who refused to renounce their religion. It is located on the main Chandni Chowk road, just opposite the Baptist Church. Visitors must cover their heads and leave their shoes outside. There is an information office near the entrance for those who want a more formal tour. The main worship room has the Sikh Holy Book, the Guru Granth Sahib under a beautiful golden canopy. Part of the banyan tree under which

the guru was killed is kept in a room at the gurdwara. Religious hymns are sung throughout the day and everyone receives karah (a sweet made of wheat and ghee that has been blessed) upon leaving. The food is made hygienically so don't worry about sampling it. A few rupees can be given as offering but it is not required.

>On the main Chandni Chowk road, just opposite the Baptist Church, before Sunheri Masjid (Old Delhi)
Nearest Metro: Delhi main
Entry: Free
Time required: 1 hour
Nearby sights: Red Fort, Chandni Chowk, Jama Masjid, Kashmere Gate, St James Church and Rajghat
Nearby places to eat: Karim's, Ghante Wala Sweet Shop, food stalls near Jama Masjid, Paranthe Wali Gali, Chor Bizarre of Broadway Hotel, Moti Mahal

Humayun's Tomb

When children see a picture of Humayun's Tomb, they tend to confuse it with the Taj Mahal in Agra. The construction of the tomb began in 1572, more than 80 years before the Taj, by Hamida Banu Begum, the wife of Mughal Emperor Humayun. The beautiful arched entrances and domes are surrounded by expansive, well manicured formal gardens. The tomb was designed in a Persian 'charbagh' or square 4-garden style enclosed by high walls on 3 sides and the Yamuna river on the other. The gardens are 348 square metres and are divided into 36 squares by a network of water channels and fountains. The beautiful structure was built of red sandstone and red and white marble. In addition to Humayun, the graves of several rulers of the Mughal dynasty lie in the vaults below the platform in the mausoleum. These include the graves of Dara Shikoh, Shah Jahan's favourite son and Bahadur Shah II, the last Mughal emperor of Delhi, who took shelter in Humayun's tomb and was later captured here by Lieutenant Hodson during the Revolt of 1857. The tomb is also called 'The Dormitory of the House of Timur' because of the known and unknown graves entombed. Humayun's Tomb was named a UNESCO World Heritage Site. Kids will enjoy the inlaid water channels that they can skip over, taking photos behind the inlaid panels and actually being able to go inside a crypt. Boo! Bus loads of tourists visit the tomb daily but the sheer size of it doesn't ever make it feel too crowded. The gardens have many benches under shady trees so the family can take a break and have a snack. No food is sold inside.

>On Mathura Road, near the crossing with Lodhi Road (South Delhi)
Nearest Metro: Kendriya Terminal
Timings: Open on all days from sunrise to sunset
Entry: Rs 10 for Indians / Rs 250 for foreigners; free on Fridays
Parking: Rs 10 for 4 hrs (Rates are subject to change)
Time for sight-seeing: About 1.5 hours
Nearby places to eat: Khan Market
Nearby sights: Lodhi Gardens, Delhi Zoo, India Gate

India Gate

No other monument in Delhi would epitomize a memento of a visit to the city but India Gate. Built by Edwin Lutyens in 1931, India Gate commemorates the Indian soldiers who died during World War I and the Afghan Wars. Originally called the All India War Memorial, the names of the soldiers who died in these wars are inscribed on the walls. At 42 metres in height, it can easily be compared to the Arc de Triomphe of Paris. In 1971, an eternal flame or Amar Jawan Jyoti, was lit under the arch of India Gate to honour the 'Unknown Soldier'. The flame is never put out and is guarded by soldiers. Near the flame, is a rifle with a helmet on it which is in tribute to the soldiers who died during battle. The best time to visit India Gate is after sunset when it is flooded with light and looks really beautiful. There is a domed kiosk with a red sandstone roof just a few metres from India Gate. A marble statue of George V once stood there. It was also designed by Sir Edwin Lutyens and was built in 1936. The statue was removed post independence and is in the Coronation Memorial Park in North Delhi. Be sure to check out the nearby Children's Park (see *Playground Paradise*, p.73) with an array of playground equipment, and pay Rs 30 for a 15-minutes paddle boat ride on the little lake next to India Gate. Republic Day is marked every January 26 with a grand parade along Rajpath replete with colourful floats, and the participation of folk dancers and children from across India. The president of India places a wreath at the Amar Jawan Jyoti in honour of all the soldiers in the Indian armed forces. Ice cream cones, water and other snacks are sold on the grounds, and a bevy of toys and balloons that will probably break before the kids even reach the car.

>Less than a mile from Connaught Place (Rajiv Chowk), at the eastern end of Rajpath (Central Delhi)
Timings: Daily, 24 hours
Entry: Free
Time required: 1 hour
Nearby sights: Children's Park, Rashtrapati Bhavan, Parliament House, the National Museum, National Gallery of Modern Art.
Nearby places to eat: Ice cream vendors on the lawns; hotels Le Meridien, Imperial; Connaught Place restaurants (McDonald's, Pizza Hut, Parikrama, Ruby Tuesday, Barista and Café Coffee Day)

Jama Masjid

Yet another magnificent structure built by Emperor Shah Jahan, the Jama Masjid is the largest mosque in India and one of the last to be built by him. It is also called the Friday Mosque as the word Jama means Friday, a holy day for Muslims. However, the original name was Masjid-i-Jahanuma or 'The Mosque Commanding a View of the World'. Completed in 1656, the mosque is built from red sandstone and white marble and is located 500 metres west of the Red Fort. The mosque was built on a high platform with 3 gateways, 4 towers and 2 minarets, and it is a replica of the Moti Masjid in Agra. One was exclusively reserved for the emperor and other royalty. Today, visitors can enter the mosque from the northern or southern gates. Non Muslims are allowed inside the mosque all day long except from 12:30 pm to 2 pm. Both men and women must remove their shoes and cover their heads. Moderate dress is mandatory. While there, visitors can see 2 very old copies of the Quran, the Muslim holy book, made of deerskin and one long hair said to be from the Prophet Mohammed's beard, his sandals and a footprint of his in marble. Inscriptions throughout the structure detail the history of the mosque. Visitors can climb the southern minaret, but the space on the top is small. This is not advisable for small children. One can see the Red Fort and all Old Delhi from the top.Women are not allowed to go alone to the top of the minaret. During Muslim festivals of Id-ul-Fitr and Id-ul-Zoha, thousands of devotees at a time offer their prayers in the courtyard.

>500 metres west of Red Fort, near Chandni Chowk in Old Delhi
Timings: Daily sunrise to sunset

Nearest Metro: Kashmere Gate
Entry: Free and open to all except during prayer timings. Tourists should cover their knees as well their arms and remove their shoes before entering the mosque. Cloth to be draped around your limbs or feet, is available at the entrance and is provided on request.
Photography charges: Rs 20 for Indians / Rs 150 for foreigners
Charges to climb the southern minaret: Rs 10
Time required: 1 to 2 hours
Nearby places to eat: Karim's, McDonald's, Paranthe Wali Gali, Ghantewala sweet shop, food stalls near Jama Masjid
Nearby sights: Red Fort, Chandni Chowk, St James Church and Rajghat

Jantar Mantar

Located near Connaught Place, the Jantar Mantar, sometimes called Yantra Mandir (literally, the 'temple of instruments'; also 'yantra' and mantra mean instruments and formula respectively), was built in the year 1724 by Maharaja Jai Singh II of Jaipur and was operational for 7 years. The primary purpose of the observatory was to compile astronomical tables, calculate the time and track the movements of celestial bodies. It comprises several salmon coloured structures, called the Samrat Yantra, the Ram Yantra, the Jai Prakash and the Mishra Yantra. The Samrat Yantra is a huge sundial that dominates the complex. It was used to measure the time of the day and is accurate to within half a second. In the age of digital this and that, children are likely to be in awe of the sundial alone. The Ram Yantra and the Jai Prakash were also used for the study of heavenly bodies. For calculating the shortest and the longest days of the year, the 2 pillars on the southwest portion of Mishra Yantra were used. In December of each year, one of these pillars covers the other with its shadow. The Ram Yantra helped determine the position of the sun, moon, planets, stars and other heavenly bodies. For measuring the zodiacal sign or the group of the stars on the meridian, the Jai Prakash was used. Kids take it for granted that time-keepers are these tiny, practical things that fit nicely on their wrists. It would be important to teach them that these instruments were important in helping to determine seasons and when and what to plant for sustenance as they chronicled the passage of time accurately. The instruments are spread over an open area, and a stroller is advisable for little kids who are likely to get tired. There are toilets and drinking water. Parking can be found about 200 metres away. Although the instruments were quite accurate, the tall buildings that have been built around the observatory have diminished their accuracy. The Jantar Mantar is among several astronomical observatories built by Maharaja Jai Singh II. The other observatories are in Jaipur, Varanasi, Ujjain and Mathura, and have fallen into disrepair. The one in Mathura was demolished and the Ujjain and Varanasi observatories are decaying. The Jaipur observatory was refurbished and is the best of the lot.

>Parliament Street (Central Delhi)
Timings: Sunrise to sunset
Nearest Metro: Rajiv Chowk
Entry: Rs 5 Indians / Rs 100 foreigners
Time required: 1 hour
Web: www.jantarmantar.org
Nearby sights: Rashtrapati Bhavan, India Gate, Gurudwara Bangla Sahib and Hanuman Mandir
Nearby places to eat: Hotel Le Meridien, Imperial Hotel, Hotel Inter-Continental, Parikrama, Delhi Darbar, Nizam's Kathi Kebabs, McDonald's, Pizza Hut, Domino's Pizza, Nirula's, Ruby Tuesday, Barista, Café Coffee Day and the food stalls at Dilli Haat

Lodhi Tomb

Lodhi Tomb is located in Lodhi Garden and is one of the many mausoleums in the city that have been built inside a garden. Lodhi Tomb entombs Sikandar Lodhi as well as the Tomb of Muhammad Shah, Shish Gumbad and Bara Gumbad. Sikandar Lodhi's tomb is shaped like an octagon and is representative of Mughal architecture. The first garden tomb to be built in Delhi, it has a double dome top and dates back to the early sixteenth century. The fact that the tomb is in the middle of the beautiful Lodhi Gardens is just a bonus. There's also a small petting zoo. On any given day, one can see yoga classes, take a guided tour, try to catch butterflies or just chill in the shade. There are vendors selling water and ice cream at the gates outside the gardens.

>Lodhi Garden on Lodhi Road (South Delhi)
Timings: Sunrise to sunset
Entry: Free
Time required: As long as you want. Have a picnic under a big tree afterward
Nearby sights: India Gate, Humayun's Tomb, Safdarjung's Tomb

Nearby places to eat: India Habitat Centre, Khan Market, Basil and Thyme in Santushti Shopping Complex

Lotus Temple

The Bahai House of Worship is popularly known as the Lotus Temple because of its shape like a lotus flower. Located opposite Kalkaji Mandir, East of Nehru place, the temple is one of the most visited edifices in India, attracting more than 70 million people since it opened, surpassing the number of yearly visitors even to the Taj Mahal. Maybe the temple has such appeal because it is the only Bahai House of Worship in Asia, with 7 worldwide. The temples are also famous for their architectural beauty and 9-sided design representing the manifestation of God and are open to all regardless of religion. Sitting on 26 acres of beautifully landscaped pools and gardens, the concrete and white marble structure was completed in 1986 at a cost of Rs 10 million. The uniquely designed temple, constructed by 700 workers, has won many architectural awards. There is an information centre on the grounds that provides information on different aspects of the Bahai faith, however, it seems to be closed most of the time. The 9 walkways represent the 9 unifying spiritual paths of the Bahai faith. The 9 doors of the Lotus Temple open onto a huge hall that can hold up to 2,500 people. Silence is a prerequisite inside the New Delhi Lotus Temple, so no talking and please put the mobile phones on silent. Also, one needs to take off one's shoes before entering. There is a shoe collection point and tickets are given. Don't tell the kiddies that the inside doesn't look like a lotus flower, too, let them find out for themselves.

>Opposite Kalkaji Mandir, East of Nehru Place (South Delhi)
Timings: Tue to Sun 10 am to 12:30 pm; 4:30 pm to 7:30 pm
Entry: Free
Parking: Rs 40 (subject to change)
Prayer session timings: 10 am to 10:15 am; noon to 12:15 pm; 3 pm to 3:15 pm; 5 pm to 5:15 pm
Time required: 45 minutes due to the long lines
Nearby sights: Kalkaji Temple and Nizamuddin's Shrine
Nearby places to eat: Hotel Park Royal; Inter-Continental Nehru Place, Yum Yum Tree and Ego Thai in New Friends Colony Community Centre, restaurants in Greater Kailash I Market

Parliament House

Parliament House was designed by Sir Edwin Lutyens and Sir Herbert Baker, the architects of New Delhi. The building accommodates the 2 Houses of Parliament, the Lok Sabha (House of the People) and Rajya Sabha (Council of States). His Royal Highness, the Duke of Connaught, laid the foundation stone of Parliament House in the year 1921. It took 6 years to complete the Delhi Parliament House and it was inaugurated in the year 1927 by the then Governor-General of India, Lord Irwin. The transfer of power from British rule to Indian rule took place in the central hall on the night of 14 August 1947.

Parliament House is located at the end of Parliament Street in a regal circular building which has many columns as part of its design. It is where the representatives of world's largest democracy meet to govern the more than 1.5 billion people of India. At just one storey tall, the building—made of blocks of sandstone—is 75 feet high and 570 feet in diameter. It houses ministerial offices, a number of committee rooms and a brilliant library. It was originally supposed to be an extension of the Viceroy's House (Rashtrapati Bhavan), but was designated as a Parliament House or Legislative Assembly of the country in 1919, with the foundation stone laid by the Duke of Connaught in 1921. The Chambers house Lok Sabha (Lower House of Parliament), the Rajya Sabha (Upper House of Parliament) and the Parliament library are attached by galleries. The meetings are held in the domed circular central hall and the 3 semi-circular buildings. The 3 semi-circular chambers are surrounded by a circular corridor or an open verandah with 144 pillars, which along with the 28 m central dome give the whole building a majestic look. Parliament House is surrounded by beautiful lawns, gardens, fountains and waterways. Enclosing the Parliament House Estate is an attractive red sandstone wall or iron grill with iron gates.

Of the 550 seats in the Lok Sabha, 530 members are elected representatives of the Indian states and 20 elected members represent Union Territories (territories governed by the Central (Federal) government). The Rajya Sabha has 250 members, 238 of whom represent states and Union Territories and the 12 nominated members are nominated on the basis of eminence in the fields of arts, sciences, literature and other disciplines. Parliament is in session 3 times a year: summer, monsoon and winter. Prior permission has to be taken before visiting the Parliament House. Indians need to get permission by applying at the Parliament Secretariat and foreigners through their Embassies or High Commissions.

> Northwest of Vijay Chowk, next to the Secretariat buildings at the end of Parliament Street (Sansad Marg) (Central Delhi)
Metro: Central Secretariat
Timings: Entry requires official permission, whether Parliament is in session or not. Visitors can enter the public galleries with prior permission, after receiving an official pass.
Entry: Free, but prior permission required (foreigners/citizens: from their embassies or High commissions/from the reception office on Raisina Road)
Time required: 2 hours
Nearby sights: India Gate, Rashtrapati Bhavan, Jantar Mantar
Nearby places to eat: Hotel Le Meridien, Imperial Hotel, restaurants in Connaught Place

Purana Qila
East of India Gate and north of Humayun's tomb, the Purana Qila (Old Fort) is said to be constructed on an ancient mound, which possibly conceals the ruins of the city of Indraprastha (dating back to 900 BC).
It was built by Emperor Humayun and Sher Shah who captured the city before it was recaptured by Humayun. At about one mile long, the 18-metre high walls of the fort have 3 gates and are surrounded by a moat fed by the Yamuna river, which once flowed on the eastern side of the fort. The wall was built by Humayun while the buildings in the fort are attributed to Sher Shah. Unlike other forts built by the Mughals, the Old Fort does not have a complex of palaces, recreational or administrative buildings. Pieces of pottery known as Painted Grey Ware and relics dating to around 1000 BC were excavated from the site. An archaeological museum in the main gate gives a brief history of Delhi and the Purana Qila, and has a few artifacts found during excavation. Visitors should check out the mosque built by Sher Shah in 1541, Sher-Mandal, a 2-storey, red sandstone and marble octagonal tower and boating on the lake. The top of the mosque offers a great view. Purana Qila

also has a sound and light show that showcases 5,000 years of Delhi's history. There are toilet facilities and snacks and drinks can be purchased.

>Mathura Road, to the East of India Gate and north of Humayun's Tomb (South Delhi)
Nearest Metro: Pragati Maidan
Timings: Daily sunrise to sunset
Entry: Rs 5 Indians / Rs 100 foreigners
Time required: Two-and-a half hours
Nearby sights: The Delhi Zoo is within walking distance, India Gate, Humayun's Tomb
Nearby places to eat: Restaurants at Sunder Nagar Market including Baci, Hotel Oberoi, Flavors in Defence Colony, India Habitat Centre
Boating/shikara rides/water scooter rides: Rs 40 for 30 minutes / Rs 100 for two rounds / Rs 50 for two rounds in the lake adjacent to the Old Fort. It has a separate entry just before the main entrance of Purana Qila if you come from the Pragati Maidan exhibition grounds.
Timings: Noon to 7 pm in summer; 11 am to 6 pm in winter

At the Old Fort, Delhi Tourism organizes a **sound and light show** every evening.

>**Tel:** 011 2462 9365; 011 2460 3178
Entry: Rs 25
Timings: Tue, Thu, Sat and Sun; Sept to Oct: 7 pm to 8 pm (Hindi), 8:30 pm to 9:30 pm (English); Nov to Jan: 6 pm to 7 pm (Hindi), 7:30 pm to 8:30 pm (English); Feb to April: 7 pm to 8 pm (Hindi), 8:30 pm to 9:30 pm (English); May to Aug: 7:30 pm to 8:30 pm (Hindi), 9 pm to 10 pm

Qutab Minar

The Qutab Minar, said to be a tower of victory to commemorate Muslim rule in India, is the highest stone tower in the country at a height of 73 metres. Construction of the five-storied minaret made of red sandstone and marble began in 1193 by Qutab-ud-din Aibak after he defeated Delhi's last Hindu kingdom. It could not be completed in his lifetime so later rulers made additions to the tower. Three storeys were constructed by Iltutmush, and the rest by Firoz Shah Tughlak.

Each of the storeys has a balcony with their diameter ranging from 15 m at the base to 2.5 m at the top. It is adorned with inscriptions and elaborately decorated brackets. There is also the Quwwat-ul-Islam Mosque, the first mosque built in India, which is at the base of the Qutab Minar.

Inside the courtyard of the mosque is a 7 m high iron pillar. It is believed that if you are able to encircle it with your hands while standing with your back to it, your wish will be granted. However, the iron pillar now has a fence around it so visitors can see and not touch, unless of course they have very long arms. An inscription near the eastern gate notes that the stones used for the Qutab Minar came from the demolition of 27 Hindu temples. The toilets are located down a long passageway near the entrance, and the Western style toilet is relatively clean as it is unlocked only on request. There are a few tables near the concession stand where sandwiches, sodas, water, chips and candy are sold. Snacks are also sold outside the entrance along with film and batteries. Many trees provide shade so a picnic can be had on the grounds.

>Mehrauli
Timings: Daily sunrise to sunset
Entry: Rs 10 Indians; Rs 250 foreigners; children free
Time required: 1 hour
Nearby sights: Mehrauli Archaeological Park
Nearby places to eat: Restaurants along Aurobindo Marg

Rajghat

Rajghat is the resting place of Mahatma Gandhi, the Father of the Nation. His cremation took place there in 1948. The memorial has a simple square platform made of black stone, with the words 'Hey Ram', his last words before he died, inscribed near it. As homage to the Mahatma, an eternal flame, in a copper urn, burns 24/7. Enclosing the memorial is a simple low wall. Every Friday, a remembrance ceremony takes place. Gandhi's birthday (2 October) and his death anniversary (30 January) are marked by prayers at Rajghat. The memorial is set in a lovely garden with trees that bear labels naming the famous dignitaries who planted them. Visitors must remove their shoes when approaching the Rajghat Samadhi as they have to do when entering a temple. Next to Gandhi's cremation site are those of other leaders: Indira Gandhi (called Shakti Sthal); Rajiv Gandhi (Vir Bhumi); Jawaharlal Nehru (Shanti Vana) and Lal Bahadur Shastri (Vijay Ghat).

>Opposite Red Fort (Central Delhi)
Tel: 011 2332 0005
Metro: Kashmere Gate
Timings: Daily 5 am to 8 pm
Entry: Free
Time required: 45 minutes

Nearby sights: National Gandhi Museum, Red Fort, Chandni Chowk, Old Delhi
Nearby places to eat: Karim's, Ghantewala sweet shop, Moti Mahal, Lalit Hotel

Rashtrapati Bhavan

Rashtrapati Bhavan is the official residence of the President of India. It was the former residence of the Viceroy of India during the days of British rule. Rashtrapati Bhavan was designed by Sir Edwin Lutyens, who designed the city of Delhi. It took 18 years to build the 200,000 square feet, 340-room palace, which has 54 bedrooms, 37 salons, 74 lobbies and loggias, 18 staircases and 37 fountains. Kids will be in awe that someone could actually live in a structure this big. Rashtrapati Bhavan has a large court in the front and a 145-metre column, the Jaipur Column, given as a gift by the Maharaja of Jaipur stands in the middle of the main courtyard. There is a Mughal style garden in the rear. Popularly known as the Mughal Gardens or Butterfly Garden, this garden behind Rashtrapati Bhavan is designed after the terraced gardens of Kashmir and spreads over an area of 130 hectares. Visitors can access the Mughal Gardens (see *Beauty and the Beast*, p.14) only 5 weeks every year when it is open to the public from 16 February to 23 March. It has a number of rare species of flowers especially roses, which are found nowhere else in India. The only way visitors can enjoy the inside of Rashtrapati Bhavan and not just the gardens, is by booking ahead for a tour. With the exception of the White House, the Kremlin and Buckingham Palace, rarely can visitors see the homes of their official or ceremonial leaders of countries. Even the Palais de l' Elysée in Paris is not open to the public. Many of the homes, which also serve as meeting places for official government business, are closed due to security reasons. But this is one of those rare opportunities of a structure that has housed leaders from colonial rule to the present.

>Built on Raisina Hill, western end of Rajpath (Central Delhi)
Tel: 011 2301 5321 to book a tour
Nearest Metro: Central Secretariat
Entry: Free, but permission is required
Special event/Annual event: Republic Day Parade and Change of Guard ceremony every Saturday

between 10:35 am to 11 am in winter and 8:30 am to 9:15 am in summer
Nearby sights: India Gate, Parliament House, National Museum, Jantar Mantar
Nearby places to eat: Parikrama, Delhi Darbar, Nizam's Kathi Kebabs, Bengali Market, Wenger's, McDonald's, Pizza Hut, Domino's Pizza, Nirula's and Ruby Tuesday

Red Fort

Lal Qila, also known as the Red Fort was named a World Heritage site by UNESCO in 2007. Located on the banks of the Yamuna river, the Red Fort is the largest and one of the most important monuments in all of India and the world's largest non-functional fort. The prime minister addresses the nation from the fort every 15 August, which marks the country's independence from British rule. The whole structure is made of red stone. The fort was built in 1648 by Shah Jahan, the Mughal king who also built the famous Taj Mahal. Shah Jahan shifted his capital from Agra to Delhi and the Red Fort was the seat of the new capital. Lal Qila stands at the eastern side of Shahjahanabad and its name comes from the huge wall that encloses the whole structure. The wall is 2.5 km long and the height varies from 16 metres on the river side to 33 metres toward the city. The city was built with 14 gates for people and the royal procession to enter and exit. Just 5 of the gates survive today. The path through the Kashmere Gate, located at the northern end of the Walled City of Delhi, led to Kashmir. Built in the late 1650s, the Turkman Gate was the southern entrance to the old Walled City. It is now in one of the most densely populated areas of the capital. The Ajmeri Gate is one of the gates of Shahjahanabad, which would open onto the western side of the Walled City. Shah Jahan's mosque is situated in Ajmer. The biggest tourist draw is the huge wall that surrounds the entire fort. The walls have 2 entrances, one at the Delhi Gate (the southern gateway), and the other at the Lahore gate (named as such because it faces west toward Lahore in Pakistan), which leads to a long covered bazaar called Chatta Chowk. The walls are lined with shops. The Lahore Gate is the main entrance point of the fort. Chandni Chowk, one of the most bustling markets in Delhi, is across from the gate.

There are 3 museums at the Red Fort. The Indian Archaeological Museum, Indian War Memorial, Swatantra Sanghralaya and Senani Smarak contain artifacts from the Mughal period to India's freedom movement. The Archaeological Museum displays a collection of objects from the Mughal period and old maps, engravings, arms and paintings from that period (see *Make the Most of Museums*, p.90). A new 400-car parking lot for private cars makes visiting the Fort much easier. Since visitors are not allowed to enter through Delhi Gate, free shuttle buses take visitors from the parking lot to the Lahori Gate entrance of the fort. Car parking is Rs 10 and Rs 5 for scooters and motorcycles.

>Old Delhi, banks of Yamuna river (Old Delhi)
Metro: Chandni Chowk
Tel: 011 2327 3703 (Archaeology); 011 2327 5569 (Arms and weapons)
Timings: Tue to Sun 9:30 am to 4:30 pm
Entry: Rs 10 Indians/Rs 250 foreigners
Entry for Sound and Light Show: Rs 50. Tickets are available at a kiosk at the fort
Time required: 2 to 4 hours
Timings of sound and light show: Nov–Jan: 7:30 pm; Jan–Apr: 8:30 pm; May–Aug: 9 pm; Sept–Oct: 8:30 pm

Safdarjung's Tomb

Considered the poor, underrated cousin of Humayun's Tomb, Safdarjung's Tomb entombs Muqim Abul Mansur Khan, also known as Safdarjung. He was the viceroy of Awadh under Mughal Emperor Mohammed Shah and later became prime minister.
In 1754, Nawab Shuja-ud-Daulah, Safdarjung's son, built the tomb, which holds the distinction of being the last garden tomb built in Delhi. Despite its historical importance, the tomb sometimes doesn't register on the must-see sights radar. Located near the Safdarjung Airport on Aurobindo Marg, the tomb was built on a high terrace in a grand garden with high walls and a central domed mausoleum. The 2 graves inside the tomb are of Safdarjung and his wife. The tomb, typical of Mughal architecture, is made of red sandstone and buff stone and has several pavilions, a courtyard, mosque and a madrassa (Muslim school) inside the premises. There is a library over the main gateway, maintained by the Archaeological Survey of India (ASI). There are toilets and drinking water for visitors.

>Intersection of Safdarjung Road and Aurobindo Marg, near the Safdarjang Airport

(Central Delhi)
Nearest Metro: Central Secretariat
Timings: Daily sunrise to sunset
Entry: Rs 10 Indians, Rs 100 foreigners
Time required: 1 hour
Nearby sights: Dilli Haat, Lodhi Garden, India Gate
Nearby places to eat: Food court at Dilli Haat, Eatopia, restaurants at Khan Market

Zafar Mahal

Zafar Mahal was the part-time home of the late Mughals. Believers in the powers of the Sufi saint Qutubuddin Bakhtiyar Kaki, his followers built a little palace next to his dargah (tomb) in Mehrauli. At the site, one also finds the Moti Masij and some graves that are in dire need of upkeep. Those buried here include Bahadur Shah I, Shah Alam II (who was blinded by the Rohillas), his son Akbar Shah and Prince Mirza Fakhru (son of Bahadur Shah II, also known as Zafar).

> From Adham Khan's tomb, next to the Mehrauli bus stand, walk down the main street toward Bakhtiyar Kaki's dargah. Bring a plastic bag as you will have to remove your shoes and carry them with you through the dargah.
Timings: Daily sunrise to sunset

No. 1: Agra. Explore three World Heritage Sites within a short distance from each other including the grand monument to love, the Taj Mahal.

There is plenty to see and do just a few hours drive from Delhi. Experience nature, calming lakes, and places where we just want to relax. The Taj Mahal in Agra should top the list, but also buy crafts at the Surajkund mela; watch the birds at Sultanpur Bird Sanctuary and soar over the city in a hot air balloon from Damdama Lake. If forts get the pulse racing, there's Neemrana Fort Palace, Kesroli Fort and the Mud Fort in Kuchesar. Picnics in parks outside the city, boating and horseback riding can easily be managed with some pre-planning and snacks for the road. However, if sometimes just a day in picturesque surroundings won't do, there are lots of hotel/guest house options nearby.

A Peep into History

Agra

The Taj Mahal in Agra needs no introduction. It was built as a mausoleum of Shah Jahan's favourite wife, Mumtaz Mahal. It is probably one of the world's most photographed monuments. One of the New Seven Wonders of the World, it is just 4 hours away by car (if you leave Delhi by 7 in the morning, that is); and 2 hours by train. The Taj and its surrounding lawns are magnificent—children will enjoy the hokey photos that make it look like they have the Taj Mahal in the palm of their hands, but the guides are nothing like the hilarious rendition by the kids in *Slumdog Millionaire*! Located on the banks of the Yamuna river in the northern state of Uttar Pradesh, Agra was once the capital of India from 1526 to 1658, before Emperor Shah Jahan shifted the capital to its current home. The Taj Mahal, Agra Fort and Fatehpur Sikri are all UNESCO World Heritage Sites. Have lunch at the Oberoi Amarvilas, then hit the road back to Delhi. For security reasons, you have to call beforehand to make a lunch reservation. But you don't have to pin down a specific time as the dining room is never packed. After lunch, hit the road back to Delhi and you'll be home for dinner. A round trip can be done in 12 hours.

>**By car:** About 200 km from Delhi. Take Mathura Road to the NH-2 and follow the signs to Agra. There's a McDonald's on the way, at the half-way point. Stop for breakfast, coffee or a bathroom break.

>**By train:** Indian Railways: Check www.indianrail.gov.in for train times and fares. Go to www.irctc.co.in for online booking.
Places to eat in Agra: Oberoi Amarvilas, Taj East Gate Road. Numerous other budget options.
Tel: +91 562 223 1515
Web: www.amarvilas.com/Hotel/Hotel-Overview.aspx

Kesroli Hill Fort
Palaces and forts seem to sprout out of the hillsides around Delhi and the Kesroli Hill Fort is no exception. What only appears in fairytales for kids in the rest of the world (except Europe), a real life climb-and-imagine-you're-a-warrior-or-heroine-waiting-to-be-rescued is do-able in a day. The driving distance to the fort is no big deal once you've been to Agra and back in a day. Located in Rajasthan, the distance of 155 km takes about 3 hours. The fort is on a hill overlooking the village of Kesroli. Built in the fourteenth century, the heritage property is just 15 km away from Alwar. It also offers easy access to the Sariska Tiger Sanctuary and Siliserh Lake. The property is owned by the Neemrana group, but visitors are welcome to take in the view from the fort. The hotel has one restaurant and bar.

>Kesroli village, near MIA post office, Bahala, Alwar, Rajasthan
Tel: 01468 289 352 or the Neemrana shop at 011 4358 7183
Web: www.neemranahotels.com

Kuchesar Mud Fort
With the holy Ganges River just 24 km away from the Mud Fort in Kuchesar, the 60 km drive offers a two-for-one visit. Set amid mango orchards and lush greenery, the 7-turreted fort was built in the eighteenth century by the Jat rulers to defend against cannon attacks from the British. A moat was also constructed around the palace. Beautiful gardens can be seen from 3 sides of the fort. The resort offers a bullock cart safari and horseback riding, both of which you don't need to be a guest to enjoy. Be sure to also explore the bustling Bulandshahr Market along Ansari Road.

>Delhi–Moradabad Road
Tel: +91 573 627 3038
Web: www.mudfortkuchesar.com

Neemrana
Neemrana is an ancient historical town in the Alwar district of Rajasthan, located just 133 km from Delhi on the Delhi–Jaipur highway. The splendid Neemrana Fort Palace is the main attraction here. Kids won't tire of exploring it. Built in the fourteenth century, the beautifully restored fort has spectacular views of the countryside. Converted into a 40-room hotel, there are 2 restaurants in which to eat after taking in the stunning views. Because the fort is now a hotel, only public areas are open to visitors. But they provide wonderful views of the hillside.

> Neemrana, Alwar district
Tel: 95 1494 24 6006 or the Neemrana shop in Khan Market at 011 4358 7183
Web: neemranhotels.com

Call of the Wild

Camp Wild
Nestled in the Aravalli Valley, Camp Wild at Dhauj offers adventure and fitness activities. There's an endless list of activities for kids who love to move-it, move-it, such as rock climbing, mountain biking, zorbing, parasailing and cliff jumps. Those who err on the side of caution can play volleyball, cricket and football. There's a fun obstacle course for kids to channel their inner Georges of the Jungle.

>Holiday Moods
3/6 DB Gupta Road, Paharganj
Tel: 011 4300 0800
Entry: Overnight packages from Rs 1,400 for shared room
Web: www.holidaymoods.net

Damdama Lake
Damdama Lake is one of the biggest natural lakes in the Haryana, covering 300 acres. It is located about 20 km from Gurgaon on the Gurgaon–Alwar road. Surrounded by the Aravalli Hills, it is a popular picnic spot to spend the weekend. Those who are into adventure sports will feel that this place is downright paradise because of the boating, rowing, fishing, kayaking, cycling, hot air ballooning and parasailing facilities. Nature walks should also be on the agenda as the lake attracts more than 190 species of birds, both migratory and native during the winter, which runs from November to March. Numerous resorts have sprung up along the lake if plans are afoot to spend the weekend

instead of heading back to Delhi.

>45 km from Dhaula Kuan on Delhi–Alwar highway
Best time to go: Oct to March

The Ballooning Club of India
The club organizes hot air balloon rides over Damdama Lake (see *Playground Paradise,* pp.57–8). Balloon rides are best suited for children 5 and older. They will have to be accompanied by an adult. Taking off and landing are a thrilling experience. Regular rides last one hour and cost Rs 10,000 for 10 people. However, a 15% discount is given for groups of 10.

>**Office:** 8-B Bahadur Shah Zafar Marg
Tel: 011 2371 6665; Mr Gupta (chairman) 98100 11382
Departure point: Damdama Lake, Haryana
Timings: From Sept to March
Entry: Rs 300 per child; Rs 500 for adult with a minimum of 10 people
Other options: The Saras Tourist Complex in Haryana also offers paragliding, rock climbing, parasailing and for those in the know, there's sphering or zorbing, a sport that involves rolling down a hill in a plastic ball. Eat lunch post your balloon ride. A group of at least 30 is required for the activities, so rope in more adventurous family and friends. Parasailing is Rs 12,000 per day for 30 to 50 people; paragliding Rs 1,700 per flight with a minimum of 8 flights per day; rock-climbing Rs 5,500 per day for 30 to 40 people; sphering Rs 6,500 per day for 30 people. Booking has to be made 3 days ahead of time.

Keoladeo National Park
Keoladeo National Park in Bharatpur has over 300 species of birds and animals. The best time to visit this park is October to February. Migratory birds fly in from China, Central Asia and Siberia. Bharatpur was founded by a local ruler in the 1870s and is named after a Keoladeo (Shiva) temple within its boundaries. It was made a World Heritage Site in 1985. Pythons can frequently be seen sunning themselves around the park. Tigers are also a big attraction in the park. Other animals that can be spotted include antelopes, nilgai, sambhar, chital, wild boar, porcupines, jackals, leopards, jungle cats and marsh crocodiles. Vehicles are only permitted up to a certain point. The van provided by the forest department can be hired in the sanctuary, although the best way to explore the park is on foot or bicycles which are available on hire. Cycle rickshaws can also be hired. Restaurants

are very basic so if you plan on spending an entire day in the park, it is best to pack a picnic. Situated at the border between Rajasthan and Uttar Pradesh, at 215 km away from Delhi, the drive will take about 3 hours.

> Keoladeo Ghana is situated just 2 km from the town of Bharatpur, which is connected by train and road to Delhi (200 km away). There are regular buses to Bharatpur from Delhi. A map of the park's walking trails can be obtained from the reception counter at the entrance.
Entry: All visitors to Keoladeo Ghana, Bharatpur, need to obtain an entry permit from the Warden or Ranger at the entrance to the park. Foreigners pay an entry fee of Rs 200; Indians pay Rs 25. Extra charges are levied for cameras and photographic equipment.

Siliserh
A popular picnic spot, Siliserh is situated on the Jaipur road, 15 km from Alwar in Rajasthan and just 164 km to the west of Delhi. The Siliserh Lake that surrounds the wooded hills is tranquil. Few places are worth the visit not only for the views they offer but more so for the convenience of going by car, and Siliserh fits the criteria. Maharaja Vinay Singh built Siliserh Lake for his queen Sheela in 1845 AD. In order to build this lake, 2 earthen dams were constructed between 2 hills. Siliserh Lake is on the forested slopes of the Aravallis and various migratory birds often frequent this lake, so this is also a bird watcher's haven. The lake offers boating facilities so the family can row, row, row their boats, and many sportsmen also bring their fishing poles. Motor boats can be rented at Rs 300 for 15 minutes. It is an ideal family getaway in the summer.

> Siliserh District, Alwar
Leave early in the morning, starting at Dhaula Kuan and taking the NH-8 for Gurgaon. Continue south on NH-8 for Dharuhera past Manesar. At Dharuhera, turn left on State Highway for Alwar via Tijara. At Alwar, take the local road for Siliserh.
Places to stay: The Siliserh Lake Palace is a great option. Operated by Rajasthan Tourism Development Corporation, the Hotel Lake Palace has 10 rooms. The in-house restaurant serves Indian and regional cuisines.
Tel: 011 2435 6145

Sultanpur Bird Sanctuary
At any given time, there are about 5,000 migratory birds, 50 to 100 different

species, in the Sultanpur Bird Sanctuary and that number can soar to 50,000 from October to December. Species from Europe, Siberia and even central Asia come to the lake within the sanctuary. There are 4 watch towers (machans) at various locations and binoculars for use. Located about 50 km outside Delhi, the park has parking, toilet facilities, drinking water, and a children's park in the reserve. A popular spot for picnics during the day, if you're interested in an overnight stay, there is a resort near the entrance that provides food as well as lodging. The onsite educational Interpretation Centre has more than 50 photos of various bird species with detailed descriptions of the many birds you may spot on the walk around the perimeter which takes about 2 hours.

>50 km from Delhi, 15 km outside Gurgaon, District of Haryana
Gurgaon Farukh Nagar Road
Tel: 0124 6322057
Entry: Rs 50 per person

There's More to Gurgaon

Gurgaon should not only be known for its massive malls and concrete jungle. It has historic towns such as Farrukh Nagar, Pataudi, Firozpur Zhirka and Tauro. Named after the Mughal ruler Farrukk Siyar, Farrukh Nagar was founded by a Baluch chief Faujdar Khan. The town has a Sheesh Mahal, Baoli (bath place) and 5 gates built in 1711 AD and railway station built during the colonial era. About 50 structures have been identified by INTACH as having some kind of historical significance.

Dhankot

Dhankot is believed to be the place where milk was supplied to Guru Dronacharya and his followers. According to Buddhist teachings, Dhankot, also known as Thullkottiha, was visited by Lord Buddha. It is located 11 km west of Gurgaon. Best for older kids who have been exposed to various religions and want to get a bit more first-hand information.

>Gurgaon–Farrukhnagar Road

Farukhnagar

Farukhnagar was built by the local Nawab Faujdar Khan in the 18th century. The town is named after its ruler. Points of interest include the Sheesh Mahal and the Jami Masjid. Built by Faujdar Khan, the Jami Masjid was constructed with red stone from Agra. Two slabs of red sand stone are also affixed in the court yard. While there, visit the village of Mubarakpur, 5 km away, which has the shrine of Budho Mata. Thousands of people flock to the temple every year to take blessings from the goddess, especially newly married couples, and babies get their first haircuts here. For children, a visit to this town is noteworthy because it really is a sight to behold what many kids themselves have probably gone through as babies experiencing their first haircuts.

>21 km from Gurgaon's centre

Nuh

Most people don't think of Nuh without thinking of salt, which used to be manufactured and traded from nearby villages. Nuh, pronounced 'Nu-hu', not 'nah' (the likely response you are likely to get when you ask the kids if they are ready for bed), is centrally located for visiting places of historical interest. To the west of Nuh is a tank made of red sandstone that is decorated with beautiful floral designs. Sheikh Musa's tomb, built with both Muslim and Rajput influences, can be found 2.5 km from town. In Kotala village, about 7 km south of Nuh, is a mosque and tomb of Bahadur Khan Nahir. The gateway to the tomb has 2 pillars called shaking minarets. A fun exercise to show the kids, that will prove that not only do parents have eyes on the back of their heads as they believe, but also Superman's superhuman strength, is to actually shake them. The secret is to hold one of the pillars at the top of a minaret and push it. This action will cause the adjacent minaret to move.

>45 km from Gurgaon on the Delhi–Alwar Road

Sanghel

Sanghel is one of the highest mounds in the area. There are many mounds in Gurgaon, but Sanghel towers over them. Historians differ whether the mound is hundreds of years old or thousands of years old. The mound has a rich archaeological history as gray ware paintings and other artifacts have been found inside it. Points of interest include several stone sculptures with the images of Varaha and Narasimha and the Goddess Lakshmi. Another attraction near Sanghel is the Ujina village that is famous for its picturesque lake. It affords the perfect opportunity for kids to walk along the lake shore and take photos beside the sculptures.

>13 km south of Nuh on Nuh–Hodal Road

Et cetera

Badhkal Lake

A great spot for a picnic outside the city is Badhkal Lake near Faridabad. The name is a bit of a misnomer as the lake dried up years ago, but the lawns are beautiful and well manicured. A swim can be had in the pool for Rs 100 per hour and camel and horse riding is a bargain at Rs 20 per ride. There's something here for every member of the family, with boating, water sports such as canoeing and kayaking, and a chilren's park which the kids will enjoy. Snack kiosks and a restaurant keep the hunger at bay, and there's a motel with a fitness centre too. (Also see *Beauty and the Beast,* p.12–13.)

>Haryana Government Tourist Bureau for details
36 Janpath, Chanderlok Building
Tel: 011 2332 4910/11
Entry: Rs 20 per car
Web: http://haryanatourism.com/destinations/r_badkhal.asp

Sohna

The village of Sohna is located on top of the Aravalli Hills in Haryana, about 60 km from Delhi. Sohna got its name from a nearby stream whose sands are said to have been littered with 'sohna', the Hindi word for gold. Sohna is also famous for its sulphur spring. The water supposedly has medicinal benefits in curing skin diseases. This town is well known for its hot springs where the temperature of the spring ranges from 46°c to 51°c. The spring comes from the base of a rock, which is covered by a dome. This dome is believed to have been built in the 14th century. The springs can only be accessed on foot, as the lanes in the town are too narrow for a vehicle to pass. Hindus consider the tank sacred and come for a dip in its water on solar/lunar eclipses and Somavati Amavasya. A ruined old fort can be explored on an adjoining hill. Every February, a Statesman Vintage Car Rally is held in the area. The Haryana Government set up a Barbet resort for tourists. One can choose from a 4-bed dormitory, camper huts or family huts. The facilities include a restaurant, health club with steam, sauna and sulfur baths. There's also a small splash pool.

>Barbet Resort
Tel: 0124 2362 2256

>The Westin Sohna
Tel: 0124 450 8888
Web: www.starwoodhotels.com/westin/index.html

The Delhi Tourism Development Corporation conducts parasailing flights at Kanwarshikha near Sohna. The minimum number of people required is 10. The flight lasts 5 to 7 minutes. Participants must weigh between 45–70 kg (99 and 154 pounds). Activity is geared for older kids and parents.

>Central Reservation Office, DTDC,
Baba Kharak Singh Marg, opposite Hanuman Mandir
Tel: Ashok Kakkar at 011 2341 4011
Office hours: Mon to Fri 9 am to 5 pm
Timings: To be determined dependent on the weather
Entry: Rs 600 per person

Surajkund

At barely 8 km from Delhi, beyond the old city of Tughlaqabad, Surajkund, is the epitome of a day trip that requires very little planning. The name derives from a splendid water tank that is believed to have been constructed by the Rajput king Suraj Pal in the eleventh century. The village has become quite famous for its yearly mela during the first 2 weeks in February that draws craftspeople from all over Delhi in a must-see event. A range of silver jewellery, wood carvings, puppets, carpets, silks and embroidery and fabrics are on offer. Nothing is machine made and in addition to sampling the culture you can sample various cuisines. If shopping is not your thing, the Badhkal Lake Complex, 9 km away, boasts camel rides, fishing and swimming, which the entire family can enjoy. There's even a 9-hole golf course, complete with putting greens. The lake is another attraction. The term 'lake' is a misnomer, however, as it is not a lake but a man-made reservoir. The name in Hindi means 'Reservoir of the Sun'. Surajkund, with its serene surroundings, is a popular picnic spot for Delhites. Besides exploring the lake, visitors can also have a closer look into the life of the local community. There is also a terracotta park tucked away in the hillside. The Surajkund complex has basalt rocks around it and is popular for rock climbing. Photography enthusiasts will love the grassy slopes all along the roadside. The village's natural setting has pebbled paths, dense shrubbery and bougainvillea creepers all over the place. There are small bridges that arch across rivulets and end in a pool. Flower beds are scattered here and there and when in full bloom and in season, they add greatly to the beauty of the surroundings.

> Take the Delhi–Agra highway or the approach road from the Mehrauli–Tughlagabad highway

Tilyar Lake

Situated 70 km from New Delhi in Rohtak district, Tilyar Lake is a favourite excursion for those coming from New Delhi. The lake offers facilities for boating, accommodation, restaurants, bar, children's park and a mini zoo.

>70 km from Delhi in Rohtak district

EATS

No. 1: Yum Yum Tree. Delicious Sunday brunch for the family.

Delhi has turned into quite a patchwork of culinary delights with a wide range of traditional North Indian and South Indian cuisine to Indian Chinese, Chinese, Italian and Continental and a mix of everything else thrown in between. Those who prefer the restaurants at 5-star hotels still can't resist the food cooked roadside every once in a while. Roadside fare isn't recommended for young children or the uninitiated but there are plenty of family-friendly options for all palates and price points. Locations near tourist haunts get extra treatment here, but if you happen to be staying in out-of-the-way guest houses or with family or friends, check out *Time Out Delhi*, foodiebay.com, burrp.com and justdial.com to find more outlets, restaurant reviews, scanned menus, addresses and phone numbers.

The Food and Safety Standards Authority (FSSA) has prepared a directory of safe eating establishments. It recognizes about 1,000 small and medium restaurants across Delhi (highly concentrated in the areas of Connaught Place and Chandni Chowk) that maintain hygienic kitchens and serving areas per FSSA guidelines. The establishments have an FSSA seal of approval. But even if a restaurant doesn't have the seal, it doesn't mean that it doesn't meet hygienic standards. It could just mean it wasn't on the targeted list. With thousands of eateries in Delhi, the agency concentrated on establishments that needed to be cleaned up in the first place by teaching staff about health and safety standards. The certification is a way to ensure that minimum standards are maintained all over the city. These standards include head and beard covering for kitchen staff and separate storage and preparatory areas for raw meat and poultry. The list—not yet published at press time—will be posted at www.fssai.gov.in. *Bon appétit!*

Rise and Shine

All-day breakfast options will go a long way for parents of children who don't like to try anything new, don't like their food to touch and who don't like to eat. At least seeing pancakes with smiley faces will get something in their stomachs. A few of the breakfast items listed are not served after 11 am, but that hardly makes your meal a less enjoyable one. The food is great!

The All American Diner
The owners could not have picked a more appropriate name for the diner. Everything Americana is found on the extensive menu at the All American Diner. Wear your pants with the elastic at the waist. Choose from doughnuts, chocolate croissants, pancakes, waffles, bagels and French toast. The eggs come every which way but loose (unless you order them over easy). The kids will like the booths and the juke box. Come back for lunch, too, if you don't want to spoil them with a milkshake for breakfast. Breakfast for a family of four is Rs 1,000.

>India Habitat Centre, Lodhi Road
Tel: 011 4122 0000 / 4366 3162
Timings: 7 am to 11 pm

Choko la
With branches in Khan Market and Vasant Vihar, you have your bases covered with Choko la. The Khan Market branch is full of the expat set. Big picture windows, comfy chairs and a long fixed sofa are ideal for the kids. Menu offerings include waffles, crepes, eggs as you like and delicious homemade jam and hot chocolate made with real chocolate, not the powdered stuff. The only real downside is the steep climb up about 15 steps to get inside the first floor of the restaurant. Not ideal if you have a stroller. But there is a guard at the door so he can help you carry it up. The bathroom is located between the first and second floors and has a low toilet that is ideal for little ones. You can also take away handmade chocolates, rice crispies, cookies etc. They're all nicely packaged so you can pull out a treat for later. Menu offerings include American-style pancakes, Eggs Benedict and an array of muffins, breads, juices, coffees and tea. The prices are quite reasonable, ranging from Rs 190 to Rs 250. Choko la offers an afternoon tea that serves 2 for Rs 350 and home delivery.

>36 Khan Market, Middle Lane
Tel: 011 4175 7570
Timings: 8 am to 11 pm

>Priya Cinema Complex
Basant Lok, Vasant Vihar
Tel: 011 4166 9595
Timings: 8 am to 11 pm

Cocoa by Belgique

At Cocoa by Belgique, combos of all kinds make for a hearty breakfast. Their extensive omelette menu, American breakfast combo, classic combo and country combo leave you spoiled for choice. The restaurant serves mainly European and American foods so don't come in looking for spice. Prices start from Rs 600 for two. (See also restaurant listings, pp.134–5.)

>Select Citywalk Mall,
Ground Flr, Saket
Tel: 011 4265 8279
Timings: 10 am to midnight

The Coffee Bean & Tea Leaf

The Coffee Bean & Tea Leaf will make you pop into Select Citywalk Mall even if you have no shopping to do. Spread over nearly 2,000 square feet, there are well over 150 seats, both comfy and café shop regimented, and a menu filled with a variety of sandwiches, salads, pies, desserts and an all-day breakfast menu. It is also reasonably priced; pastries begin from Rs 50 and sandwiches from Rs 250. Of course, there's a fine selection of teas and coffees. Take a seat on the terrace so the kids can run across the spacious lawn and throw coins in the fountain. The establishment overlooks a spacious lawn so the kids can run about under your watchful eye.

>Select Citywalk Mall, Saket
Tel: 011 4059 7571
Timings: Daily 9 am to 11 pm

Eggspectation

Some Westerners may have already sampled the breakfast options at Eggspectation franchisees across the US and Canada. Obviously eggs in every preparation are on the menu, but the restaurant also offers a selection of crepes and pancakes. This place is open 24 hours so you can stick around for a proper meal too. The average cost is Rs 800 for 2.

>Jaypee Vasant Continental
Basant Lok, Vasant Vihar
Tel: 011 2614 8800
Timings: Daily 24 hours

Hare Krishna Guest House

In the heart of the main bazaar in Paharganj, Hare Krishna Guest House offers rooftop dining for a very reasonable price; the average cost is Rs 200 for 2. Breakfast is served around the clock and includes Thai food. There's a pool table too.

>1572–73 Main Bazaar, Paharganj, near Khanna Cinema
Tel: 011 4154 1341
Metro: New Delhi Railway Station
Timings: Daily 24 hours

Market Café
Market Café in Khan Market will satisfy your cravings for Western fare. Spanish omelettes, scrambled eggs on toast, eggs Benedict and freshly squeezed orange juice rule the menu. Located above women's designer store Maanan, you're sure to feel better about dropping several thousand rupees on the slow walk down. There's an outdoor balcony if you'd like to brace yourself for a day of sightseeing.

>8 Khan Market
Tel: 011 4175 7703
Timings: Daily 10:30 am to 11 pm
Cost: Rs 800 for 2

McDonald's
McDonald's has already made inroads with our waistlines with the Maharaja Mac. Now they are taking on breakfast staples of Hot Cakes, sausage patties, eggs and hash browns at a few select outlets around the city. There are 14 combination platters on the breakfast menu.

>42 Janpath, Connaught Place, Delhi
Tel: 011 2331 8931, 011 2331 8906
Breakfast timings: 7 am to 11 am

>P-16, Sector 18, Atta Market, Noida
Tel: 95120 4312623
Breakfast timings: 7 am to 11 am

>Karma Lake Land, Naurangpur, Manesar
Tel: 0124 325 4539
Breakfast timings: 7 am to 11 am

Mrs. Kaur's Crepes & More
Crepes & More, located at Khan Market, lives up to its name: it is a place dedicated to crepes. The restaurant serves up a dizzying array of crepes and all-day breakfast options of omelettes and other breakfast staples and healthy options such as the Berry Bowl which is a bowl full of berries. Simplicity is taken to an art form here. Also on offer are sandwiches, soups, salads, smoothies and great service for non-breakfast meals. Average cost is Rs 600 per person.

>1st Flr, 66, Khan Market, Middle Lane
Tel: 011 4352 8300/ 9818900005
Timings: Daily 8 am to 10:30 pm

Sam's Café
With a garden-like setting

for its rooftop dining and a covered area, Sam's Café is popular with backpackers for its typical Western breakfast fare and prices starting from Rs 200 for 2. The café also serves pizza, milkshakes, salads, falafel, lasagna and schnitzel.

>Vivek Hotel, 1534–50 Main Bazaar, Paharganj
Tel: 011 4154 1436.
Metro: New Delhi Railway Station
Timings: 8 am to 11 pm

Saravana Bhavan
The south Indian eatery, Saravana Bhavan, has mini tiffins for Rs 75 that include 5 mini idlis, a mini dosa, rawa khichdi, chutney and sambhar. You can regular-size these, of course. Other items on the menu include uttapams, vadais and pooris. Ghee pongal is also a must-try breakfast special made of generous helping of ghee, rice and moong dal.

>46 Janpath; P-15 Connaught Circus
Tel: 011 2331 7755
Timings: 8 am to 10 pm

Ten
Ten get high marks for their breakfast combos that include traditional Western fare and vegetarian cutlets and paranthas. The price just cannot be beat, starting at just Rs 75.

>10 International Guest House, Sansad Marg, Connaught Place
Tel: 011 2374 8026
Timings: 7 am to 10 am

Yellow Brick Road
This restaurant screams Americana from the name to the bright yellow interiors. Breakfast, starting at Rs 250, draws big crowds, probably because of the generous helping of pancakes, bacon, sausages and eggs and waffles.

> The Ambassador Hotel, Sujan Singh Park, Cornwallis Road
Tel: 011 6601 1825
Timings: Daily 24 hours

Good Takeaway / Budget Options for Breakfast in Old Delhi

Al Jawahar
>Opposite Gate No. 1, Jama Masjid
Tel: 011 2326 1341
Nearest Metro: Chawri Bazaar
Timings: Daily 7 am to midnight
Cost: Paya and nahari from Rs 40; and rotis from Rs 4

Café
>1575/80, Main Bazaar, Paharganj
Tel: 011 3255 4470
Timings: Daily from 7 am to 11 pm
Cost: Rs 50 for Spanish

omelette; Rs 15 for coffee and many choices of freshly baked breads

Indian Coffee House
>Mohan Singh Place, Connaught Place, Delhi
Tel: 011 2334 2994
Timings: 9 am to 9 pm
Cost: Rs 7 for coffee; Rs 35 for non-veg dosa

Mohan Ram
>Shop 4, Tiraha Kinari Bazaar, Milwada
Nearest Metro: Chandni Chowk
Timings: Daily 8 am to 8 pm
Cost: Bedmis from Rs 10

Pandit Devi Dayal
>First shop on Paranthe Wali Gali
Metro: Chandni Chowk
Timings: Daily 9:30 am to 10 pm
Cost: Bedmis from Rs 10, aloo gobi and matar paranthas for Rs 8 to Rs 10

Triveni Tea Terrace
>Triveni Kala Sangam, 205 Tansen Marg
Tel: 011 3771 8833
Timings: Daily 10 am to 3 pm; 4 pm to 7 pm
Cost: Cheese toast from Rs 30 and paranthas from Rs 13

Brunch Options

All American Diner
(See extended review *Eats*, p.124.)
>India Habitat Centre, Lodhi Road
Tel: 011 4122 0000; 011 4366 3162
Sunday brunch timings: 7 am to 11 pm
Cost: Rs 445 per person for a la carte menu items

Amigo
Hola Amigo! Mexican food is a great option for brunch especially if you're not big on Western breakfast fare. The tacos, quesadillas (both veg and non-veg) at Amigo will have you saying *otra vez* (again). No kitchy fried ice cream or churros for dessert, but the ice cream roll cake is nice enough.

>3 Local Shopping Centre, Masjid Moth, GK II
Tel: 011 2921 6220
Sunday brunch timings: 12:30 pm to 4 pm
Cost: Rs 750 per person plus tax for mocktails and kids rate; unlimited margaritas Rs 1,000 per person plus tax

Asia Kitchen
If you and the kids are in the mood for 5 courses of a set 'oriental meal', Asia Kitchen in Noida fits the bill. Unlimited drinks including Jacob's Creek wine and beer—that's not for the kids though!

>H-1A/33 Sector 63, Noida
Tel: 0120 421 8555
Sunday brunch timings: 12:30 pm to 3:30 pm

Cost: Rs 395 per person plus tax including unlimited wine and beer; kids Rs 325 plus tax

Café G

While the adults are chomping down on the kebabs, Brazilian grills, international and Asian cuisines at Café G, the kids will feel the brunch was their idea because of the children's corner. Replete with a children's buffet, movies, clowns and games, this brunch can easily stretch into a 3- or 4-hour affair.

>Crowne Plaza Today Gurgaon
Tel: 95124 453 4300
Sunday brunch timings: Noon to 4 pm
Cost: Rs 2,450 plus tax per person, including alcohol; children 5 and under free; children 6 to 12 Rs 1,250 plus tax

Café Uno

Café Uno's menu changes weekly so choices are endless if you're a frequent diner. With 12 live cooking stations and nearly 100 dishes on offer, make a plan to get there when the brunch begins and to be the last people leaving 3 hours later. There's even a chaat station. A separate section for the kids lets them make pizzas and cookies alongside the chefs. They even get to wear little aprons and hats. Adults can drink an unlimited amount of champagne and choose from a fine selection of wines, too.

>Shangri-La Hotel
19 Ashok Road
Tel: 011 4119 1010
Timings: Noon to 3 pm
Cost: Champagne brunch Rs 2,700 plus tax with unlimited Veuve Cliquot champagne; Non-alcoholic brunch Rs 2,550 per person; kids Rs 1,350 plus tax

Epicentre

It's worth the drive to Gurgaon to pay so little for the brunch at Epicentre. Jazz music wafts through the room during brunch at the Apparel House. Menu items include eggs, pancakes, chaat and other fare. There are kid-centric activities including a puppet show, face painting and jugglers.

>Epicentre, Apparel House, Sector 44, Gurgaon
Tel: 98999 27626
Timings: Sun 11:30 am to 2:30 pm
Cost: Rs 475 for adults; Rs 275 for kids below 12

Olive Beach

Known for its grills and jumbo prawns, Olive Beach's brunch includes a huge buffet; non-vegetarian and vegetarian cold cuts and salads; soups, fish, homemade pizza, pastas and a dessert section that will make you wish you wore pants with elastic around the waist. The 'Beach' in the name is spot on as it is outdoor dining at its best. The 'picnic on the beach' comes with a picnic basket filled with a baguette, homemade bocconcini, cheese and a bottle of wine. Mediterranean dining at its finest. There's a 'breakfast martini' shaken with orange marmalade that will have you hanging around till lunchtime. The pizzas and pastas on the menu will satisfy the kids while you can indulge in the fresh oysters.

>9 Sardar Patel Marg, Diplomatic Enclave, Chanakyapuri
Tel: 011 4604 0404
Sunday brunch timings: Noon to 4 pm
Cost: Rs 1,895 plus tax per person including alcohol; kids under 10, Rs 895 plus tax

Patio

World class international cuisine can be found underneath one umbrella, so to speak, at Patio at the Metropolitan Hotel. Take a culinary journey that will take your stomach on a tour from Bangkok to Venice to Calcutta and back. Great option for parents who want to shy away from the fast food for both themselves and the children.

>The Metropolitan Hotel Bangla Sahib Marg, Connaught Place
Tel: 011 4250 0200
Sunday brunch timings: Noon to 4 pm
Cost: Rs 600 including champagne; pricing is the same for kids

Pickwicks

The brunch buffet is just an offshoot of the regular, always good and satisfying fare at Pickwicks. The spread includes European, Indian and Chinese food along with organic salads, soup, cheeses, seafood, and a live dim sum station with little elbow room 30 minutes into the brunch. A variety of desserts top the buffet. Unlimited select drinks are also included in the price. The Sunday brunch is in the extensive gardens with the pretty blossoming flowers as a backdrop. There's organic salad, red snapper, imported cold cuts, and king prawns for grilling. The live dim sum station's thronged by noon.

>The Claridges
12 Aurangzeb Road
Tel: 011 4133 5082
Sunday brunch timings: Noon to 3:30 pm
Cost: Rs 1,650 per person plus tax including alcohol;

Rs 1,200 per child plus tax for children under 15

Potpourri

Potpourri has one of the most affordable, value-for-your-money weekend buffets. Part of the Nirula's family of restaurants, the Western breakfast buffet spread consists of pancakes, hashed brown potatoes, eggs, cereals, juices, cheeses and fruit. The Indian options include paranthas, omelettes and sambhar vada.

>N-64 Outer Circle,
Connaught Place
Tel: 011 4151 7070
Timings: 7 am to 11 am
Cost: Rs 275 per person plus tax

Punjabi by Nature

Punjabi by Nature's brunch is not for the faint-hearted and only serious meat eaters need cross over the threshold. There are lots of vegetarian options but the sheer gluttony of the offerings for the non-vegetarians may be a bit disconcerting. There is every kind of tikka or kebab and nans and curries to satiate diners at least until dinner.

>11 Basant Lok, Vasant Vihar
Tel: 011 4151 6666
Timings: Sat and Sun 12:30 pm to 4:30 pm
Cost: Unlimited veg platter Rs 399 per person plus tax; non-veg unlimited platter Rs 499 per person plus tax. Both platters include unlimited beer.

Sartoria

Italian restaurant Sartoria serves live music along with thin-crust pizzas, pastas, bruschettas and champagne to wash it all down.

>A-18, Basant Lok Market,
Phase I
Vasant Vihar
Tel: 011 4168 3305; 011 4168 3306
Sunday brunch timings: Noon to 4 pm
Cost: Rs 699 per person plus tax; children free up to age 5

Yum Yum Tree

Yum Yum Tree restaurant, broadly translated to mean celebration or tree of life, has taken Chinese food to a whole new level with its offerings. From dim sums, to sushi, to soups and grills, a leisurely lunch, brunch or dinner can turn into a 3 or 4-hour affair. Sunday brunch especially will have you coming back mid-week to sample other items on the menu. The menu includes several varieties of seafood, vegetable platters, curries, noodle dishes and meats. There is an unlimited supply of Grey Goose Martinis, Mai Tais, Carlsberg beer and Giant Mojitos and sparkling wine. A special Kiddie Buffet, which includes honey chicken, shredded potatoes, stir-fried vegetables, vegetable noodles and spring rolls, is arranged on the adjoining terrace of one of the dining areas. The high point of this brunch is the special area where children can take part in art and craft activities such as handbag designing, T-shirt or kite-making, sand art, colouring or aero-modelling, finger painting and colouring. There is also a play area within the play area for the under-2-year-old set complete with soft toys, balls, boxing gloves and toys that make them and the parents smile. Don't forget the takeaway bag on the way out.

>1st Flr, Community Centre, New Friends Colony
Tel: 011 4260 2020
Timings: Sundays Noon to 5 pm
Cost: Rs 1,200 for adults; Rs 450 for kids up to 12 (activities included)
Web: www.theyumyumtree.in/

Worth a Visit

Angels in My Kitchen

Known for their desserts, but the food offerings are also satisfying. A great place for afternoon tea since there's a huge selection of tasty treats to choose from.

>Shop No. 7, Main Market, Defence Colony Market, Delhi
Tel: 011 4155 1122, 011 41556474
Timings: Daily 11 am to 10 pm

Aqua

Sample everything from sirloin to seafood from the barbecue grill on the weekends. Aqua takes the word 'lounge' to a new level. Guests can also eat poolside. No one frowns on kids who want to dip their toes in the water, though they will if they try to cannonball inside.

>The Park New Delhi
15 Parliament Street
Nearest Metro: Rajiv Chowk
Tel: 011 2374 3000
Timings: Daily 11 am to 1 am; Fri to Sun outdoor 8 pm to 1 am
Cost: Rs 2,000 for 2

Arora's Shake 'n' Juice

Multi-flavoured ice cream with a dollop of fruits and nuts are the order of the day. Aptly named the 'traffic jam', it can be had for only Rs 30.

>Shop 6, H-15 Vijay Nagar Road
Tel: 98680 96687
Timings: Daily 10 am to 11 pm

Baci

Upscale Italian food. The

décor and the set-up isn't particularly kid friendly, but the food is very good and you cannot go wrong with delicious pasta any day of the week. It is best to go at lunch time if you're in the area after visiting the Zoo or after going to the Crafts Museum.

>23 Sunder Nagar Market
Tel: 011 4150 7445
Timings: Daily 11 am to 11 pm
Cost: Rs 2,000 for two

Basil and Thyme
European cuisine, but has a really nice pasta the kids will love. The menu changes to reflect seasonal offerings. And its location in Santushti Shopping Complex means a huge lawn to run around on while waiting for the food to arrive. Santushti Shopping Complex has the cleanest free bathrooms in all of Delhi.

>Santushti Shopping Complex, New Wellington Camp, RK Puram, Delhi
Tel: 011 2467 4933; 011 2467 3322
Timings: Daily 10:30 am to 6 pm
Cost: Rs 750 per person

The Big Chill
American-style food, but with lots of Indian-style sauces. For picky eaters, it is best to say 'hold the sauce' several times. Indoor and outdoor seating options, though you have to walk up a flight of stairs to get to the first floor and yet another to the second floor. Outdoor dining options if it is not crowded. Delicious desserts and ice cream. The bathroom is located on the left of the landing before the ascent to the second floor of dining. It's really tiny. So if you're helping your little one, hold off on your dessert until after the pit stop. There are 357 (really) items on the menu. The eatery wants you coming back for more every day of the year.

>62-A Khan Market
Tel: 011 4175 7588
Timings: Daily noon to 11:30 pm
Cost: Rs 1,000 for 2

There's a smaller Big Chill facing the parking lot in Khan Market with about 8 tables. This is also an option for parents with small children as you won't have to worry about navigating stairs. No bathroom though.

>35 Khan Market

>F-38, East of Kailash, Delhi
Tel: 011 2648 1030; 011 2648 1020
Timings: Daily 12:30 pm to 11:30 pm

Bikanervala
Vegetarian meals, snacks to

desserts. The restaurant is upstairs.

>A-2/43, Rajouri Garden, Delhi
Tel: 011 2593 5288
Timings: Daily 11 am to 11 pm
Cost: Rs 200 for 2

Café Turtle
Located inside Full Circle book stores (see *Shopping*, pp.174–5), Café Turtle is worth a visit, even if you don't want to buy a book. Its vegetarian menu consists of salads, pastas, sandwiches, quiches and cakes. The Khan Market and GK outlets have balconies so outdoor seating is a great option.

>Saket, MGF Metropolitan Mall, Shop No. 13, 1st Flr.
Tel: 011 4059 7541/2
Timings: Daily 10 am to 9:30 pm
Cost: Rs 600 for 2

>5-B Khan Market
Tel: 011 2465 5641/43

>N-8, GK I, N Block Market
Tel: 011 2924 5641/44

China Garden
Authentic Chinese cuisine.

>M-73, Greater Kailash II, Delhi
Tel: 011 2922 3456/9
Timings: Daily 12:30 pm to 3:30 pm, 7:30 pm to midnight
Cost: Rs 1,500 for two

Choko la
Choko la seems to do everything right when it comes to families so you're going to see it mentioned quite a few times in this guide. We've already covered the fabulous all-day breakfasts. Lunch and dinner options are also memorable. Menu items include mezze platters, bruschetta, soups, salads, pizzas and pastas. These can be followed up by some of their signature desserts or the selection of chocolates. This is not a place for meat-lovers as you won't get any pepperoni on your pizza or a side of bacon with that egg order. They also offer an array of fresh fruit juices. Even the kids will like the Red Defender, a blend of strawberries and grapes. The name alone can be a selling point.

> 36 Khan Market, Middle Lane
Tel: 011 4175 7570
Timings: Daily 8 am to 11 pm
Cost: Rs 700 for 2

> Choko la Vasant Vihar
Basant Lok Market
Near Hotel Vasant Continental
Vasant Vihar, Delhi
Tel: 011 4166 3787

Cocoa by Belgique
If a business can have prime real estate at a mall, this

would be it. Located on the ground floor of upscale Select Citywalk Mall in Saket, this café has outdoor seating that overlooks the huge garden pathways of the mall. You can enjoy burgers, sandwiches, soups, pastas, salads and all-day breakfast, including waffles, while keeping an eye on the kids as they run around the lawn. (See also *Rise and Shine*, p.125.)

>Select Citywalk Mall, Ground Flr, Saket
Tel: 011 4265 8279
Timings: Daily 10 am to midnight
Cost: From Rs 600 for two

Colonel's Kebabz
>29, Defence Colony Market, Delhi
Tel: 011 2433 8137; 011 2433 0136; 011 2433 3124
Timings: Daily noon to midnight
Cost: Rs 700 for 2

Dilli Haat
Dilli Haat isn't just for shopping. The food stalls offer everything from momos and fish to organic thalis and grills, and cover the best of Indian cuisine from across 25 states. The prices are reasonable and the kids can walk and explore as they eat. (Also see *Shopping*, pp.185–6.)

>Sri Aurobindo Marg, Opposite INA Market
Tel: 011 2611 9055, 2467 8817
Timings: Daily 10:30 am to 10 pm
Entry: Rs 15 adults, Rs 5 children

Eatopia
Five express food counters with multi-cuisine, mainly Indian food in a food court setting make up Eatopia. However, there's a kid's platter of burger, fries and a soft drink. To keep them stimulated post meal, there is a cyber café, video arcade and a play area. The restaurant regularly hosts special events on the weekend.

>India Habitat Centre
Tel: 011 5122 0000
Timings: Daily noon to 11 pm
Cost: Rs 300 for 2

>Sri Aurobindo Marg (opposite INA Market)
Timings: Daily from 10:30 am

English Dairy
Strictly vegetarian Indian fare

>A-22, Connaught Place, Delhi
Tel: 011 4151 6700
Timings: Daily 10:45 am to 10:45 pm
Cost: Rs 250 for 2

Ego Thai
Some of the best food outside

of Thailand according to some under sevens who really like Thai food. There's a library on the top floor of Ego Thai where kids can peruse books while waiting for the order. Spacious with big sofas and 2 floors, the kids will feel free to roam. The sticky rice and coconut ice cream is a great ending to a satisfying meal.

>53, Community Centre, New Friends Colony
Tel: 011 2633 1181/2
Timings: Daily 12:30 pm to 3:30 pm; 7:30 pm to 11:30 pm
Cost: Rs 1,700 for 2

Flavors
Quite popular with locals, Flavors serves up Italian food, Indian style. There are definitely better Italian restaurants to choose from, but the ice cream offerings are great and there's plenty of outdoor seating overlooking a park. Reservations are recommended as it tends to fill up quickly. However, if you have a tendency to eat lunch on the early side, you're unlikely to have a problem getting a table.

>52-C Moolchand Flyover Complex
Defence Colony
Tel: 011 2464 5644
Timings: Daily noon to midnight
Cost: Rs 1,500 for 2

Food Court, EDM Mall, Kaushambi, Ghaziabad
Whatever you fancy, it can be found here. From kebabs, street food, Chinese, pizza and 69 different kinds of paranthas at Parantha 69, there are lots of choices. Bribe the kids with a promise of bowling at the mini alley afterward. At just Rs 50 an hour, it is well worth a trip.

>Kaushambi, Ghaziabad, 201010
Timings: Daily 10 am to 11 pm
Cost: Rs 300 for 2

Gulati
Traditional north Indian, Mughlai and tandoor food. There's a children's play area and outside seating.

>6 Pandara Road Market (Behind Bikaner House)
Tel: 011 2338 8836; 011 2338 8839; 011 2378 2949
Timings: Daily noon to midnight
Cost: Lunch buffet starts at Rs 299 per person
Web: www.gulatirestaurant.com

Haldiram's
Really satisfying vegetarian Indian fast food. They are everywhere. You're bound to stumble across one.

>B-1, H/8, Mohan Cooperative Industrial Estate,

Main Mathura Road
Tel: 011 2889 8004; 011 2889 8017
Timings: Daily 8 am to 10 pm
Cost: Rs 200 for 2
Web: www.haldiram.com/ for more locations

Hotel Metropolis
The rooftop restaurant has a menu that offers an eclectic mix of food. Open since 1928, it is surprisingly quiet given its location in the main bazaar of Paharganj.

>1634 Main Bazaar, Paharganj
Tel: 011 2356 1782
Nearest Metro: New Delhi Railway Station
Timings: Daily11 am to 11:45 pm
Cost: From Rs 75

The Imperial
Royal options galore at the Imperial. A range of dining options can be had on the beautiful lawns. The buffet at 1911 La Brasserie offers a feast that feels like it hits almost every region across the world. There's foie gras, seafood, Italian and Indian fare. The menu changes weekly and you get a chance to sit out on the lawns which are huge. At any given time, you see little kiddies scurrying after the birds and squirrels. The courtyard at the Spice Route serves up Far Eastern fare. It's a bit on the pricey side so it's best to share your food with the kids or order an entrée for them to share. A gazebo and lion fountain will keep them busy while you eat in the Paradiso Divino courtyard at San Gimignano. There's also a spacious patio area on offer here.

>The Imperial, Janpath
Tel: 011 2334 1234
Nearest Metro: Rajiv Chowk

It's Greek to Me
The name says it all. Greek food in Delhi. Try it, you'll like it.

>B6/4, Commercial Complex, Safdarjung Enclave, Delhi
Tel: 011 4101 2240; 011 4101 2241
Timings: Daily 12:30 pm to 3:30 pm, 7 pm to midnight
Cost: Rs 2,000 for 2

Kachori Jodhpuree
No, you don't have to go all the way to Jodhpur to satisfy your taste for kachoris. Kachori Jodhpuree sells 3 varieties of kachoris and 2 kinds of pakodas from Jodhpur. Priced at just Rs 10 each, they will satisfy the palate and the pocket book. Kachoris made of channa dal, potato and onion with robust spices and other menu items including mirchi bada and an onion and garlic kofta make dropping in worthwhile. The air-conditioned restaurant has

about a dozen counter-type seats.

>NP-160 Mangal Bazaar Road Pitampura (near Gopal Mandir)
Tel: Daily 011 4755 2580
Timings: Daily 9 am to 10 pm

Karim's

A long-time favourite of the meat-eating set and purveyor of probably the best kebabs in town, Karim's, officially named Karim Hotel, claims it was started by the descendants of cooks who fed Mughal royalty. But the restaurant legendary for lots of flavourful meat dripping with oil, was established in 1913, long after the last emperor, Bahadur Shah Zafar was dead. Menu offerings include mutton, tandoori rotis, koftas and Mughlai chicken. There are several locations around Delhi to choose from. Vegetarians need not shy away. There are curries, dals and paneer offerings that are satisfying. The place can get crowded, not every Karim's has a bathroom and the ones that do aren't the best, so takeout is a great option.

>Karim's
16 Gali Kababian
Tel: 011 2326 9880; 011 2326 4981; 011 2324 3343
Timings: Daily noon to 3.30 pm; 6 pm to 11 pm
Cost: Rs 700 for 2
Web: www.karimhoteldelhi.com

>Dastarkhawan E Karim, 168/2, JHA House Basti Hazrat Nizamuddin West
Tel: 011 2435 0018; 011 2435 0024; 011 2435 8300
Timings: Daily 7 am to 10 pm

>26 A/4a, Bungalow Road Jawahar Nagar
Tel: 011 6542 1051; 6542 1052
Timings: Daily 7 am to 10 pm

>A-18, Kailash Colony Greater Kailash II, Delhi
Tel: 011 6565 3801; 011 6565 3802; 011 2647 2561
Timings: Daily 7 am to 10 pm

>Opposite Sagar Complex Preet Vihar, Delhi
Tel: 011 2251 9517; 011 2250 6311
Timings: Daily 7 am to 10 pm

>18/85/1, Zakir Nagar Opposite New Friends Colony, Delhi
Tel: 011 2698 1619; 011 2698 0565
Timings: Daily 7 am to 10 pm

Khan Chacha's Kebab Corner

Kebabs. Both veg and non-veg. Walk and eat and shop around the market. They are

HOT, so spring for a bottle of water. There are always throngs of people 15 deep milling about despite there being 3 other kebab joints in the market. One, which will remain nameless, is on the same lane.

>75, Middle Lane, Khan Market, Delhi
Tel: 98106 71103
Timings: Daily noon to 10 pm, closed on Fri
Cost: From Rs 75

The Kitchen
How can one describe this eatery without saying it has something for everyone while blending Vietnamese and Thai with Mexican and Italian and a proper fish n' chips which comes wrapped in paper, the British way, thank you very much. Cool postcards for the kids to pocket at a newspaper rack and a clean toilet at the rear is all one can really ask for. The food is good, the warm chocolate cake with ice cream is divine and fizzy drinks in tall glasses really hit the spot.

>75 Khan Market (next to Khan Chacha)
Tel: 011 4175 7960/1
Timings: Daily 11 am to 11 pm
Cost: Rs 800 for 2

Laxmi Dairy
Famous for the kalakand, lassi and milkshake varieties, this sweet shop has been around for nearly 50 years.

>14 Edward Line, Kingsway Camp
Tel: 011 2713 4966
Timings: Daily 6 am to 10 pm
Cost: Rs 250 for 2

Lebanese Point
Lebanese. Veg and non-veg Inexpensive.

7, PVR Saket
Tel: 011 4166 4440
Timings: Daily 11 am to 11 pm
Cost: Rs 800 for 2

Lodhi – The Garden Restaurant
The restaurant's garden is a great and we mean, great, place for families for Saturday and Sunday lunch and brunch. Lodhi – The Garden Restaurant is going to make an encore appearance throughout this guide. With comfy sofa seating, shaded table and chairs, misty sprays throughout, old carriages and a stone waterfall, the kids have plenty of space to run around and just be kids. There's a swing that can't be resisted and feathered friends can be seen in the adjacent fenced yard. There's inside seating too, but only choose this option when it's unbearably hot and you

want the benefit of fans and AC. Though the menu is Mediterranean leaning, a generous portion of fish and chips, tasty soups, starters and entrees are also featured. The bar is fully stocked with Cosmopolitans and Green Apple Martinis and fresh fruit juice options. The waiters are friendly and no one gives you the eye hoping you will leave to free up the table. Desserts include chocolate mousse, apple pie and various ice creams with honey. Of course there is a nice fresh fruit platter with a mix of seasonal fruit for a healthier option. The toilet is inside the restaurant and is also kid size so you won't even have to pick them up. Make a reservation, ask for the sofa and justify the request by telling them you have kids with you.

>Lodhi Garden, near Gate 1
Tel: 011 2465 2808
Timings: Brunch daily 11:30 am to 4 pm; 6:30 pm to 11 pm
Cost: From Rs 800 for 2

Mainland China
For many years it was the de facto place to go to for great Chinese food. Mainland China still has its fans, though cheaper and as tasty options can be had elsewhere. The menu has something for everyone and you won't walk away from the meal disappointed. You will be a bit poorer, yes. But, disappointed, no.

>E-4 Local Shopping Complex Masjid Moth, GK II
Tel: 011 2922 2123/7
Timings: Daily noon to 3:15 pm; 7 pm to 12:30 am
Cost: Rs 1,200 for 2

Market Café
Walk upstairs to have a delicious Mediterranean meal in a wi-fi enabled café with outdoor seating. Menu choices at Market Café include hummus, dips, pesto pasta, pizza, sandwiches and chicken and lamb dishes. The pastry bar at the exit is a big draw for kids and adults alike, and the restaurant also has a clean and spacious bathroom.

>8 Khan Market
Tel: 011 4175 7703
Timings: Daily 10:30 am to 11 pm
Cost: Rs 800 meal for 2

Moti Mahal
With over 70 outlets across the country known for its famous tandoori chicken that has had people from the Shah of Iran to the King of Nepal smacking their lips for over 60 years, Moti Mahal is still a favourite. Menu offerings include Indian dining staples like butter chicken and dals and rotis. Butter chicken was

apparently invented here. Go to http://motimahal1947.com/ for locations.

>11 Defence Colony, Delhi
Tel: 011 2433 0263/4/5
Timings: Daily noon to 3:30 pm, 7 pm to midnight
Cost: Rs 800 for 2

>M-30, M Block Market, Greater Kailash I
Tel: 011 2641 2467; 011 2628 0480
Timings: Noon to 3:30 pm, 7 pm to midnight

>3703, Netaji Subhash Marg, Daryaganj
Tel: 011 2327 3011; 011 2327 3661
Timings: Daily noon to 3:30 pm; 7 pm to midnight

> 20/48, Diplomatic Enclave Malcha Marg, Chanakyapuri, Delhi
Tel: 011 2611 8693; 011 2687 2760
Timings: Daily noon to 3:30 pm; 7 pm to midnight

Nirmal Restaurant
Another Old Delhi restaurant that has earned raves from its perch on Paranthe Wali Gali.

>756 Chandni Chowk, opposite Town Hall
Timings: Daily 6:30 am to midnight

Nirula's
Restaurant and ice cream shop that serves up tasty, less expensive food. There's a huge selection of ice creams and the kids get balloons. Go to www.nirulas.com for more locations.

>N-64, Connaught Place
Tel: 011 41517070; 98731 83643
Timings: Daily 10:30 am to 11 pm
Cost: Rs 400 for 2

>23, Basant Lok Vasant Vihar, Delhi
Tel: 011 2614 7756, 011 2615 4096
Timings: Daily 10:30 am to 11 pm

>B/H, Chanakya Cinema Chanakyapuri, Delhi
Tel: 011 2687 1712; 011 2467 3100; 011 2467 1598
Timings: Daily 10:30 am to 11 pm

Not Just Paranthas
Paranthas of all kinds.

>A-24, Vishal Enclave, Rajouri Garden
Tel: 011 2544 2434
Nearest Metro: Rajouri Garden
Timings: Daily noon to 4:30 pm; 7 to 11:30 pm
Cost: Rs 600 meal for 2; discount for takeaway orders

>M-84 GK II, M Block Market
Tel: 011 2922 3366

>V3S Mall, Plot 10, Vikas

Marg, Laxmi Nagar
Tel: 011 6450 6888

>Cyber Greens, DLF Phase II
Tel: 0124 411 4777/8/9

>West Gate Mall, Raja Garden
Nearest Metro: Rajouri Garden

Oh! Calcutta
Not keen on a train ride to Calcutta to satisfy cravings for Bengali food? Look no further than Oh! Calcutta. Located in the premises of The Park Plaza in Nehru Place, it is a favourite place for a Sunday lunch with the family because everything scores high marks from the food, to the décor and the service. The restaurant scores on every item on the menu. Stick to fish, which comes all the way from Kolkata, and prawn, which is heavy on mustard oil and there's no going wrong. Do try the crab appetizer wrapped in banana leaf. The food is pricey, however, a buffet lunch consisting of Bengali delicacies like koshan mangsho (mutton, slightly spicy with a very thick red gravy); maacher jhaal (mustard fish), mustard prawn and selections for vegetarians included cholar daal (chana dal), begun bhaja (brinjal fry) and other common items with rice and puri (luchi in Bengali). You have to really love fish to enjoy the buffet. Some Bengali sweets top off the meal.

> Park Royal Hotel, International Trade Tower, Ground Flr, Nehru Place
Tel: 011 2646 4180/2/4
Timings: Daily 12:30 pm to 3:30 pm; 7 pm to 11 pm
Cost: Rs 2,500 for 2; however there's a buffet lunch for Rs 450

Paranthe Wali Gali
The paranthas of various fillings just cannot be beat here.

>Chandni Chowk, near Ajmeri Gate
Tel: 98116 02460

>4th Flr, Cafe Terrace, City Square Mall, Rajouri Garden
Tel: 011 3291 7920
Timings: Daily 11 am to 11 pm
Cost: Rs 250 for 2

Parikrama
Kids will be so fascinated by the city moving around them at Parikrama, the revolving restaurant. This way, they really won't pay attention to the food you're slipping into their mouths on the sly. Nowhere else can the family take a trip around Delhi in a little over an hour. However, the food is pretty good on its own with a choice of tandoori chicken,

kebabs and fish tikkas for non-vegetarians; paneer tikka, bharwa aloo and dal makhani for vegetarians. Order a tutty frutty for dessert.

>Antariksh Bhavan, Kasturba Gandhi Marg
Tel: 011 2372 1616; 011 2372 1617
Timings: Mon to Sat 12:30 pm to 11:30 pm
Cost: From Rs 600 for 2

Park Balluchi
Located in the middle of the deer park in Hauz Khas, Park Balluchi is surrounded by forest, manicured lawns, and deer. The ambience is enough to draw throngs. Kids can do some bird spotting. That aside, the restaurant serves the most distinctive barbecue dishes in Delhi. Among them is Murg Potli (marinated chicken breast wrapped around minced mutton and served flambeed) and Mewa Paneer Tukra (farmer's cheese stuffed with mushrooms, almonds, walnuts, and sultanas, marinated in cream and then roasted). The house creations, such as Banarasi Seekh Kabab (minced vegetables and cheese rolled onto a skewer) and Lazeez Karela Mussalam (bitter gourd stuffed with cottage cheese and herbs, cooked in the tandoor), are also recommended.

>Inside Deer Park, near Hauz Khas Village, Hauz Khas
Tel: 011 2696 9829
Timings: Noon to 11 pm
Cost: Rs 1,000 to 1,500 for 2

Piccadelhi
One can find a little bit of London's Piccadilly Circus at Piccadelhi. Kids can ride on a mini-bus and watch Charlie Chaplin's antics on a TV screen. The multi-cuisine offering includes pizza, pastas, onion rings, Indian food and an extensive offering of desserts including a chocolate fountain.

>Plaza Cinema Building, Connaught Place
Tel: 011 2331 6344/9
Timings: 11 am to 11 pm
Cost: Rs 400 for 2

Ploof
It's seafood and good seafood. There's a courtyard upstairs so outdoor dining is nice and kids can focus on greenery other than the vegetation on their plates. Menu options also include north Indian, Chinese and Thai food.

>13 Lodhi Colony, Main Market
Tel: 011 2464 9026
Timings: Daily lunch noon to 4 pm; dinner 6:30 pm to 1 am
Cost: Rs 2,500 for 2

Priviledge Punjab
Indo-Chinese fare and a variety of soups and rice dishes.

>A-12, Vishal Enclave
Rajouri Garden
Tel: 011 2515 5163/4/5
Timings: Daily 11 am to 5 pm; 7 pm to 11 pm
Cost: Rs 800 for 2

Punjabi by Nature
Amazing kebabs, but not much choice for vegetarians.

>11, Basant Lok Community Centre, Priya Cinema Complex, Vasant Vihar, Delhi
Tel: 011 4151 6666/7/8
Timings: Daily 12:30 pm to 3:30 pm; 7:30 pm to 11:30 pm
Cost: Rs 1,200 for 2

>P-19, Sector 18, Noida (Near McDonald's)
Tel: 95 120 425 0111
Timings: Daily 12:30 pm to 3:30 pm; 7:30 pm to 11:30 pm
Cost: Rs 1,200 for 2

Rajdhani
Known for its thalis and sweet dishes. The weekend thali can be had for Rs 200 per person.

>P/90 Daulatram House,
Connaught Place
Opposite PVR Rivoli
Tel: 011 2334 6300
Cost: Rs 350 for 2

>The Great India Place Mall, Noida, Sector 38A, 3rd Flr
Tel: 95 120 648 8933
Timings: Daily noon to 11 pm

Rendezvous
Good pasta, salads and Mexican food.

>T-540 Panchsheel Park, Malviya Nagar, Delhi
Tel: 011 2668 2222, 011 2668 4444
Timings: Daily noon to 11:45 pm
Cost: Rs 1,200 for 2

Rodeo
Multi-cuisine. But the Tex-Mex food is a stand-out. The place has saddles for chairs so that's likely to keep the kiddies in their seats as they eat.

>A-12, Connaught Place, Delhi
Tel: 011 2371 3780/1
Timings: Daily noon to midnight
Cost: Rs 1,200 for 2

Route 4
After a long day of seeing the sights and sounds of Delhi, Route 4, may just be the ticket for several hours of (American) comfort food and relaxation. Open practically all day long, the restaurant serves up generous portions of typical American food which is heavy on the size and low on the spice. Prices are reasonable at about Rs 400 per person.

>No. 4 Khan Market, Middle Lane
Tel: 011 4352 1811/10
Timings: Daily 8 am to midnight
Cost: Rs 1,200 for 2

Sagar
South Indian vegetarian food at its finest. Always crowded.

>18 Defence Colony Market
Tel: 011 2433 3110; 011 2433 3440; 011 2433 3658; 011 4155 1097; 011 2668 1308
Timings: Daily 8 am to 11 pm
Cost: Rs 450 for 2

>C-2, Malviya Nagar, Delhi
Tel: 011 2668 0088; 011 2667 7941; 011 6565 7499
Timings: Daily 8 am to 11 pm

>A-2/40, Rajouri Garden, Delhi
Tel: 011 2510 7746; 011 2516 6848
Timings: Daily 8 am to 11 pm

Sagar Ratna
The all-veg restaurant specializes in South Indian cuisine. The breakfast combo of dosa, idli, upma, vada and a strong cup of South Indian coffee can be had for about Rs 200 per person.

>Ashok Hotel
50-B, Chanakyapuri
Tel: 011 2688 8242 Ext: 1456
Timings: Daily 11 am to 11 pm
Cost: Rs 450 for 2

Sancho's
This is what Mexican food should taste like when you're outside Mexico. Feast on burritos, fajitas, quesadillas, enchiladas, tacos, refried beans, tortillas and a host of traditional desserts.

>E-3, South Extension II, 3rd and 4th Flrs
Tel: 011 4607 6422
Timings: Daily noon to 12:30 am
Cost: Appetizers start from Rs 99, main courses from Rs 275

Saravana Bhavan
Great South Indian vegetarian food. The place is always crowded, but the service isn't too good.

>46, Janpath, Connaught Place, Delhi
Tel: 011 2331 7755; 011 2331 6060
Timings: Daily 8 am to 11 pm
Cost: Rs 200 for 2

Sethi's
Heavy Punjabi food. Lots of oil. If the shopping at near Rajouri Garden didn't tire you out, after a meal here, you will be racing back to your hotel room for a nap.

>Shop No 8-9, DDA Market, Community Centre
Opposite Surya Hotel, Rajouri

Garden, Delhi
Tel: 011 6575 3939; 011 6575 9700
Timings: Daily noon to midnight.
Cost: Rs 300 for 2

Shalom
Lebanese, Mediterranean. Great lunch option after shopping in the Greater Kailash I market.

>N-18, N Block Market, Greater Kailash I, (Near Lady Sri Ram College)
Tel: 011 4163 2280; 011 4163 2283
Timings: 12:30 pm to 3:30 pm, 7:30 pm to midnight
Cost: Rs 1,200 for 2

Spaghetti Kitchen
Pizzas and pastas. A bit overpriced, but tasty nonetheless. Desserts are yummy. (There's a play area on the same floor with slides, Little Tykes cars and balls. Ideal for kids ages 2 to 4. The rate is Rs 150 for one hour.)
>Select Citywalk Mall, Saket, 2nd Flr
Tel: 011 4265 8430
Timings: Daily noon to 3:30 pm; 7 pm to 10:45 pm
Cost: Rs 2,000 for 2

Spice World Mall food court
The food court at Spice World Mall is more mini bazaar than food court so the kids can't say there's nothing to eat. When the eating's done, check out the 4D arcade, movie theatre and gaming centre. Tickets for the 4D movies cost Rs 100.

>Spice World Mall, Sector 25, Noida
Tel: 0120 436 6400
Timings: Daily 10 am to 11 pm
Cost: Rs 300 for 2

Sushiya
Authentic Japanese restaurant.

>Neb Sarai, Saket, Delhi
Tel: 93124 44086
Timings: Daily noon to 9:30 pm
Cost: Rs 600 for 2

Swagath Restaurant
South Indian specialties abound.

>No.1, Community Centre, Naraina
Tel: 011 6469 1357/58
Timings: Daily 11 am to 11:30 pm

>14, Defence Colony Market
Tel: 011 2433 0930; 011 2433 7538; 011 2433 4537
Timings: Daily 11 am to 11:30 pm
Cost: Rs 800 for 2

>C-8, Malviya Nagar, New Delhi
Tel: 011 5183 0622; 011 5183 0613
Timings: Daily 11 am to 11:30 pm

>J-57, Sector 18, Noida
Tel: 95120 2516066; 95120-4240619
Timings: Daily 11 am to 11:30 pm

>Logic Cyber Park, Sector 62, Noida
Tel: 95120 6483744
Timings: Daily 11 am to 11:30 pm

TGI Friday

As average as the fare in the US. Nothing better, nothing worse. Mexican and American food. Avoid Friday evenings and lunch hour rush unless you make a reservation. And who really wants to make a reservation at a Friday's?

>F-16, Inner Circle, Connaught Place, Delhi
Tel: 011 2371 1991/2
Timings: Daily noon to 11 pm
Cost: Rs 900 for 2

Wenger's

The Connaught Place restaurant was started by a Swiss couple in 1926. It fell into local hands nearly 20 years later, and this pastry shop has an array of delicious offerings from the main course to dessert. Tasty shami kebabs share space on the menu with chocolate éclairs. Extremely affordable.

> A-16, Connaught Place, Delhi
Tel: 011 2332 4403; 011 2332 4594; 011 2332 4373
Timings: Daily 10:30 am to 8 pm
Cost: Rs 250 for 2

Yum Yum Tree

Yum Yum Tree will make multiple appearances because it also gets points for not just the kids' brunch on Sunday, but for making its okra dish satisfy the veggie quotient for those little people who are veggie adverse. From spring rolls to dim sum to not spicy chicken, the menu offers innovative Chinese dishes. The conveyor belt will dazzle the kids while you're waiting for your order.

>Community Centre, 1st Flr, New Friends Colony
Tel: 011 4260 2020
Timings: Daily noon to 4 pm; 6:30 pm to 1 am
Cost: Rs 1,400 for two

Bread Feast

Why settle for the grocery store variety of bread for sandwiches or a quick bite as the family explores Delhi? There are several fantastic options for freshly baked bread that just could rival some of the patisseries in Europe.

Bread & More

An array of choices on offer from wheat, multi-grain, rye, corn and olive oil in the form of rolls, baguettes and loaves. Coffee and other baked goods are also available. Dine in or take away.

>N-17 GK 1
Tel: 011 2923 0575; 011 2924 6301
Timings: Daily 8 am to 10 pm (same for all outlets)
Cost: Rs 200 for 2

>30 Central Market, West Punjabi Bagh
Tel: 011 2522 6417

>23-E/15, East Patel Nagar
Tel: 011 6529 5527

>Shop No. 214, DLF City Centre Mall, Gurgaon
Tel: 95 124 404 4042

Chocolate Wheel
Lots of breads in a lineup that includes cakes and 33 kinds of chocolates. But remember, it's the bread that you're there for.

>55 Sanjay Gandhi Green Lane, Jor Bagh (Near Jor Bagh market)
Tel: 011 2464 7520; 011 2462 3844
Timings: Daily 8 am to 8 pm

Daily Bread
No worries in finding something for everyone with the 30 kinds of European and Indian breads available.

>Shop 6, G13, Community Centre, New Friends Colony
Tel: 011 4652 0857
Timings: Daily 10:30 am to 11 pm

Defence Bakery
Started in 1962, today the bakery serves more than 60 kinds of breads and focaccia. The sundried tomato bread is a signature offering. Rolls and coffee from the café round out the experience.

>34 Defence Colony Market
Tel: 011 2433 8119; 011 1433 3178
Timings: Daily 10 am to 10 pm

Ego Café
Some of the best croissants and baguettes outside of Belgium. You can order baguette and loaves of bread, fresh from the oven. Lots of pastries, coffee and other stuffed treats.

>33 Community Centre, New Friends Colony
Tel: 011 4167 2326
Timings: Daily 11 am to 11:30 pm
Cost: Rs 500 for 2

German Bakeshop
Just as its name suggests, the German Bakeshop serves a variety of German breads including sesame, potato, sauerteig, bretzel, raisin rolls and chewy mini baguettes.

>ITA Group Building
162-A/9 Kishan Garh Main

Road, Vasant Kunj
Tel: 011 2612 4421
Web: www.german-bakeshop.com

Gourmet Shop
Interesting name choices such as the Dagwood, cheese burger and parsley caper garlic bread headline the list of truly scrumptious breads.

>The Metropolitan Hotel, Bangla Sahib Road, Connaught Place
Tel: 011 4250 0200
Timings: Daily 10 am to 10 pm

Patisserie Petunia
This bakery is definitely worth the drive all the way to Gurgaon. Multi-grain, oat, garlic and raisin breads are the favoured choices.

>C-132, The Shopping Mall, Arjun Marg
DLF City Phase I, Gurgaon
Tel: 95124 4105758
Timings: Daily 11 am to 11 pm

Red Moon Bakery
It's hard to find a good bagel in Delhi. Many places claim to have them, but essentially they are pieces of bread with holes in the middle. That isn't the case at Red Moon Bakery. A Canadian couple does the baking of the aforementioned bagels in several varieties; cookies, cakes, pastries, breads (including focaccia, pita and Grissini). The bakery offers delivery or you can stop in to see what's there.

>Shop No. 32 Pocket D and E Market, Sarita Vihar
Tel: 011 4053 4797
Timings: Mon to Sat 9 am to 7:30 pm
Web: www.redmoonbakery.net

Ye Old Bakery
This pastry shop in The Claridges Hotel has an exotic menu of sunflower seed, corn, oatmeal and multi-grain breads. The shop also features a 'bread of the month' that will offer pleasant surprises throughout the year.

>The Claridges
12 Aurangzeb Road
Tel: 011 4133 5133
Timings: Daily 11 am to 9 pm

Fast Food / Cheap Eats

No vacation is complete without some greasy burgers, fries, kebabs, pizza or chicken. Most, if not all, of these places offer delivery. Some of these blink-and-you-miss-it places don't have great ambiance and are crowded if they do offer seating. The portions are small and manageable so doing a takeaway is a good option. Eat while you walk to the next touristy spot. (There are numerous locations so check out delhiburrp.com for addresses of other outlets.)

Diamond Café

Most of the items on the menu cost less than Rs 100. The relatively clean restaurant offers everything from Indian to Israeli food and a great mix of Continental cuisine.

>5066 Main Bazaar, Paharganj, opposite Vivek Hotel
Tel: 98108 18456
Metro: New Delhi Railway Station
Timings: Daily 7:30 am to 1 pm
Cost: Rs 200 for 2

Domino's

Pizza, soft drinks, salads, garlic bread and chicken wings. Delivery is available. Outlets in Connaught Place, Kamla Nagar, Preet Vihar, Green Park, Greater Kailash, Patel Nagar, Saket, Pragati Maidan, Rajouri Nagar and a number of shopping complexes. Go to www.dominos.co.in to find more locations.

>M-42, Connaught Circus, Connaught Place
Tel: 011 2341 5879/6880/6876
Timings: Daily 11 am to 11 pm

>Shop No 6–7, Shanti Niketan Market, Chanakyapuri
Tel: 011 2411 9120/23
Timings: Daily 11 am to 11 pm

>Kalkaji, opposite Nehru Place
Tel: 011 2642 1601/2/3
Timings: Daily 11 am to 11 pm

Frontier Samosa

Around since 1947, the price cannot be beat at Rs 6 per samosa. No ambience to speak of, so it is definitely buy and go. The samosas are served with spicy chhola.

>Panchkulan Road (near Lady Harding Medical College), Connaught Place

Kachori Jodhpuree

The only authentic Marwari restaurant in town.

>NP-160, Mangal Bazaar road,
Pitampura (Near Gopal Mandir)
Tel: 011 4755 2580
Timings: Daily 9 am to 10 pm
Cost: Jodhpurees from Rs 10 a piece

Kentucky Fried Chicken (KFC)

Fried chicken and side orders that go nicely with crispy fried chicken. Outlets in Noida, Connaught Place, Dwarka, Saket, Vasant Kunj and Ansal Plaza. Go to www.kfc.com for more locations.

>A-12 Inner Circle, Connaught Place (Near Palika Bazaar)
Tel: 011 4151 6307
Timings: Daily 11 am to 11 pm

Malhotra Restaurant
Serves good Indian and Continental food. The place is spacious and there's seating for about around 40 people.

>1833–34 Laxmi Narain Street, Paharganj, (opposite the Hotel Cottage Yes Please)
Tel: 011 2358 9371
Metro: New Delhi Railway Station
Timings: Daily 7 am until 11 pm
Cost: Rs 200 for 2

Manohar's Japani Samosa
It tastes like a samosa although it's shaped more like a patty than a triangle. The samosas have layers of potatoes and peas and are served with chhola.

>Between Lajpat Rai Market and Moti Cinema

McDonald's
Burgers, fries, milkshakes, cold coffees and ice cream. Delivery is available. Go to www.mcdonaldsindia.com to find more locations.

>B-24, Inner Circle, Connaught Place
Tel: 011 2373 7121/2
Timings: Daily 10 am to 11 pm

>42 Janpath, Connaught Place
Tel: 011 2331 8931/06
Timings: Daily 10 am to 11 pm

>P-14 Connaught Place
Tel: 011 2331 8931; 011 2336 3422/5146
Timings: Daily 10 am to 11 pm

>34-A Khan Market
Tel: 011 2464 5261
Timings: Daily 10 am to 11 pm

>ISBT DMRC Railway Station, Kashmere Gate, ISBT
Tel: 011 2386 3159/6413
Timings: Daily 10 am to 11 pm

>Ansal Plaza, Khel Gaon Marg, Siri Fort
Tel: 011 2625 5325
Timings: Daily 10 am to 11 pm

>13-A, Jor Bagh Market Dr Zakir Hussain Marg, Delhi
Tel: 011 2460 4047
Timings: Daily 10 am to 11 pm

The Metropolis Bar and Restaurant
Located on the rooftop of the Metropolis Tourist Home, this

is one of the best restaurants in Paharganj. Both Indian and Western dishes are prepared.

>Metropolis Tourist Home
1628 Main Bazaar, Paharganj
Tel: 011 2356 1782
Timings: Daily 8 am to 11 pm
Cost: Rs 750 for 2

Pizza Hut
Serves up vegetarian and non-veg pizzas, salads and garlic bread. Go to www.pizzahut.co.in for more locations. Outlets in Connaught Place, Defence Colony, Greater Kailash I, Shanti Niketan, Grandlays Cinema Complex, Sonia Cinema Complex, EDM Mall, Pacific Mall and Sector 18 in Noida

>E-3, Inner Circle, Connaught Place
Tel: 011 2341 4366
Timings: Daily 11 am to 11 pm

>N-14, Outer Circle, Connaught Place
Tel: 011 4152 3236; 011 4152 3237
Timings: Daily 11 am to 11 pm

>B-112 Ansal Plaza
Tel: 011 4175 4034
Timings: Daily 11 am to 11 pm

>CDA, opposite IIT, Hauz Khas Village, Hauz Khas
Tel: 011 4165 7111/2
Timings: Daily 11 am to 11 pm

Subway
Sandwiches, both vegetarian and non-veg. Cookies, chips and drinks. Save money on the daily special. Outlets in Saket, Basant Lok, San Martin Marg, Connaught Place, TDI Mall, Safdarjung, Greater Kailash (GK), Defence Colony, Ansal Plaza, Khan Market and a number of other places. Go to www.subway.com for more locations.

Thank God It's Friday (TGIF)
American style food, heavy on pasta, burger, fries, cocktails and loud music. Outlets in Vasant Vihar, Connaught Place, Noida, West Gate Mall and Gurgaon. Go to www.tgifindia.com for more locations.

>F-16 Inner Circle, Connaught Place
Tel: 011 2371 1991
Timings: Daily noon to midnight

Wimpy's
Burgers, fries, pizzas and milkshakes. Outlets in Hauz Khas, Janpath, Lajpat Nagar, Pitampura, Rajouri Garden, Connaught Place and New Delhi Railway Station, Platform No. 12.

>New Delhi Railway Station, Platform No. 12, Paharganj

Tel: 011 2322 1375; 011 3258 0555
Timings: Daily 10 am to midnight

>N-6 Connaught Place
Tel: 011 2331 3910

>31 Ground Flr, Hauz Khas
Tel: 011 2651 2763

>1221 Devika Tower, 12th Flr, Nehru Place
Tel: 011 3256 0634

Yellow Brick Road
Breakfast isn't all that Yellow Brick Road serves. The truly multi-cuisine menu also offers Indian, Thai and continental dishes. The Thai curry chicken and Titanic burger will have you moving slowly to the exit. The food is pretty good, especially the desserts.

> The Ambassador Hotel, Sujan Singh Park, Cornwallis Road
Tel: 011 6601 1825
Timings: 24 hours
Cost: Rs 1,000 for 2

Street Food

Sometimes, the aromas emanating from street food just seem to call out to your stomach, despite what your brain is telling you. Street food comprises chaat (the quintessential food of North India that is made up of an assortment of crisp, fried wafers sprinkled with masala powders and assorted chutneys and a dash of yogurt) to Chinese food, South Indian idlis and dosas, the vada-pau made famous by Maharashtra's Shiv Sena, kababs and biryanis, sweets like jalebis, balushahis, and gulab jamuns, snacks such as puri-bhaji or stuffed parantha. Even Tibetan momos served with steaming hot soup can be bought from stalls on the street. Of course none of this food will be complete without some hot sweet chai to round out the meal. Different varieties of omelettes, pork fry, paranthas served with curry are also available at minimal prices. When the temptation is too great to resist street food, head to Chandni Chowk in Old Delhi. But don't throw caution to the wind. Avoid anything covered in flies, any cold meats or food that has a layer of dust. Ask the vendor when the food was made. The following places are known for their chaat and most importantly, the hygiene.

Bishan Swaroop
Bishan Swaroop is hard to find as it is hidden in one of Chandni Chowk's winding streets. The menu is not extensive, but it is only a snack after all. Try the aloo kulla (boiled potatoes with chickpeas).

>1421 Chandni Chowk
Tel: 98183 64070
Timings: Daily 9 am to 7 pm
Cost: Rs 50 for 2

Jugal Kishore Ramji Lal
This place is renowned for its fruit chaat (fruit salad with a twist).

>13, Dujana House, Chawri Bazaar, Chandni Chowk, Old Delhi
Tel: 98113 53076
Timings: Daily 10 am to 10 pm
Cost: Rs 60 for 2

Lala Babu Chaat Bhandar
Good value for the money for authentic chaat. Try the gobi muttar samosas (crispy pastries stuffed with cooked cauliflower, peas, and spices)

>77, Chandni Chowk, Old Delhi (opposite McDonald's)
Tel: 011 2328 2806
Timings: Daily 11 am to 9 pm
Cost: Rs 80 for two

Prince's Paan and Chaat Corner
One of the few chaat places outside Chandni Chowk worth a visit. One would consider upmarket for what is on offer. Expats give it major points for location and hygiene. Try the gol gappas (fried crispy shells filled with a watery mixture of potato, chilli, and tamarind), also known elsewhere in India as pani puri.

>29, M Block Market, GK I
Tel: 011 2923 6364.
Timings: Daily 10 am to 10 pm
Cost: Rs 250 for 2

Samosa wallas
Sure it's not chaat, but samosas are as ubiquitous in Delhi just like its famous cousin. Find samosas worth eating from the samosa wallas in front of Scindia House. Small cocktail-size samosas are priced at 4 for Rs 4. They are cooked right in front of you so the turnover is high and freshness is ensured.

>14 Scindia House, Kasturba Gandhi Marg, Connaught Place

Shree Balaji Chaat Bhandar
Very popular with locals due to the delicious snacks. Try the papri chaat (crispy fried dough wafers, served with boiled potatoes, boiled chick peas, chillis, yogurt and tamarind chutney).

>1462, Chandni Chowk
Tel: 011 2328 0579
Timings: Daily noon until 10 pm
Cost: Rs 80 for 2

Street Foods of India
Chaat and other snacks in hygienic mall food-court settings.

>Ambience Mall, DLF Phase 3, Gurgaon
Tel: 011 4350 3716/17/18
Timings: Daily noon to 10 pm
Cost: Rs 200 for 2

>Metropolitan Mall, 3rd Flr Food Court
Mehrauli Gurgaon Road, Gurgaon
Timings: Daily noon to 10 pm
Cost: Rs 200 for 2

>Great India Place, Sector 18, 3rd Flr, Noida
Tel: 011 4350 3716/17/18
Timings: Daily noon to 10 pm
Cost: Rs 200 for 2

>City Square Mall, Raja Garden
Tel: 011 43503 716/17/18
Timings: Daily noon to10 pm
Cost: Rs 200 for 2

Sweet Endings

Once the family has sampled its way through Delhi's eateries, satisfy the sweet tooth with an array of desserts.

Ice creams

Baskin Robbins
With at least 31 flavours to sample, how can you go wrong? Rs 40 per scoop. Go to www.baskinrobbins.com for more locations.

>Defence Colony Market
Tel: 011 2433 3849
Timings: Daily 10 am to 11 pm

>New Friends Colony Market
Tel: 011 6450 9366

>Vasant Kunj Market
Tel: 011 6510 8662

>Connaught Place
Tel: 011 2371 3921

>Kamla Nagar
Tel: 98180 01139

>Pitampura
Tel: 011 2735 5971

>Ansal Plaza
Tel: 98713 13716
Timings: Daily noon to midnight

Gelato Italiano
Most of the flavours are 96% fat free and 100% vegetarian. The chain also offers 100% fat-free and dairy-free sorbets.

>M-34, Greater Kailash I
Tel: 011 4658 8556
Timings: Daily 11 am to 11 pm
Price: Rs 65 per item

>6 G13, Community Centre, New Friends Colony
Tel: 011 4652 0857

>A-302, The Great India Place Mall, 3rd Flr
Sector 38A, Noida
Tel: 0120 422 6556

Gelato Vittorio
Find a bounty of delicious and not run-of-the-mill flavours to satisfy your sweet tooth.

>West Gate Mall, 1st Flr, Rajouri Garden
Tel: 011 3254 3577
Timings: Daily 11 am to 11 pm
Price: From Rs 90 per item

>Ansal Plaza, Ground Flr, C Block, Khel Gaon Marg
Timings: Daily 11am to 11 pm

>Select Citywalk Mall, Ground Flr, Saket
Timings: Daily 11am to 11 pm

>Basant Lok, Vasant Vihar
Tel: 98185 47242
Timings: Daily 11 am to 11 pm

Giani Di Hatti
This place is famous for its kesar kulfi faluda and fruit ice creams.

>A-3, DDA Market, Paschim Vihar
Tel: 011 6579 8586
Timings: Daily noon to 11 pm

Nirula's
Nirula's seems to do everything at a reasonable price. After you've had a thali, choose from a robust selection of ice creams. Check the Web for an outlet nearest to you.

>**Timings:** Daily 10:30 am to 11 pm
Web: www.nirulas.com

For die-hard sweet tooths

Brownie Cottage
This is a chocolate lover's paradise. Over 1,000 brownies are baked and sold daily. Customers can also choose chocolate toffee which start at Rs 12 a piece.

>Select Citywalk Mall, Saket
Tel: 98202 91196
Cost: Brownies Rs 45 to Rs 85; cakes Rs 550 to Rs 1,350 per kg.

Chaina Ram Sindhi Confectioners
Open for over 100 years, this sweet shop is famous for its Karachi halwa

>Chandni Chowk
Tel: 011 2392 7585; 011 2395 0747
Timings: Daily 7:00 am to 8:30 pm
Cost: From Rs 20 per item

Choko la
Handmade chocolates, rice crispy treats, cookies, pastries and cakes that are so beautiful, they should be photographed.

>36 Khan Market, Middle Lane
Tel: 011 4175 7570

> Choko la Vasant Vihar
Priya Cinema Complex, Basant Lok, Vasant Vihar
Tel: 011 4166 9595

Cookie Man
Who stole the cookie from the cookie jar? The Cookie Man stole the (ginger, almond, coconut, walnut and many more) cookies from the cookie jar. Cookies, cookies and well, more cookies. There are several outlets to choose from including IGI Airport.

>F-14 Metropolitan Mall, 1st Flr, Gurgaon (near Sahara Mall)
Tel: 0124 410 0788
Cost: Rs 40 per cookie

>L-1, Upper Atrium, Centre Stage Mall, Sector 18, Noida (near The Great India Place)
Tel: 0120 420 5921

>Centrestage Mall, Ground Flr, Sector 18, Noida (near Radisson Hotel)
Tel: 0120 431 2708, 0120 302 6555
Timings: Daily noon to midnight

Defence Bakery
This is the place for pastries galore.

>34 Defence Colony Market
Tel: 011 2433 8119
Timings: Daily 10 am to 10 pm

Mad Over Donuts
It's hard to find a good doughnut in Delhi but this place delivers. Choose the regular sugar and chocolate varieties or snack on a mushroom and cheese doughnut.

>The Great India Place Mall
A-2 Sector 38A, Noida
Tel: 95120 4271438
Timings: Daily 10 am to 8 pm
Cost: Rs 25 to Rs 30; Rs 250 per dozen
Web: www.madoverdonuts.com

> Select Citywalk Mall, Saket
Level 2 Food Court
A3 District Centre
Tel: 011 4059 7517

Mrs. Kaur's Premium Cookies
With two (blink and you will miss them) outlets in Khan Market and one in East Patel Nagar, Mrs. Kaur's definitely gives the Cookie Man a run for its money. There are 30 to 40 choices and a microwave to make the outlet's famous brownies warm and gooey. Free delivery for the die-hard cookie fans.

>73-A Khan Market (Middle Lane)
Tel: 98189 0005
Timings: Daily 10:30 am to 10 pm

>Arcade E, Inside Gallery, Khan Market
Tel: 98189 0005
Timings: Daily 10:30 am to 10 pm

>29/6 East Patel Nagar
For delivery: 011 4248 0808; 011 4248 2345; 98189 00005
Cost: From Rs 35 per cookie; brownies Rs 50 to Rs 60 each
Web: http://www.mrskaurs.com/

Sugar 'n' Spice
There's a huge selection of cakes, cookies, doughnuts, pastries and imported chocolates at reasonable prices, so it may surprise you that you're actually standing in Khan Market. Imported cheeses and meats also are available.

>58-A Khan Market
Tel: 011 2464 0741
Timings: Daily 10 am to 8:30 pm

Traditional Indian sweets

Annapurna Mistanna Bhandar
This shop holds the distinction of being the only shop that caters to Parliament when it is in session. The majority of offerings at Annapurna Mistanna Bhandar are made of chhena, not khoya. However, you can still get rosogullas and sandesh here. Opened in 1929, the sweetshop is famous for its kancha golla that sells for Rs 250/kg.

>1463, Chandni Chowk, Delhi
Tel: 011 2396 2050; 011 2386 8466
Timings: Daily 8 am to 8:30 pm

Bengali Sweet House
Bengali Sweet House, one of the oldest shops in the Bengali Market, opened in 1942. It offers a wide variety of sweets and namkeens from the traditional North Indian mithai to Bengali mithai. There is also a snack bar serving south Indian dosa (pancake), chaat and golgappas.

>27–37, Bengali Market, Connaught Place
Tel: 011 2331 9224; 011 2331 1855
Timings: Daily 8 am to 11 pm
Cost: From Rs 30

Ghante Wala's Sweetshops
Famous for having sweetened the mouths of emperors with the always consistent jalebis, Ghante Wala's is still going strong. They guarantee no milawatt, and all of their preparations are made with desi ghee. Some must-try sweets include their balushahi, gulab jamun, kala jamun, motichoor ke laddoo, shahi laddoo and pista ki lauj. Online delivery is available.

>1862-A, Chandni Chowk
Tel: 011 2328 0490
Web: www.ghantewala.com to place an order online

Haldiram's
Look no further than Haldiram's for a mithai shop. Their soan papdi, made of almonds, pistachios and desi ghee into a flaky sweet, comes in a variety of gift boxes. More typical fare includes gulab jamuns, kalam petha, raj bhog and rasgullas dipped in saffron and rose flavoured syrup stuffed with dry fruit. Outlets can be found city wide.

>1454/2 Chandni Chowk
Tel: 011 28883 3007

>B-1/F-2 Mathura Road, Badarpur
Tel: 011 2889 8018; 011 28889 8027

>45, Ring Road, Lajpat Nagar
Tel: 011 2889 8032/3

Timings: Daily 9 am to 11 pm
Web: www.haldirams.com for more outlets

Nathu's
Typical North Indian fare that flies off the shelves every day. Some hot-selling, both literally and figuratively, items are gulab jamuns swimming in the hot syrup, rasmalai kesar, dhodha barfi and soan papri. There are sugar-free options like the kalakand. Online delivery is available.

>23–25 Bengali Market, Babar Road
Tel: 011 2371 7313; 011 2371 6326

>1 Defence Colony Market (near Mother Dairy)
Tel: 011 2433 3128; 011 2433 3127

>2 Main Market, Sundar Nagar
Tel: 011 2435 4982
Timings: Daily 8 am to 11 pm
Web: www.nathusweets.com for other outlets

Tiwari Brothers Confectioneries
Traditional Indian sweets. Pure ghee ladoos are their specialty.

>862 Chandni Chowk
Tel: 011 2392 7690; 011 2391 8326/3327
Timings: Daily 8 am to 10 am

>O-3B Lajpat Nagar II
Tel: 011 2684 9479; 011 2691 8348

Eggless treats

Most bakeries carry egg-less desserts and are labeled as such. However, it's guaranteed they can be found at the following places:

Angels in my Kitchen
>Defence Colony Market; Shop 9AB New Friends Colony
Tel: 011 5163 1239/40

Big Chill
>68 Khan Market
Tel: 011 4175 7588/99

Gelato Vittorio
>M-69, GK I
Tel: 011 3251 2527
Web: www.gelatovittorio.com for more outlets

Mrs. Kaur's Premium Cookies
>73A Khan Market
Tel: 011 4248 0808
Web: www.mrskaurs.com for more outlets

Organic Food Shops / Delivery Services

For a range of organic spices, pulses, jams, soaps, dried fruits, candy and vegetables, check out the following stores.

Bhatia Health Foods
C-16, Masoodpur, Vasant Kunj
Tel: 99681 77551; 99106 34333

Dubden Green
Seasonal selection of vegetables and fruits. Delivery is available.

>4-A Shahpur Jat
Tel: 98101 31343; 011 3290 5310
Email: dubdengreen@organicbounty.com
Web: www.organicbounty.com

Fabindia
(Also see *Shopping*, p.177.)
Web: www.fabindia.com for outlets

French Farm
A big variety of vegetables, herbs, poultry (including turkeys), lamb and pork is delivered to your door.
Tel: Roger Langbourg 98101 66196

Khadi Bhandar
>Khadi Gramdyog Bhavan 24 Connaught Place, Regal Building
Tel: 011 2336 2231

Navdanya's Organic Vegetables
There's no hard and fast rule that you can't prepare a home-cooked meal while you're on vacation. According to your accommodations, you can go for a hot meal or refreshing salad. Orders have to be placed in advance and you're given a pick-up time. Only members can get their greens delivered.

>D-26 Hauz Khas, near Hauz Khas Market
Tel: 011 2653 2124; 011 2653 2460; 011 2685 3772
Cost: Rs 400 for a basket of mixed vegetables and herbs

>Organic Café, D-26, Ground Flr, Hauz Khas
Near Hauz Khas Market

>HPCL Outlet at Ashram Chowk
Delhi Ring Road, Mathura Road Crossing
Tel: 011 5162 7100; 011 5162 7500

>Stall No.18, Dilli Haat, Opposite INA Market

>HPCL Outlet, Sundar Nagar, Mathura Road
Tel: 011 2435 8611; 011 2435 8144
>Shop No.35, Vasant Arcade, Vasant Kunj
Tel: 011 4178 3205

Tribes Shop
>9 Mahadev Road (near Gol Dak Khana)
Tel: 011 2373 1214

SHOPPING

No.1: Central Cottage Industries Emporium. One-stop shopping for everyone in the family and the household, too. Multiple floors, AC, and a restaurant mean that one can easily spend a half-day here.

In addition to soaking up the rich history of Delhi, putting aside an afternoon or several afternoons for shopping is a must. Check out the many mega malls and the high-end and low-end markets and numerous bazaars. Handicrafts, fabrics, woodwork, trinkets, baubles, leather, toys, clothes, shoes, accessories and electronic goods can all be found here.

The government emporiums and stalls and shops all over the city carry items that will be envied at home. Fixed prices are never really fixed when you buy enough, except for the government emporia, but if you don't mind haggling and are willing to walk away, till you get to the next stall selling something similar, that is, bargains can be found from Sarojini Nagar to Paharghanj and Chandni Chowk to Connaught Place. Even the hotels have expansive shopping arcades that sell marked up trinkets and designer duds. Look out the car window at traffic stops and the latest novels along with Indian flags, toys, magazines, pens and even glittery Ganesh statues can be bought after a few minutes of bargaining. If there is any hesitation on the part of the vendor after asking the price, offer a quarter of the quoted price and start the bargaining from there. Pay what you should be paying.

Remember, the airlines weigh the suitcases, not you. So stack those bangles on your arms, layer those scarves around your neck and put on a funky T underneath the Anokhi tunic.

Markets

Delhi's markets come crammed with goods, people and smells. Although it seems as if a billion malls have cropped up around Delhi in the last several years, markets continue to thrive as regulars shop at the places where their parents and grandparents have shopped. The markets offer everything from household goods, daily food staples and the trinkets that tourists and locals can't seem to get enough of.

The closing days for the shopping complexes in Delhi are as follows. However, some shops in all of these places sometimes keep hours different from the rest of the complex:

- Sundays: Connaught Place, Janpath, Baba Kharak Singh Marg, Jor Bagh, Khan Market, Malcha Marg, Nehru Place, Sunder Nagar, Yashwant Place, Chandni Chowk, Sadar Bazaar.
- Mondays: Defence Colony, INA Market, Jangpura, Karol Bagh, Lajpat Nagar, Sarojini Nagar, South Extension.
- Tuesdays: Greater Kailash, Green Park, Hauz Khas, Kalkaji, Safdarjung Enclave, Vasant Vihar, Shahdara, Yusuf Sarai.

Chandni Chowk

The magnificent bazaars of Chandni Chowk are open daily and piled high with sarees, beads, unique silver jewellery, gold, nuts, spices, pulses, silks, carpets and perfumes that are worth visiting to stimulate your senses. The large cycle market is a draw for those passionate about anything on wheels. Chandni Chowk is also famous for its cloth market, bed linen, photographic materials and photo albums. The Chowk is the major street in the walled city of old Delhi, which includes the Red Fort. It also has several religious shrines, the Jama Masjid being the most famous. Once among the most prestigious markets of Delhi, today mainly regulars and tourists flock to the shops. What really makes Chandni Chowk stand out is the variety of markets where everything can be found in a jumble of winding and crowded streets. There really is no point in shopping in Chandni Chowk if you don't round out the experience by eating at Karim's (see *Eats*, p.138), known to be a meat lover's paradise; or Paranthe Wali Gali (see *Eats*, p.142), famous for its paranthas.

> Old Delhi, near the Red Fort
Timings: Mon to Sat from 10 am to 7 pm

Connaught Place

Located at the heart of New Delhi, the shopping district is also called CP, but officially it has been renamed Rajiv Chowk. (The Metro stop is named Rajiv Chowk so don't start wondering why you can't find Connaught Place.) Built in 1932, it is the commercial hub of the city. Most shops in this tourist mecca are open 7 days a week. The markets and shops are structured on an inner and outer ring and are distinguished by blocks A to F in the inner ring and G to P in the outer ring. Framed by Janpath's famous stalls, everything from knick-knacks to restaurants, jewellery and handicrafts can be found here. The infamous underground Palika Bazaar is also located here. It is the grandfather of all things from the grey market with about 400 stores selling cheap electronic goods and clothing. Frequent raids by the police close it down, but the stores are usually up and running in a few days' time.

Most international and national retails brands and food outlets can be found here including Adidas, Benetton, Puma, Raymond's, Bata, Nirula's, KFC, TGIF and McDonald's. For a complete list of stores, divided by blocks, go to www.connaughtplacemall.com. The majority of the shops are closed on Sundays but some remain open for the inevitable foot traffic.

Daryaganj
Books, books and more books. Some first editions of the classics have found their way onto the tables.

>**Timings:** Sundays from 7 am to 5:30 pm

Greater Kailash M and N Block Markets
Sure to give Khan Market a run for its money and a run on the money in your wallet, these markets are becoming more upscale by the day with all the international and national brands present and lots of restaurants to choose from including Moti Mahal, McDonald's, Pizza Hut and the Smoke House Grill.

>South Delhi
Timings: 10 am to 7 pm; closed Tue

Gujarati Market
The lane off Janpath that primarily offers saris, cushion covers, bags, beads and the like from Gujarati traders. Though Janpath is closed on Sundays, you can still shop here for bargains.

>**Timings:** Daily 11 am to 8 pm

Hauz Khas Village
Art galleries, high end designer boutiques, antique stores selling lots of old pieces that have been turned into interesting furniture and several nice family restaurants including Park Balluchi in the Deer Park; Naivedyam, a South Indian eatery or the Village Bistro.

>Hauz Khas Village (near deer park), South Delhi

Timings: Mon to Sat 10:30 am to 8:30 pm

Hanuman Mandir

If it is a Tuesday, then the place to go is Hanuman Mandir. According to priests, one lakh devotees throng the temple on Tuesdays. It was built by Maharaja Jai Singh in 1724 and is believed to be the only place where Hanuman appeared in his childhood avatar. Devotees come to have their wishes fulfilled and others come because a flea market of sorts has sprung up around the temple over the years. Over 70 stalls sell bangles from Hyderabad and Jaipur and do brisk business during the wedding season. There's something here to fascinate every mom and her little princess. Also popular here are the mehendiwalis who charge a nominal Rs 10 per hand. Compare this to prices starting at Rs 275 per hand in Khan Market. Food is also a big draw here. Aam papads and choorans and deep fried pakoras served with mint chutney, can be bought for Rs 10. Astrologers can read your fortune for Rs 101.

>Baba Kharak Singh Marg
Timings: Tue market from 10 am; closed Sun

Janpath

Located near Connaught Place, it is open 7 days a week. Also, known as the Tibetan market, the shopping district has its origins after partition in 1947. Refugees from Pakistan began selling goods along this road. Go here for export surplus and rejects from international labels, cheap chic, contemporary clothing, ethnic jewellery, bags and handicrafts. Real antiques from Tibet can be found in the jumble of stores as well as real junk. So be wary of 'authentic' labels. It is also close to the metro.

>Near Connaught Place
Timings: Daily 10 am to 7:30 pm
Nearest Metro: Rajiv Chowk

Jor Bagh Market

Why head to Jor Bagh Market? For pottery at C Lal & Sons; books at The Book Shop and cheeses and meats at The Steakhouse. Pop into other stores too.

>Near Safdarjung's Tomb
Timings: Daily 9:30 am to 7:30 pm

Karol Bagh Market

One of the oldest shopping areas in the city is also very close to many monuments including India Gate and the Zoo. Kids are likely to be fascinated by the cycle market at Jhandewalan. Moms ought to go to Karol Bagh with bare fingers, ears and necks as fabulous jewellery can be had from the stores. Furniture, fabrics, clothes, spices and teas can also be found here. You'll also find a wide variety of imported goods at Gaffar Market in Karol Bagh.

>Central Delhi, 2 km from New Delhi Railway Station
Timings: Tue to Sun 10 am to 8 pm

Khan Market
Pull out the movie star sunglasses and the designer bags as Khan Market is *the* most upscale place to shop in all of Delhi (Emporio Mall excluded). It is one of Delhi's most expensive markets (in the top 20 internationally as far as retail space goes). Diplomats, Bollywood stars, expats and young politicians-in-waiting have been spotted casually strolling on the sidewalks along with the requisite entourage. Sure, the parking lot is pure chaos and the middle lane needs to be paved over, but the retail outlets, salons and restaurants will make you forget all of that in seconds. There are a wide variety of stores including Fabindia, Anokhi, Nike, Reebok, Hi-Design, Good Earth, Benetton and Kriti Creations. The Big Chill, McDonald's, Café Turtle, Khan Chacha, Route 4, Blanco, The Kitchen, Market Café, Barista and Café Coffee Day are some of the eateries found here. Everything you can find in Janpath or the Cottage Emporium can also be found here at a premium. All of the eateries and some of the stores have toilets and there's a free, though smelly toilet located near the McDonald's. Also check out the Bombay Fruit Store for imported fruits and other goods and Sugar n' Spice for meats, cheeses and baked goods. Khan Market is located very close to Lodhi Gardens, the India International Centre and the India Habitat Centre.

>Close to India Gate, South Delhi
Timings: Daily 11 am to 8 pm; some stores open on Sun

Lajpat Nagar Central Market
Where the locals shop to get everything from cushion covers to household appliances. Home decor, fabrics and other items to add pizzazz to your dream house can and should be bought here. You get excellent deals on electrical goods.

>South Delhi between Greater Kailash and South Extension
Timings: Tue to Sun; 11 am to 8:30 pm

Mohan Singh Place
Stores here stock 'authentic'

labels for those who are fashion savvy but a bit light on the funds. Jeans can be had for as little as Rs 400.

>Near Connaught Place
Nearest Metro: Rajiv Chowk
Timings: Daily 10:30 am to 8:30 pm

Nai Sarak

The first and last stop for discounted and second-hand books. Most publishers can be found in the narrow lanes. It is very popular with students who buy textbooks here. Books in all languages spoken in India can be found in the stalls. Prices are low so no need to haggle. In many cases, there is no rhyme or reason to how the books are stacked so be prepared to search if there is something in particular you are looking for. Nai Sarak is also particularly well known for its musical instruments shops.

>Near Chawri Bazaar
Nearest Metro: Chawri Bazaar or Chandni Chowk on the yellow line
Timings: Mon to Sat

Palika Bazaar

The only air-conditioned underground market near Connaught Place is famous for cheap electronics and clothing—much of which is imported. Frequently raided by the cops, it offers a huge collection of 'not always legal' DVDs, video games, kids' playstations, iPods and other electronics. This is as grey of a market as you are going to get. Dating back to the 1970s, the market has nearly 400 shops. Although it is a bargain-hunter's playground, prices quoted are always high and you have to haggle to get the best deals. Be prepared to walk away as there will be 50 or more stores selling relatively the same things so you can leave with what you want and the price you are willing to pay.

>Under Connaught Place
Timings: 10 am to 6 pm

Paharganj

Across from the New Delhi Railway Station and within walking distance of Connaught Place, Paharganj divides Old and New Delhi. The stores in this area are mainly thronged by the budget minded tourist looking for funky T-shirts and affordable souvenirs. Bargaining here is a must, but the prices are so reasonable compared to Khan Market and even Janpath, don't sweat it too much. Some great buys here include leather sandals, body art, bindis and bangles. Many handicraft stores can be found in the narrow lanes also.

>Near Connaught Place
Timings: Mon to Sat 10 am to 7:30 pm

Santushti Shopping Arcade
One would insult even the birds that grace the well-appointed lawns with their presence if Santushti Shopping Arcade was called a market. The complex with the lush gardens, and meandering pathways, was conceived in 1990 by the Air Force Wives' association. It's not for bargain shoppers, but for designer, high-end wares from clothing to jewellery to home furnishings.

>Race Course Road, Chanakyapuri (near Samrat Hotel)
Tel: 011 2467 9220
Timings: Mon to Sat 11 am to 7 pm

Sarojini Nagar Market
Perfect export surplus market. Also a great place to buy shoes. Denims, shirts, dresses can be had for between Rs 50 and Rs 100.

>Near Dilli Haat
Timings: Tue to Sun 11 am to 8:30 pm

South Extension Market Part I and Part II
Yet another upmarket shopping district where national and international brands reign supreme. Divided into 2 parts, South Extension I and South Extension II, the markets are relatively easy to navigate on foot, though parking is a royal pain. There's an underground tunnel connecting the two parts which are separated by the Ring Road. Books, clothing, jewellery, mobile phones and restaurants abound. Go to Sancho's (see *Eats*, pp.145–6) at E-3 in South Extension II for Mexican food.

>South Delhi, situated on the Ring Road
Timings: Tue to Sun 11 am to 8 pm

Sunder Nagar Market
The market is located in an upscale area near the zoo and specializes in Nepali handicrafts, copper, brass, semi-precious stones, textiles and silver jewellery from Ladakh. Some interesting tea shops are also located in Sunder Nagar Market, in addition to Baci, an Italian restaurant which is a great place to have lunch with the kids before heading to the Crafts Museum (see *Co-ed*, pp.48–9). Look for the sign with the lips.

>Off Mathura Road near the zoo
Timings: Mon to Sat 10 am to 7:30 pm

Shopping Malls

Ansal Plaza

A part of HUDCO Place built on 35 acres of land, Ansal Plaza is a shopping complex situated near South Extension, one of the posh markets of rich South Delhi. Branded clothes, trendy jewellery and other designer items are some of the things that you can shop for at Ansal Plaza. It has a slew up upscale stores including Marks & Spencer, Shopper's Stop and Music World. Many restaurants and fast food outlets to choose from. Open all days. Kids will love Funkie Orbits (see *Playground Paradise*, pp.67–8) a fun indoor jungle gym with slides and plastic balls.

>Khel Gaon Marg, Andrews Ganj
Tel: 011 2625 5532
Timings: Mon to Fri 11 am to 8:30 pm; weekends 8:30 am to 9:30 pm
Parking: Underground and outside parking; Rs 10 to Rs 30
Web: www.ansalplazadelhi.com

Centrestage Mall

Wave Cinema, food court, and a small children's play area in addition to the usual mall shops.

> L-1, Sector 18, Noida
Tel: 0120 436 4600
Timings: Mon to Sat 9:30 am to 11 pm; Sun noon to 11 pm
Parking: Underground and outside parking, Rs 10 to Rs 20

DLF City Centre

Spread over 250,000 square feet. It houses all the big-name shops, a 4-screen movie theatre and a food court. Big-name eateries like Ruby Tuesday and Pizza Hut are also found here.

>DLF City Phase I, MG Road, Gurgaon
Tel: 0124 238 6296/97
Timings: 10 am to 11 pm
Web: www.dlf.in

DLF Place

Third in a row of malls located in Saket after MGF Metropolitan Mall and Select Citywalk, which annoyingly, are not really connected so you have to risk your life walking or you have to get back into your car for a one-minute journey and deal with the hassles of parking again. The DLF Place has international brands, including Debenhams and Adidas and a 6-screen theatre. Wide open spaces inside are set aside for concerts, promotional events and children's activities, so the kids will find loads to keep them entertained. The food court, which includes The Great Kebab Factory and Old World Hospitality, is so expansive, one could ideally bring a book and have breakfast, lunch and dinner there. The mall is new and plans are afoot for a Hilton hotel and cinema and other entertainment options. Parking can accommodate 900 cars.

>Press Enclave Road, Saket
Tel: 011 4601 0385/86
Timings: Daily 10 am to 9 pm

>DLF Place, Vasant Kunj
Tel: 011 4610 4466
Timings: 10 am to 11 pm

East Delhi Mall
Popularly known as EDM and opened in 2005, this was one of the first major malls in East Delhi. The mall is spread over 3 floors and carries all the big brand stores, has a 3-screen movie theatre, food court, children's play area and adjoining hotel rooms.

>1 Kaushambi, Ghaziabad
Tel: 0120 301 8004
Timings: 10 am to 8 pm
Web: www.edm.com

The Great India Place
The Great India Place is a retail and entertainment behemoth that is part of Entertainment City, an all-encompassing amusement park. It is the largest mall in Northern India. All the branded players are here along with specialty jewellery shops, restaurants, including a food court (leading off on to a children's entertainment zone and gaming area) that occupies most of the top floor, and a movie theatre. The mall takes family entertainment to a whole new level and it is easily a day-long outing. For the kids, the fun spills beyond the doors of the mall, with a variety of outdoor rides and a large fairground setting just a few metres away.

>Sector 38A, Noida
Tel: 0120 465 0300
Timings: Mon to Sat 11 am to 11 pm; Sun noon to 11 pm

Mega Mall
Five levels of shopping, entertainment and food options that span 16 international cuisines.

>Sector Road, DLF City, Phase I, Gurgaon
Tel: 0124 438 0352
Timings: 11 am to 8 pm

MGF Metropolitan Mall
With 150 stores including Shoppers Stop and Om Book Shop, one can get quite a work-out window shopping. There's also a McDonald's and PVR Cinemas. Ample parking over 3 levels, though that doesn't seem enough on the weekends.

>MG Road, Gurgaon
Tel: 0124 438 0352
Timings: Daily 9 am to midnight

Pacific Mall
One of the highlights of the Pacific Mall and something to wow the kids is the IMAX theatre, the second in India, and the fifth in Asia. Shopping in the mall is secondary, though all the brand-name shops (Globus, Westside, Spencers, Crosswords, Chunmun, Ritu Wears, Rough n Tough, Nike Adidas, Reebok and Louis Phillipe) are there. It's more amusement park, night spot and food plaza rolled into one. There's also a Clark's Inn Pacific hotel attached to the mall.

>Plot No. 1, Site 4, Sahibabad, Industrial Area, Ghaziabad
Tel: 0120 301 2301
Timings: Daily 9 am to midnight

Sahara Mall
This mall started off the mall craze in Gurgaon in 2001. It prides itself on being built to be earthquake resistant. The mall has a beautiful atrium when you enter which is framed by 80 branded stores. There are several restaurants to choose from and many entertainment options including bungee jumping and a PVR theatre.

> Mehrauli Gurgaon Road, Sector 28 Gurgaon
Tel: 0124 238 7741; 0124 4048592
Timings: 10 am to 11 pm

Shopprix Mall
Branded stores, restaurants, multiplex, a bowling alley and gaming zone including 2 pool tables, ice hockey and video games.

> C-134B, Sector 61, Noida, (opposite Flex Industries)
Tel: 120 249 0000
Timings: Mon to Sat 9:30 am to 11 pm; Sun noon to 11 pm

Spice World
The name is misleading. One's first thought is of a mall dedicated to selling turmeric and garam masala. However, the mall is aimed at adding spice to one's life with 4 floors of branded shops, a truly magnificent kids' entertainment zone, India's first 4D movie theatre, many restaurants and coffee shops.

>I-2, Sector 25A, Noida
Tel: 0120 436 6400
Timings: Mon to Sat 9:30 am to 11 pm; Sun noon to 11 pm
Web: www.spiceworld.co.in for booking movie tickets

Metro Walk Mall
It is one of the biggest malls in capital which also boasts an excellent amusement park, Adventure Island. Like

all other malls, it has also a wide selection of the leading national and international brands including Pantaloon, Reebok, Nike, etc. There is an array of food options, from chain restaurants such as McDonald's, and an extensive food court with a bounty of menu options of Chinese, chaat, pizzas and Mexican food. The USP of most malls the world over is the retail shopping. But for the Metro Walk Mall, it holds the distinction of having Adventure Island which has several rides and swings that are found in amusement parks around the world (see *Playground Paradise*, pp.59–60).

>Unitech Metro Walk Mall, Sector 10, Rohini, Adjacent to Rithala Metro
Tel: 011 2757 3480
Timings: Daily 10 am to 11 pm

Select Citywalk Mall
Another mega mall located in South Delhi, the retail space has more than 150 shops, a huge food court, stand-alone restaurants, kids' play area with Little Tykes toys for just Rs 150 an hour and movie theatres. Every weekend, there's a Weekend Club from 4 pm to 9 pm at the Kids Fountain Terrace on the second floor of the mall where kids can do finger painting, pottery, caricatures, mini-golf. There's also music and storytelling.

>Press Enclave Road, Saket
Timings: 10 am to 10 pm
Web: www.selectcitywalk.com

Flea Market
Held every Wednesday at Select Citywalk Mall in Saket, Flea@Nite offers great shopping, children's toys, books, fresh fruits, vegetables and flowers, deli products, jewellery and home linens among the many offerings. It has the feeling of Dilli Haat with live music, grills and gelatos, juice and mocktail bars, cafes and street art thrown in. It can get crowded, but the tents and big-tent feel will make for an enjoyable family outing.

>Select Citywalk Plaza, Saket
Timings: Every Wed 4 pm to 10 pm
Web: http://www.selectcitywalk.com/Flea-nite.htm

Bookstores

First-hand bookstores

Bookstores in and around town are great places to pick up city maps, guides, news magazines and books for the entire family. Some bookstores hold weekly story readings and art sessions to keep the kids entertained.

Children's Book Trust
A huge selection of books for kids in various age groups. There's a big selection in both English and Hindi.

>Nehru House, 4, Bahadur Shah Zafar Marg
Tel: 011 2331 6970
Web: www.childrenbooktrust.com

CMYK
Unique books kids would treasure. CMYK has loads of children's activities, and there's even a terrace upstairs.

> 15-16, Mehar Chand Market, Lodhi Road (near India Habitat Centre)
Tel: 011 2464 1881
Timings: Daily 10 am to 9 pm

Crossword Bookstore
> Select Citywalk
Level 1, Crossword, Select Citywalk Mall
Press Enclave Road, Saket
Tel: 011 4609 8500
Timings: Daily 11 am to 9:30 pm

Eureka!
Eureka is the city's one and only bookstore dedicated to children. Located in a little market on the main Alaknanda road, the blink-and-you-may-miss-it shop carries the latest books and classics from Indian and Western writers. Monthly workshops are held where authors read from their books and children can participate in interactive storytelling and drawing sessions.

> 6, Local Shopping Complex, Narmada Market,
Opposite Don Bosco School, Alaknanda
Tel: 011 2602 1092
Timings: Wed to Mon 10:30 am to 8:30 pm

Fact & Fiction
A nice selection of books and music to sing along to while you shop.

>39 Basant Lok Market, Vasant Vihar
Tel: 011 2614 6843
Timings: Wed to Mon 11 am to 8 pm

Faqir-Chand & Sons
The small Khan Market retailer has the latest best-sellers and will find it and hold it for you in case it is not in stock. Nothing is computerized so it can sometimes be frustrating.

>15-A Khan Market
Tel: 011 2461 8810
Timings: Mon to Sat 9:30 am to 6:30 pm

Full Circle
The Khan Market branch

of Full Circle has travel, how-to, fiction, non-fiction and general best sellers on the ground floor and a very nice children's book corner on the first floor with books from the crib to college. The store carries the classics and many interactive books, also. There's a counter selling baked goods nearby and Café Turtle (see *Eats*, p.134) is one more flight up.

>5-B Khan Market
Tel: 011 2465 5641/43
Timings: Daily 11 am to 7:30 pm

>Saket, MGF Metropolitan Mall, Shop No. 13, 1st Flr
Tel: 011 4059 7541/2

>N-8, GK I, N Block Market
Tel: 011 2924 5641/44

Mama's Little Donut
The toy store extraordinaire also has a nice selection of books that are not readily available in other stores around town. The books where a child's photo can be inserted so he/she can be part of the story are quite the novelty items. The store sometimes conducts almost weekly story telling sessions in the play area outside.

>D-6 Soami Nagar (North), near Panchsheel Enclave
Tel: 011 4174 9243
Timings: Daily 11 am to 7:30 pm

Midlands Bookshop
Discounts on books year-round. This is definitely the place for voracious readers.

>20 Aurobindo Place, Hauz Khas
Tel: 011 2696 2718
Timings: Mon to Sat 10 am to 7:30 pm

Om Bookshop
With over 100,000 books to choose from, everyone in the family can find something interesting. Check out the website for more locations.

>E-77, South Extension Part I (near Bengali Sweet Shop)
Tel: 011 2465 3792/3
Timings: Tue to Sun 11 am to 9 pm
Web: www.ombooks.com

>45, Basant Lok, Vasant Vihar (Near Priya Cinema Market)
Tel: 011 2614 3530; 011 2615 6388

>G 13-16, MGF, Metropolitan Mall, DLF, Gurgaon (Opposite Barista)
Tel: 0124 401 5585; 0124 401 5586

>3 Community Centre Anupam PVR Complex, Saket (Near PVR Saket)
Tel: 011 4166 4206

>43, The Great India Place Mall, Ground Flr,
Sector 38A, Noida (Near Atta market)

Tel: 0120 245 0066; 0120 245 0068

Oxford Bookstore

Wide selection of books, greeting cards, DVDs and CDs. Very much like Barnes & Noble in the US, there's a cosy Cha Bar which serves teas and sandwiches, snacks, salad, fries, quiches and pastries.

>148 Statesman House, 1st Flr, Barakhamba Road
Tel: 011 2376 6080
Timings: 10 am to 9:30 pm
Web: www.oxfordbookstore.com

Sunday book market

There's nothing you won't find in Daryaganj, and the sight of all those books spread out on the pavements is something the kids won't forget in a hurry. A bit flea market, a twist of madness, but there's order to the chaos or regulars wouldn't keep coming back weekly.

>1.5 km area near Golcha Cinema

The Bookshop

The store regularly has readings and the selection is quite good.

>13/7 Jor Bagh Market
Tel: 011 2469 7102
Timings: Mon to Sat 10:30 am to 7 pm

Discount / Used bookstores

Anil Book Corner

What's great about this place is you can exchange 2 books and get one book if the stall is so inclined. It's a good deal if you like to read but are not wedded to building a whole library.

>Plaza Cinema Building, H block, Connaught Place (near PVR Plaza)
Nearest Metro: Rajiv Chowk
Tel: 011 2371 3223
Timings: Daily 9:30 am to 8:30 pm

Anjali International

Books can be had for as little as Rs 50. Lots of academic work books for kids and general fiction and non-fiction in good condition.

>II-J-10 Central Market, Lajpat Nagar,
14 Central Market, opposite Bata
Tel: 98109 37779
Timings: Tue to Sun 11 am to 8 pm

Jacksons Books

Brisk business is done from foreigners as the store stocks books in 25 languages. Books can be bought at half price and resold to the store at half the price. There is something for everyone here.

>5106 Main Bazaar, Paharganj, opposite Medikos

Opticians
Nearest Metro: New Delhi Railway Station
Tel: 011 5535 1083
Timings: Daily 10 am to 11 pm

Three L Library
Excess used copies of some books can be had for half of the price listed.

>49 Main Market, Defence Colony
Tel: 011 2433 3576
Timings: Tue to Sun 11 am to 9 pm

Shopping Central

Indian clothing is synonymous with vibrant colours, silky fabrics and ornate work. From classic sarees to funky tunics, salwar kameezes and Western wear, the shopping malls, markets and stalls from Paharganj to Chandni Chowk, offer up bargains and designer clothes for everyone. Dig through the piles of denims in Sarojini Nagar or have shop assistants fawning over you in Emporio. The only dilemma would be whether or not to throw out the clothes you came with.

For the family

Fabindia
Find something for everyone and the house too at this one-stop shop. Garments, linens, rugs, accessories, organic foods, upholstery fabric and body care. Log on to www.fabindia.com for more store locations.

>Connaught Place
B-28, Upper Ground Flr, Inner Circle, Connaught Place
Tel: 011 4151 3371/72/73/74
Timings: 10 am to 8 pm daily
>Greater Kailash, Part I
14 N Block Market (garments)
Tel: 011 2923 2183/84/85

>7 N Block Market (furnishings)
Tel: 011 2924 9306

>Karol Bagh
17 A/62, Ajmal Khan Road
Tel: 011 4504 6182/3

>Khan Market
Central Hall, Above Shop No. 20 and 21
Tel: 011 4175 7142/43/44

>Lajpat Nagar, II
I/1B, Ground and 1st Fl, Central Market, Lajpat Nagar II
Tel: 011 2981 0512/13/14/15

>Saket
Select Citywalk Mall, 2nd Flr
Tel: 011 4265 8392/93/94/95/96

>Vasant Kunj
10 Local Shopping Centre, Nelson Mandela Road,

Vasant Kunj
Tel: 011 2689 9775

For the kids

Apartment 9 Kids
This store, an offshoot of hip and funky furniture and furnishings at Apartment 9, has all kinds of knick-knacks to make the friends of your kids envious. From really cute toothbrush holders to pencils and sharpeners, wooden pegs for hanging things and photo holders, the list goes on and on. Parents will definitely leave there with happy kids.

>N-18 GK I, N Block market
Tel: 011 3243 8224
Timings: 11 am to 8 pm; closed Tue

Bata
Go here for affordable and comfortable shoes and great prices. Fashionable is not No. 1 priority here, but the selection is fine and the shoes aren't too heavy.
>Go to www.bataindia.com for store locations

Benetton
Where else in the world can you get a dress from Benetton for only Rs 700? That may seem a bit high by Indian standards but if you know the dollar price, you know you're saving a bundle. Go to www.benetton.com for store locations.

>E-13 Connaught Place
Tel: 011 4151 7950
Timings: 11 am to 8 pm

Catmoss
Children's wear, mainly western at reasonable prices.

>G-1, South Extension Part I
Tel: 011 4134 9487
Timings: Tue to Sun 11 am to 8 pm

Ebony
Clothing and baby gear.

>D-4 South Extension Part II
Tel: 011 2625 9099
Timings: Tue to Sun 11 am to 8 pm

Elvy
It's a hub for all things cutesy. Both the big and little boys may want to flee the store, but there are plenty of things with the word Princess scrawled over them to make the little princess happy.

>18 Square One Mall, Ground Flr,
C-2 District Centre, Saket
Tel: 011 2956 2118
Timings: Daily 11 am to 8 pm
Web: www.elvy.in for more store locations

Esprit Kidswear
Dress your mini-me's with stylish clothes akin to what is offered for adults.

>M-64 GK I, M Block Market
Tel: 011 4173 9970
Timings: 10:30 am to 9:30 pm; closed Tue

>F-12 Select Citywalk Mall, Saket
Tel: 011 4057 5098
Timings: 10:30 am to 9:30 pm

>E-2 South Extension Part II
Tel: 011 4608 1122
Timings: Tue to Sun 10:30 am to 9:30 pm

Fabindia
Lots of kids' clothing to deck out the children and cushion covers to decorate the rooms.

>www.fabindia.com for outlets

Gift Palace
Toys galore at this store. All the brand names, doll houses, skate boards, inflatable pools, video games and DVDs. If they don't have what you're looking for, they will source it in a matter of hours or just a day or two. The Gift Palace even has catalogues to order big kids' play houses and garden toys and birthday party planning is one of their strengths. From face painters to magicians and bouncy castles, all of it can be found here. And yes, you can score an elephant, too.

>52-B Khan Market
Tel: 011 2463 2640
Timings: Mon to Sat 11 am to 7:30 pm

Fast fact: The label on the toy gives information about the percentage of toxicity, the appropriate age group and the name and address of the manufacturer. It is wise not to buy unbranded toys that are hawked by vendors at India Gate and at traffic stops which are likely to carry no useful information about the toy. Many of the toys available in India carry an official European Community (CE) symbol on the toy. The symbol means the toy meets the safety standards set out by the EC. Toys imported from the US also carry safety information.

Kroma
An art gallery strictly dedicated to art kids would love. The paintings have a heavy splash of whimsy and cute animals. Paintings range from Rs 4,600 to 1 lakh.

>113-A Shahpur Jat, 1st Flr, near Asiad Village
Tel: 011 4175 2946 or 98117 53888
Timings: Mon to Sat 11:30 am to 5 pm
Web: www.kroma.in

Lilliput
Fashionable clothing for kids newborn to 12. Accessories include shoes, bags and sunglasses.

>G-15, 2nd Flr,
South Extension Part 1
Tel: 011 4134 9411
Timings: 10:30 am to 8:30 pm; closed Tue
Web: www.lilliput-india.com for store locations

Mandira
Indian clothing, hair barrettes, baby blankets and stuffed animals and hand puppets. Not run of the mill offerings, so great gifts to take back home.

>25 Santushti Shopping Complex
Tel: 011 2410 1251
Timings: Mon to Sat 10 am to 6:30 pm

Mama's Little Donut
The name sounds like a cute little snack shop, but it's really a cute little toy shop. Mama's Little Donut stocks everything from Victorian doll houses and puppets to wooden puzzles and non-electronic toys. You can buy toys that require batteries, but they happily tend toward the learning side. Delightful costumes and play tents and a play area out back make the shopping experience fun. There's weekly story telling or activities held in the play area beside the store. Call for details.

>D-6 Soami Nagar (North), near Panchsheel Enclave
Tel: 011 4174 9243
Timings: Daily 11 am to 7:30 pm

Maya Toys
If you want to breeze in and out of Maya Toys, forget about it. And, please leave the kids at home as the shopping bags will be plenty and the wallet will be empty. Occupying 2 storefronts in Aurobindo Market, there's toys floor to ceiling and huge catalogues to order what is not available in house. The store was opened in 1947, when India gained its independence.

>11&16 Aurobindo Place Market, DDA Market, Aurobindo Marg
Tel: 011 2652 6979
Timings: Wed to Mon 10 am to 8:30 pm

Mom & Me
This South Extension store has so many sweet things for mothers and children, it just might give you a toothache. With everything one would need from pregnancy and for kids up to 9 years old, the beautifully, spacious, brightly lit store is one-stop shopping. There's even a little play area with low, colourful seating and a table for kids to play while parents shop.

>F-47 South Extension NDSE, Part I
Tel: 011 4614 2401
Timings: Daily 10 am to 8 pm

Okadi
The French label has set up shop in the Ambience Mall in Gurgaon and Select Citywalk in Saket. Parisian chic for ages 2 to 14 with prices from Rs 1000.

>S-29 Select Citywalk Mall, Saket
Tel: 011 4265 8359
Timings: Daily 10:30 am to 9 pm

Petals
The clothing here will put the spotlight on your children at any party. Really lovely selections of party wear.

>A-5 DDA Shopping Complex, Defence Colony
Tel: 011 2461 7698
Timings: 10 am to 8 pm

Ram Chander and Sons
Way before 'Made in China' became a slogan to avoid, Ram Chander and Sons has been selling quality toys since 1890. Although one can buy the latest toys, classic board games and wooden toys can still be found.

>D-1 Odeon Cinema Building, Connaught Place
Tel: 011 2341 2065
Nearest Metro: Rajiv Chowk
Timings: Mon to Sat 10:30 am to 7:30 pm

Sarojini Nagar
This is a bargain hunter's paradise. Export surplus of brand-name jeans, T-shirts, skirts and dresses. Lots of children's clothing to be had at Rs 100 or less.

>**Timings:** Tue to Sun 11 am to 8:30 pm

Smiles
With toys and more toys stacked from floor to ceiling and beyond the ceiling as there is a floor upstairs that mainly the sales people go to as they must fear that something may fall on your head before you make it to the cash register. They stock the latest trends and the classics.

>3 Tamoor Nagar, opposite Gurudwara, New Friends Colony
Tel: 011 2683 1277
Timings: 10 am to 8:30 pm

2Feet
Designer wear from newborn to age 12. Selections for girls trump the choices for boys but the clothes aren't run of the mill. It is designer Namrata Datt's own brand and the range covers baby basics including bath soaps and lotions, Indian and Western party wear. Prices range from Rs 150 to Rs 6,500. Many items can be customized.

>Santushti Shopping Complex
Tel: 011 2467 5059

Timings: Mon to Sat 10 am to 6:30 pm

>S-32, 2nd Flr, Select Citywalk Mall, Saket
Tel: 011 2688 2408
Timings: Daily 10:30 am to 9:30 pm

Toy Kingdom
One-stop shopping for toys and they organize entertainment including bouncy castles and video games for birthday parties.

>38 Aurobindo Place, Hauz Khas
Tel: 011 4175 4095
Timings: Daily 10 am to 8 pm

For mom

Anokhi
Like Fabindia, Anokhi carries bright, comfortable clothing with generous cuts. The clothes are made using traditional patterns and organic dyes. The only downside is you're likely to bump into people on the street wearing the same outfits. Just pat yourself on the back for having similar and good taste.

>32 Khan Market
Tel: 011 2460 3423
Timings: Daily 11 am to 7:30 pm
Web: www.anokhi.com

>Santushti Shopping Complex,
Opposite Samrat Hotel, Race Course Road, NWC Air Force
Tel: 011 2688 3076
Timings: Mon to Sat 11 am to 7:30 pm

>Greater Kailash Part I
N-16 2nd Flr, N Block Market
Tel: 011 2923 1500
Timings: 11 am to 7:30 pm; closed Tue

Cottons
Fabindia's more expensive and dressier cousin.

>N-11, GK I, N Block Market
Tel: 011 4163 5108
Timings: 11 am to 8 pm, closed Tue

Khadi Gram Udyog Bhavan
Pick up soaps and masalas along with the kurtas. Prices aren't bad.

>24 Regal Building, Connaught Place
Tel: 011 2341 1651
Timings: Daily 9:30 am to 6:30 pm

Manan
Designer wear at reasonable prices. The store will take orders and make something you see on the rack in your size. Also find jewellery, shoes, purses, shawls, blankets and cushion covers.

>8 Khan Market
Tel: 011 4175 7701

Timings: Daily 11 am to 8 pm
Web: www.manandesign.com for other locations

Nun
The store will bring out the little girl in Mom. Lots of frilly things and spaghetti straps. Definitely a youthful vibe. But remember, just because they sell it in your size, it doesn't mean you should buy it.

>M-53 GK I, M Block Market
Timings: 11:30 am to 8 pm; closed Tue
Cost: From Rs 350 for accessories

Sabhyata
Great designs for a third of the price of Cottons, Anokhi and Fabindia. But you'll have to venture to Lajpat Nagar II.

>E-12 Lajpat Nagar II, Central Market
Tel: 011 4172 2138
Timings: From 11 am

Santushti Shopping Complex
With clothing shops outranking silver shops, though barely, Mom can easily spend the morning here. Thirty boutiques ring the lovely gardens. Among the boutiques are Claire's, Ogaan, Tulsi, Ensemble and Rana Gill. There's also a Good Earth and Anokhi.

>Race Cross Road
Timings: Mon to Sat 10 am to 6 pm

ZingRin
The tiny store offers much in the way of accessories, belts, bangles and necklaces and the clothes have a very hip city feel. Prices start from around Rs 500.

>78 Middle Lane, Rear Entry, Khan Market
Tel: 011 4356 5455
Timings: Mon to Sat 11 am to 8 pm

For dad

Off the rack

The Raymond Shop (Factory outlet)
Quality ready to wear clothes offered at affordable prices in various textures and styles. The brand has been around since 1925. Every businessman in Delhi has probably owned a suit from The Raymond Shop sometime in his life. Made-to-order suit designs are also available.

>M-7 Connaught Place
Tel: 011 2341 6755
Timings: Mon to Sat 11 am to 8 pm
Web: www.raymondindia.com for more store locations

Fabindia (see *For the Family,* p.177)
Shirts, trousers, pyjamas and

chappals all for a good price.
Web: www.fabindia.com for store locations.

Bespoke suits

When off the rack just won't do, Dad can go for a bespoke suit, tailored just for him. It will fit to a tee and the suit will be made to order, ensuring the best possible fit. The buyer has total control over the fabric, style and tailoring. It is definitely more expensive, but there is a higher quality of customized construction.

Delhi Cloth House
>66-B Khan Market
Tel: 011 2461 8937
Timings: Mon to Sat 11 am to 7:30 pm
Cost: From Rs 6,000

Grover Cloth House
>47-A Khan Market
Tel: 011 2462 5622
Timings: Mon to Sat 10:30 am to 7 pm
Cost: From Rs 6,500

Krishna Cloth House
>65-A Khan Market
Tel: 011 2464 9126
Timings: Mon to Sat 11 am to 7:30 pm
Cost: From Rs 6,200

New Prominent Tailors
>25-K Block, Connaught Place
Tel: 011 2341 8007
Timings: Mon to sat 11 am to 7:30 pm
Cost: From Rs 7,500

Pal Zileri
>American Plaza, Ground Flr, International Trade Tower, Hotel Inter-continental Eros, Nehru Place
Tel: 011 4651 8474
Timings: Daily 10 am to 8:30 pm
Cost: From Rs 2 lakh

Paul Smith
>212 DLF Emporio Mall, Nelson Mandela Road
Tel: 011 4604 0734
Timings: Daily 10 am to 10 pm
Cost: From Rs 42,000

The Raymond Shop
>**Web:** www.raymondindia.com for the numerous outlets around the city

Savileroy
>2/9 Jangpura A
Tel: 98 1142 6261
Timings: Daily, not fixed
Cost: From Rs 8,000

Vaish at Rivoli
>Next to PVR Rivoli Cinema, Connaught Place
Tel: 011 4150 2525
Nearest Metro: Rajiv Chowk
Timings: Mon to sat 10 am to 8 pm
Cost: From Rs 15,000
Web: www.vaish.com

Vedi Tailors
>60 M Block, Connaught Place

Tel: 011 2341 6901
Nearest Metro: Rajiv Chowk
Timings: Mon to Sat 11:30 am to 8 pm
Cost: From Rs 2,500

For the house

Central Cottage Industries Emporium

The government-run Central Cottage Industries Emporium is one-stop shopping for your home. If you're not inclined to brave the heat and bargain at the Janpath stalls which are directly across the street, then this is the place. Spread over 6 floors, the air-conditioned building has items representing states across India. Popularly known as the Cottage, it was established in 1948 with the aim of preserving and showcasing traditional Indian craftsmanship. It has one of the largest ranges of accessories, linens and furniture available anywhere in India with over 20,000 handicrafts, 2,000 carpet designs and 2,000 furniture designs. There is also a clothing section which has an impressive collection of sarees, shawls and other fashion accessories with separate sections for menswear and kids. One can also shop for woodcarvings, paintings, brassware and textiles. Over the last 50 years, the Emporium has attracted several well known personalities like Queen Elizabeth II of England, Queen Farah of Iran, Jacqueline Kennedy and a host of dignitaries from across the world. It takes at least 2 to 3 hours to feel as if the place has been given justice. An elevator takes you to the level with cushion covers and bed spreads, a canteen is conveniently located in the middle of the floors which serve both veg and non-veg food and toilets are available throughout. It's really a fixed price so don't even think about haggling. Shipment of bulky furniture or rugs is available too.

>Jawahar Vyapar Bhavan, Janpath (opposite McDonald's)
Tel: 011 2332 0439; 011 2332 2936
Located about 2 minutes from Connaught Place, the best way to get there would be to take a Metro to the Rajiv Chowk station or by car as there is ample parking inside the gate.
Nearest Metro: Rajiv Chowk station
Timings: Mon to Sat 10:30 am to 7:30 pm
Web: www.cottageemporiumindia.com

Dilli Haat

Dilli Haat is an upgraded version of the traditional weekly market, housing a variety of handicrafts, shawls, clothing, toys, trinkets, food and frequent cultural activities. Hawkers come from all over India, showcasing the richness of their states through their handicrafts. Dilli Haat is a highly successful project launched by Delhi Tourism. Great gifts can be found at the ever-changing stalls, which are allotted on a rotational basis, usually for 10 days, ensuring a different variety of handicrafts for visitors at each visit. So if you like something, buy it. Whatever is quoted, offer a third of the price and start bargaining from there. You can and should bargain, but also be mindful that you are buying directly from some of the craftspeople who have made the items themselves so you may want to do a little bargaining here and save the heavy lifting for Janpath. The food plaza has some of the best cuisines that represent the 25 states of India. Toilets are located near the food plaza. The Master Crafts Fair is held in early December for 2 weeks. Award-winning artists and craftspeople sell their work during this time.

>Sri Aurobindo Marg, Opposite INA Market
Tel: 011 2611 9055, 2467 8817
Timings: Daily 10:30 am to 10 pm
Entry: Rs 15 adults, Rs 5 children

State emporia
The state emporia are located around the corner from Cottage Industries. Like the Cottage Emporium, the state emporia showcase products native to states from around the nation including Rajasthan, Gujarat, Orissa, Tamil Nadu and Kashmir. Run by the state government, the shops sell quality handicrafts, art and jewellery at great fixed prices so there's no need to bargain. Eighteen stores in all, the state emporia showcase some of the best handicrafts and handlooms India has to offer and you won't have to buy a plane, bus or train ticket to get there. Two are worth a special mention:

Bharati Delhi Emporium
One of the most prestigious of the emporia, it has a range of handicrafts, furniture, leather goods and clothing. There is also an extensive range of jewellery and loose precious and semi-precious stones. The building is air-conditioned, nicely laid out and the goods are a bit more expensive than at the Cottage Emporium.

>A-3/4 Baba Kharak Singh Marg
Tel: 011 2336 3287; 011 2334 0343

Timings: Mon to Sat 10 am to 6:30 pm
Web: http://emporium.dsidc.org

Crafts Museum Shop
This is the place to go if you want handicrafts that are found everywhere else but are of a higher quality. The selection is wonderful and you get to browse and buy without the craftsmen from the Crafts Museum putting pressure on you to do so.

>Bhairon Road, Pragati Maidan, opposite the Purana Qila
Tel: 011 2337 1269
Nearest Metro: Pragati Maidan
Timings: Daily 9:30 am to 5:30 pm

Sporting Equipment

To fully enjoy adventure sports and the like, having the right gear is in order. Several stores carry the equipment at great prices and the sales staff is super helpful so you won't be stuck with what you don't need. If you're on a budget, don't cut corners when it comes to safety. Buy proper shoes and helmets as applicable.

Adventure 18
Specializes in climbing, trekking and cycling equipment.

>18 Satya Niketan, opposite Venkateswara College
Tel: 011 2687 8888
Timings: Daily 11 am to 7 pm

Firefox Bike Station
Specialty bikes and cycling gear can be found here.

>A-12 Lajpat Nagar II
Tel: 011 4172 8067
Timings: Tue to Sun 11 am to 8:30 pm
Web: www.firefoxbikes.com

>J-13/56 Rajouri Garden Cambridge School Road
Tel: 011 4556 2852
Timings: 11 am to 8:30 pm; closed Wed

Grand Slam
All sporting equipment including cricket bats, racquets, blades and balls. The store also carries sportswear.

>M-74 Greater Kailash Part II
Tel: 011 2922 2902
Timings: Daily 10:30 am to 7:00 pm

Kalra Cycle Store
Bikes for the whole family and bike pumps, too. However, the store does not carry helmets.

>67-A Khan Market
Tel: 011 2461 8527
Timings: Mon to Sat 10:30 am to 7 pm

Zanskar Outdoor Equipment
Everything trekkers and camping enthusiasts will need.

>21 DSIDC, Scheme-3, Okhla Industrial Area II
Tel: 98116 76556
Timings: Mon to Sat 9 am to 6 pm

SLEEPS

No. 1: For value and comfort and lots of pampering thrown in, choose the Oberoi.

Hop in to hip hotels that offer real value for money—from luxurious to affordable to no-frill finds. Discover the right family hotel with ease and comfort. After a long plane ride, a long day of sight-seeing or a long luxurious spa treatment or swim, a comfortable bed for a lazy afternoon nap or a sound night's sleep beckons. Delhi is notorious for having a shortage of hotel rooms and over-charging for the ones that do exist. However, there's a hotel to fit every budget and the service provided can make for picture perfect memories. 5-star deluxe hotels often run specials so check the Web sites and call the hotel. Sometimes walk-in rates can be a boon.

Five-star Hotels

Aman New Delhi
Aman opened one of its signature properties in the heart of Delhi in 2009. Rated as the world's leading international hotel group in the 2007/2008 Zagat survey of the World's Top Hotels, Resorts and Spas, The Aman is the first city property for the luxurious hotel group. The spa features private treatment rooms, there's an award-winning hair and beauty salon and a 50-metre swimming pool, with a separate children's pool that meshes with the adult pool. If you prefer to lounge in private, the rooms have their own plunge pools, with terraces and breathtaking views. The restaurants offer international cuisines and there's also a tapas bar. The resort has a fleet of silver Ambassador cars to ferry guests around the city.

>Lodhi Road
Tel: 011 4363 3333
Rates: From US $550 low season; US $750 high season
Web: http://amanresorts.com/amannewdelhi/home.aspx

The Ashok
With more than 550 rooms, the Ashok is another luxury hotel where service is unsurpassed. It has old style charm and the rooms are

spacious. The restaurants serve good Indian food but not necessarily what children would like. However, the recreation offered at the hotel surpasses the activities offered by similar hotels in the area. Guests can enjoy table tennis, badminton, horse riding, golf, tennis and there's even a gliding club. Of course, there's a huge swimming pool and the hotel offers babysitting.

>50-B, Diplomatic Enclave, Chanakyapuri
Tel: 011 2611 0101; 011 2687 6060
Rates: From US $318
Web: www.theashok.com

The Claridges Hotel

Families will be comfortable in the double guest rooms at the Claridges. Facilities include babysitting, a big outdoor swimming pool and the restaurants. Pickwicks restaurant (see *Eats*, p.130–31) is a favourite, even for guests who aren't staying in the hotel, as it offers a range of international cuisines and calorie-filled desserts. In the winters, brunch can be had on the beautifully manicured and lush front lawns.

>12 Aurangzeb Road
Tel: 011 4133 5133
Rates: From US $133 low season; US $174 high season
Web: www.claridges.com

The Clarion Collection—The Qutab

With 96 guest rooms, the hotel has a boutique-y feel. The deluxe rooms are family sized and have pool views and a view of Qutab Minar. No, a photo of the minaret from the balcony of the room does not count as a visit. Breakfast is complimentary.

>Shaheed Jeet Singh Marg, Hauz Khas, Katwaria Sarai
Tel: 011 4120 0000; 011 2652 1010
Rates: From US $296 low season; US $360 high season
Web: www.clarionnewdelhi.com

Crowne Plaza Surya

Choose one of the 82 club rooms for the family as they provide more space. Overall the hotel has 240 super-modern guestrooms (separate from the club rooms) that come with 42-inch plasma TVs. All rooms and public areas have wireless connections. The pool is deep but on the small-ish side. Crowne Plaza caters to tourists and it shows with little touches as a separate rental car desk, tour desk, airline desk and a travel agent desk. The prices aren't great but it is convenient. The hotel also offers babysitting and the staff speak several languages. The 5 multi-cuisine restaurants will definitely satisfy even the fussiest eaters.

>New Friends Colony
Tel: 011 2683 5070
Rates: From US $148 low season; US $269 high season
Web: www.crowneplazadelhi.com

The Grand New Delhi

There are 390 rooms including 25 suites. Breakfast is complimentary and there's broadband internet access in the rooms. Guest rooms are big enough for families or suites with dining tables are a great option when you do not want to go out for dinner after a long day of sightseeing. Recreation is big at the Grand with an adult and children's pool, turf tennis courts and a jogging track. Parents can also get massages and other beauty treatments at the spa or participate in a yoga session. There are many restaurants to choose from, a family Sunday brunch and a gourmet shop selling pastries and breads that are in a league of their own.

>Nelson Mandela Marg, Phase 2, Vasant Kunj
Tel: 011 2677 1234; 011 4165 1234
Rates: From US $161 low season; US $241 high season
Web: www.thegrandnewdelhi.com

Hyatt Regency

Hyatt hotels the world over know how to entertain families with amenities that go above and beyond expectations. A club room comes with complimentary breakfast, evening cocktails and hors d'oeuvres. A family of 4 with 2 kids cannot get around the maximum of 3 per room when booking online, but you can if you telephone. There's a lovely bakery, swimming pool, fitness centre and spa. Sunday lunches at the various restaurants are decadent, but so are the prices, with a range of Rs 1,650 to Rs 3,800 depending on the restaurant and alcohol vs without alcohol.

>Ring Road, Bhikaji Cama Place
Tel: 011 2679 1234; 011 2679 1122
Rates: From US $200 low season; US $400 high season
Web: www.delhi.regency.hyatt.com

The Imperial

The Imperial hotel is an old-style grand hotel with dining options near the beautiful lawns which are great for the kids to unwind after a long day of sight-seeing. Built in 1931 and refurbished in the 1990s, the magnificent white hotel in the centre of Delhi is a remnant of India's imperial past. Opulent rooms, expansive lawns and a choice of multi-cuisine restaurants and a Chanel boutique in the lobby may make you want to extend your stay; that is, if you haven't maxed out the credit card.

>1 Janpath, Connaught Place (Opposite Cottage Emporium)
Tel: 011 2334 1234; 011 4150 1234
Rates: From US $271 low season; US $364 high season
Web: www.theimperialindia.com

ITC Maurya
This hotel's location is a tourist's delight. The Red Fort, National Gallery of Modern Art, Jantar Mantar, Delhi Golf Club, Qutab Minar, Crafts Museum, Dilli Haat and Rashtrapati Bhavan are all nearby. The award winning restaurant, Bukhara, hosted President Clinton and his daughter Chelsea. There are 440 rooms including 29 suites. The Maurya has a swimming pool, spa, babysitting and can arrange for other activities.

>21, Diplomatic Enclave, Sardar Patel Marg, Chanakyapuri
Tel: 011 2611 2233; 011 2611 3333
Rates: From US $247 low season; US $449 high season
Web: www.itcwelcomgroup.in

InterContinental Nehru Place
Within a stone's throw of the ITC Maurya, the InterContinental Nehru Place is also centrally located to many tourist attractions. There are 218 guest rooms, all with broadband internet access and there's wireless connectivity throughout the hotel. Geared toward the business and leisure travellers, 170 newspapers are delivered daily, the staff is multi-lingual, the restaurants are multi-cuisine and there's a multitude of recreational activities to participate in, including a 24-hour fitness centre.

>S-2, International Trade Tower, Nehru Place
Tel: 011 4122 3344; 011 4133 1700
Rates: From US $188 low season; US $326 high season
Web: www.intercontinental.com

The Lalit New Delhi
(previously known as the Intercontinental Grand)
Located about 15 miles from Indira Gandhi International Airport, the Lalit is near India Gate, Parliament House, the National Museum, Lodhi Gardens, Rashtrapati Bhavan, Jama Masjid, the Red Fort and the Lotus Temple. The 457-room super luxury hotel has 24-hour room service, babysitting

and 7 restaurants. There's an outdoor all-weather swimming pool with a special kids dip pool.

>Ground Flr, Barakhamba Road, Connaught Place
Tel: 011 2341 1001, 011 4444 7777
Rates: From $336 in low season; $396 high season
Web: www.thelalit.com

Leela Kempinski
The Leela is out of the way from the heart of Delhi, but it is only 5 kilometres from the international airport. The rooms, even the most basic ones, are deluxe with a capital D. The restaurants serve Indian, international and Italian cuisines. The hotel offers babysitting, has a luxurious spa and a state of the art fitness centre. It is recommended that families of 4 book into a double room or the executive room. Baby cots and/or a rollaway bed can be provided.

>Ambience Island NH-8, Gurgaon
Tel: 0124 477 1234
Rates: From US $283 low season; US $403 high season
Web: www.theleela.com/hotel-gurgaon.html

Le Meridien
The hotel is 2 kilometres from Rashtrapati Bhavan, Parliament House, India Gate and Connaught Place. Le Meridien's location puts tourists in the centre of the action. The list of amenities is endless, the restaurants offer superior food, the spa is world class and the stay will be memorable.

>Windsor Place, Janpath, Connaught Place
Tel: 011 2371 0101; 011 2371 4545
Rates: From US $161 low season; US $339 high season
Web: www.lemeridian.newdelhi.com

The Metropolitan
Located near Connaught Place, this hotel is in a shopper's and foodie's haven. With 185 rooms, the Metropolitan is super modern and has 3 fabulous restaurants to choose from. The Japanese restaurant, Sakura, serves the best authentic Japanese food in town. There's a travel desk as well.

>Bangla Sahib Road
Tel: 011 4250 0200; 011 2571 8433
Rates: From US $212 low season; US $666 high season
Web: www.hotelmetdelhi.com

The Oberoi
The award-winning luxury hotel, The Oberoi, overlooks the prestigious Delhi Golf Club and is a stone's throw from Humayun's Tomb. The

Oberoi's top-end service, décor, cuisine and both the outdoor and indoor pools may make the family give up on sight-seeing altogether, though the location puts guests within minutes of Lodhi Garden, India Gate and Connaught Place. Odd-numbered rooms face Humayun's Tomb. Threesixtydegrees, the coffee shop that has all of Delhi patronizing at least once a week, will make guests carve out some serious gym time. The young staff, who probably don't even have kids yet, treat the littlest guests like they are the ones with the credit cards. Great value, even better service and definitely worth a repeat visit on another Delhi jaunt.

>Main Road, Dr Zakir Hussain Marg
Tel: 011 2436 3030; 011 2436 0484
Rates: From US $285 low season; US $489 high season
Web: www.oberoidelhi.com

The Park

Close to Connaught Place is the luxury boutique hotel, the Park. Unlike the other luxury hotels that are heavy on ornamentation and gilded everything, the Park is modern and simplistic in its approach to decadence. It is conveniently located near Jantar Mantar and The Cottage Emporium (see *Shopping*, p.185) and many eateries. The rooftop pool is best for lounging and not lapping as it is a bit on the small side.

>15 Parliament Street, Connaught Place
Tel: 011 2374 3000; 011 2373 3737
Rates: From US $142 low season; US $155 high season
Web: www.theparkhotels.com

The Radisson Hotel

Billed as a business hotel, the Radisson still has all the amenities that a family would enjoy, plus a swanky business centre for those who feel the Blackberry is just not enough. The Radisson has won numerous awards for the hotel layout, the rooms, quality of service, spa and swimming pool and the location near the airport also gets top marks. The rooms are spacious, the restaurants offer so many choices and you truly feel like you're the only guest present because of the individual attention of the staff.

>National Highway 8, Mahipalpur (near airport)
Tel: 011 2677 9191, 011 2677 9090
Rates: From US $167 low season; US $276 high season
Web: www.radisson.com/newdelhiin

Radisson MBD Hotel
This Noida Radisson hotel has all of the amenities of its Gurgaon cousin, but the location in Noida puts it near The Great India Place (see *Shopping*, p.171) and a bevy of amusement parks.

>L-2, Sector 18 Noida
Tel: 0120 430 0000
Cost: From US $194 low season; US $372 high season
Web: www.radisson.com/noidain

Shangri-La Hotel
Located near the Purana Qila, Qutab Minar, Humayun's Tomb, Jantar Mantar, Red Fort, India Gate and Rashtrapati Bhavan, all of the 323 guest rooms in the Shangri-La Hotel offer a view of Connaught Place. The hotel is also very close to New Delhi Railway Station and about a 45-minute drive from the airport. The amenities include in-room refrigerators and a mini bar, broadband internet access, 24-hr room service, baby sitting, an outdoor swimming pool and a spa that is bliss in a bottle. Sunday brunch may well be the highlight for the kids as they can don chef's hats and aprons and cook with the chefs.

>19 Ashoka Road, Janpath, Connaught Place
Tel: 011 4119 1919; 011 4119 1110
Rates: From US $358 low season; US $443 high season
Web: www.shangri-la.com/en/property/newdelhi/shangrila

Siddharth Hotel
This 5-star hotel is often overlooked in favour of other more advertised brands, but it is truly a gem right in the middle of the city. Located near Connaught Place, New Delhi Railway Station and not far from the airport, the 98-room Siddharth hotel offers opulence on a smaller scale. It has all of the bells and whistles of the other places, but one thing that stands out is the menu at the Resto Café which offers more than 170 items! The restaurant frequently has live music.

>3 Rajendra Place
Tel: 011 2576 2501
Rates: From US $189 low season; US $443 high season

Taj Mahal Hotel
The hotel is a city landmark, nestled in one of the most posh neighbourhoods in Delhi among government offices and diplomatic missions. It is within walking distance of Khan Market (see *Shopping*, p.167), a short drive from Lodhi Garden, Connaught Place, India Gate, India Habitat Centre, the zoo and the National Train Museum. There's babysitting,

travel services, an on-call doctor; 24-hr room service, cyber-butler and gym and a big swimming pool. The 6 restaurants at the Taj Mahal Hotel leave you spoiled for choice and provide a range of cuisine in casual to formal settings.

>1 Man Singh Road, Defence Head Quarter
Tel: 011 2302 6162
Rates: From US $263 low season; US $422 high season
Web: www.tajhotels.com

Taj Palace Hotel
Just a 10-minute drive from the airport, even in heavy Delhi traffic, the Taj Palace Hotel is as beautiful as the Taj Mahal in Agra. From the sweeping lobby to the deluxe guest rooms and multi-cuisine restaurants, a week's stay just isn't enough. The staff is one of the friendliest, if not the friendliest in the city, with the exception of the staff at the Man Singh Road property. Recreational activities include a 9-hole putting green and a huge swimming pool. The property is close to Purana Qila, the Red Fort and Qutab Minar.

>Sardar Patel Marg, Diplomatic Enclave
Tel: 011 2611 0202
Rates: From US $205; US $358 high season
Web: http://www.tajhotels.com

Trident
The Trident is another Gurgaon hotel that is worth a mention because of the proximity to the airport and the super-modern sleekness of the rest of the area. The deluxe rooms or suites are ideal for a family of 4 and the views are great with a choice of a garden or pool view. The hotel offers baby-sitting, wired and wireless access, multi-cuisine restaurants, currency exchange and there are rooms for guests with special physical needs.

>443 Udyog Vihar, Phase 5, Gurgaon
Tel: 0124 245 0505
Rates: From US $177 low season; US $477 high season
Web: www.tridenthotels.com/gurgaon/index.asp

Uppal's Orchid
Delhi's only eco-friendly hotel, the Orchid, is spread over 10.5 acres of greenery and is located very close to the International Airport. The hotel prides itself on recycling and water conservation where possible, so don't throw those towels on the bathroom floor after one use. The rooms are comfortable and the gardens are lush with a huge variety of trees, bushes and shrubs that beg for a walk or a frolic while birdwatching. The pool is huge and has a

swim up bar. The Chef and I restaurant is aptly named as guests can interact with the chef to have meals prepared exactly to their liking.

>National Highway 8
Tel: 011 2506 1515
Web: www.orchidhotelnewdelhi.com

Vasant Continental
The separate kids' swimming pool in the shade which also has spouts that spray water that allow kids to do a rain dance, is the highlight for this hotel, for the kids anyway. Although, climbing down the 2 flights of stairs with swimming gear can get tricky. The adults would love the spa and the dining options at the Vasant Continental including the round the clock Eggspectation restaurant (see *Eats*, p.125) with more than 170 vegetarian and non-vegetarian options. The entire brood will delight in the hotel's location next to the Basant Lok Market which has a Choko la (see *Eats*, pp.124–125, p.134, p.157), Sony store, Le Marche grocery store that stocks imported goods of all kinds including meats and cheeses, and a McDonald's.

>44 Community Centre, Basant Lok, Vasant Vihar
Tel: 011 2614 8800, 011 2614 1177
Rates: From US $199 low season; US $520 high season
Web: www.jaypeehotels.com

Four-star Hotels

What separates the 5- and 4-star hotels in Delhi is negligible. The 4-star hotels are a 4-tier warm chocolate cake and the 5-star hotels have a cherry on top. There are plenty of 4-star hotels that could have gotten a mention here, but for the fact they were not worth the money spent for the services and/or amentities offered. Some were dated in appearance and upkeep; had unfriendly harried staff, no windows that opened to the outside but into the hallway instead, or had no pool. The following 2 made the cut, mainly because they have swimming pools. Kids are more manageable and usually ready to nap after a good swim in the hot sun.

Ambassador
Choose a deluxe suite for a family as they are roomier. The Ambassador Hotel has the same quality standards for a Taj brand with white-glove service and a wonderful staff. Amenities include broadband and wireless internet access, mobile phones that can be rented, multimedia computers, baby-sitting, a swimming pool and book shop. There

are three restaurants: the most popular, The Yellow Brick Road (See *Eats*, p. 153) is open 24 hours and is a slice of Americana, though that shouldn't be held against the quite good eatery.

>Sujan Singh Park, Cornwallis Road
Tel: 011 2463 2600
Rates: From US $293 low season; US $584 high season
Web: www.tajhotels.com

Sheraton New Delhi
The family can definitely become mall rats due to the location of the Sheraton. It is located in Saket right near Select Citywalk Mall, DLF Place and MGF Metropolitan Mall (see *Shopping*, pp.171–2). It is also 15 minutes away from Qutab Minar and 35 minutes from the airport. There are 220 rooms that are spacious and modern and come with DVD players. The hotel has a large swimming pool with a tropical island feel with the greenery and fake rocks and all. The restaurants are OK, but the food courts and restaurants at the nearby malls are a great option.

>District Centre, Saket
Tel: 011 4266 1122
Rates: From US $229 low season; US $927 high season
Web: www.itcwelcomgroup.in

Guest Houses

Guest houses and Bed & Breakfast inns are a great option for those families who don't need the bells and whistles of deluxe hotels such as pools, restaurants and bars. But they provide an economical and homey place to stay for families who do not want to pay the price associated with fancy hotels. It is a great option if you want to experience local hospitality and cuisine at affordable rates. Most advertise themselves as boutique hotels, with daily tariffs of between Rs 1,200 and Rs 10,000. Many, if not all, are child friendly and often the owners themselves have a pet or young child who could be great company for your kids. A list of Bed & Breakfast accommodations that are certified by the Ministry of Tourism is available at www.incredibleindia.org. The list, however, is limited to the NCR area. A good place to check for guest house listings is Cleartrip.com (www.cleartrip.com) which has over 150 home stays across India and (www.bharathomestay.com). Often, the owners stay on the property, prepare the meals, interact with the guests and offer a personal touch that sometimes cannot be found at bigger properties. Though a swimming pool is likely not an option, the price is worth it. See *Playground Paradise*, pp.76–8 for swimming pool options.

Ahuja Residency
Located in the heart of South Delhi in Golf Links, the Ahuja Residency is a well-appointed guest houses ideal for a long-term stay. The rooms are nicely furnished and several rooms have attached balconies. Some amenities include breakfast, laundry facilities and 24-hour Internet access. There's a second property in Defence Colony, also.

>193 Golf Links
Tel: 011 2461 1027
Rates: Rs 5,100 a night double occupancy
Web: www.ahujaresidency.com

>C-83 Defence Colony
Tel: 011 2461 1027

Amarya Garden
Once a mansion, the 4-room Amarya Garden now lives another splendid life as a boutique hotel. With 2 suites and 2 deluxe guest rooms, each unique in layout and design, guests would probably book in for a few days and stay a lot longer due to the modern amenities, calm oasis of the lawns and general vibe of the place. Meals to order are available 24 hours a day. Other facilities include currency exchange, free wireless broadband and satellite television.

>C-179 Defence Colony
Tel: Reception 011 4656 2735; Alex 98716 73666 or Mathieu 99100 01409
Rates: Rs 9,250 for suites; Rs 8,200 for deluxe rooms, breakfast included and free wi-fi.

BNineteen
Guests of BNineteen can check Humayun's Tomb off the list as the bed & breakfast is located directly across from the monument. The 5 rooms are big, have all the modern amenities and there's a terrace and numerous balconies. All meals are charged at a nominal fee. There's also a kitchen on each floor with a refrigerator for stocking bubbly, baby food or some Delhi delicacies.

>B-19 Nizamuddin East
Tel: 011 4182 5500
Rates: Rs 6,000 low season; Rs 6,750 high season
Web: www.bnineteen.com

Eleven
Located a 5-minute walk from Humayun's Tomb, free internet and wi-fi, satellite TV, sumptuous breakfast included (other meals on request).

>11 Nizamuddin East
Tel: 011 2435 1225
Rates: Rs 3250 to 3500 for double occupancy; Rs 750 for extra bed.
Web: www.elevendelhi.com
Email: elevendelhi@gmail.com

Jorbagh 27

Jorbagh 27 is in desperate need of a furnishings makeover, but that does not take away from the hospitality, warmth and personal attention. The double deluxe room will easily accommodate a family with room to spare. Each room has a TV with cable and a sitting area. There are 3 lounge areas and a huge beautiful lawn. Guests also have access to free Internet. Children below age 6 are not charged if sharing a room with the parents. It is located right down the street from Lodhi Garden; Lodhi—The Garden Restaurant, India Habitat Centre and Khan Market.

>27 Jor Bagh
Tel: 011 2469 4430
Rates: From Rs 4,300 per night for a double room; Rs 5,000 for suites
Web: www.jorbagh27.com

Jukaso Inn

50 rooms, 24-hour room service, restaurant, same-day laundry, AC, telephone, TV, rooms with attached bath.

>49–50 Sunder Nagar
Tel: 011 2435 0308
Rates: Rs 3,000 superior single; Rs 4,000 double; Rs 3,000 club executive single; Rs 3,100 double

Kailash Inn

16 rooms; 24-hour room service, laundry, car hire, AC, rooms with attached bath, TV, telephone.

>10 Sunder Nagar
Tel: 011 2435 3634
Rates: Rs 1,800 single; Rs 2,000 double; Rs 2,500 deluxe double

La Sagrita

19 rooms, 24-hour room service, laundry, safe, sightseeing tours, car hire, AC, rooms with attached bath, TV and telephone.

>14 Sunder Nagar
Tel: 011 2435 9541
Rates: Rs 1,700 single standard room; Rs 2,290 double; Rs 2,000 deluxe single; Rs 2,390 deluxe double; Rs 2,590 regal single; Rs 2,790 regal double

Maharani Guest House

Suburban guest houses always seem to provide a hidden treat. One, you get the feel of a real neighbourhood with people going about their everyday lives, and housekeeping is not breaking down the door to replenish the little shampoo bottles. With 19 AC rooms, 24-hour room service, same-day laundry, book shop, in-room TVs and an open terrace garden, a stay at the Maharani Guest House is like a stay with family members you actually like and get along with. Children under 12 stay free. It is about a 20-minute drive from the main tourist hub.

>3 Sunder Nagar
Tel: 011 2435 9521/3
Rates: Suites from Rs 6,600
Web: www.mymaharani.com

The Manor
Developed as a small country hotel in the 1950s in one of Delhi's now posh suburbs, Friends Colony, The Manor has evolved into a 2-storey, 16-room contemporary boutique hotel that is set in landscaped gardens. There's a rooftop terrace bar and yoga classes are held daily on the lawns. Feel free to customize orders for the picky eaters in the brunch at the hotel's in-house restaurant, Seventy Seven, which serves Mediterranean and traditional Indian fare. The chef will be more than happy to oblige. It is 15 minutes drive from Humayun's Tomb.

>77 Friends Colony West (Near Friends Club)
Tel: 011 2692 5151 / 7510
Rates: Rs 9,000 per night
Web: www.themanordelhi.com

Nirula's Hotel
Guests at the 29-room Nirula's Hotel can have their cake and ice cream and eat it too. Located at Noida Sector 2, it's located near the Delhi-Noida toll gates and about 30 minutes by car from Connaught Place. Close proximity to malls, shopping, cinemas, the Akshardham Temple and restaurants. Though dining at the in-house restaurant, Potpourri, is a great option. There's a breakfast buffet, live pasta station and continental cuisine. There's also a play area at the restaurant. Of course don't forget about the ice creams and oodles of pastries and cakes from the pastry shop. Guests of the hotel get preferential access to the golf course at Sector 17, Noida.

>C-135, Sector 2, Noida
Tel: 0120 244 5260 to 67; 0120 432 3444, 0120 432 3445
Rates: From Rs 4,500 standard double to Rs 8,500 superior deluxe
Web: www.nirulas.com/noida-hotel.html

Sai Villa
The 4 rooms include AC, TV, free unlimited broadband wi-fi connection, personal butler, complimentary breakfast

and fresh fruit basket daily; airport pickup Rs 850, but free transportation to airport or rail station from the villa. It is one of the best furnished as many B&B tend to be a bit overdone with elaborate brocades and the like.

>E-578, Greater Kailash II
Tel: 98110 69943
Rates: Rs 2,750
Web: www.saivilla.com

Sherwani Fort View
16 rooms, room service, AC, travel services, TV, telephone, attached bath.

>11 Sunder Nagar
Tel: 011 2435 9670; 011 2435 5831
Rates: Rs 1,850 single; Rs 2,500 double; Rs 2,800 deluxe suite

Shyama International
22 rooms; 24-hour room service, fax, laundry, car hire, TV, telephone, rooms with attached baths.

>C5/32 Safdarjung Development Area
Tel: 011 2656 2306
Rates: Rs 1,450 single; Rs 1,800 double; Rs 2,200 suite

Shalimar House
What a treat to find a guest house with a roof top swimming pool! With 6 bedrooms and one suite spread over 3 floors of a private home, there are balconies galore, well-appointed bedrooms, wi-fi Internet, tasteful art and yummy meals. There's an elevator so strollers won't be a problem on the stairs. Located in Green Park, the South Delhi residence is surrounded by shopping markets.

>H-43, Green Park Extension
Tel: 98992 28164
Rates: Rs 5,500 for double; Rs 7,000 for suite; Rs 9,000 for a one- or 3-bedroom apartment in high season; Rs 4,950 for double; Rs 6,300 for suite; Rs 8,100 for apartment in low season
Meals: Rs 200 breakfast; Rs 250 snacks; Rs 450 dinner
Web: www.shalimarhouse.com/

Tej Abode Home stay
Sanctioned by the Ministry of Tourism under the Gold category for Bed & Breakfast establishments, the Tej Abode can stand on its own without any awards. Opened since 2007, the property, located in GK II in South Delhi, is steps away from one of the best shopping districts and really good restaurants. The rooms range in size from 250 to 350 square feet and are appointed with refrigerators, TVs with cable, DVD players and writing desks. Most likely, families will have to book

2 adjoining rooms or the superior deluxe room. An extra bed can be placed in the room for a charge of Rs 500. The guest house stocks books and movies; a music library and board games for children and wireless broadband are available. Airport pick up and drop off and a car on hire can be arranged. The rates include the room, tea and breakfast. Other meals can be had at the Tej Abode from Rs 250 per person.

>S-309 Ground Flr, GK II
Tel: 011 4052 0173; 98181 89771
Rates: From Rs 5,000 per day for Superior deluxe room; Rs 500 per day for an extra bed

The Estate

There are 7 rooms (including one family suite) and all have private balconies and face the lawn. The rooms are spacious with modern touches. The guest house is separate from the owner's house so it does allow for more privacy. It is located 20 minutes from the airport and most major tourist attractions. Complimentary breakfast, wi-fi and really nice toiletries.

>House No. 29, Sultanpur Estate, Mandi Road, Mehrauli
Tel: 011 2680 2828
Rate: From Rs 4,800 low season for a double; Rs 5,800 high season
Web: www.theestatebnb.com

Thikana

Opened in 2008 by a young couple, the bed & breakfast reflects their youth as it has vibrant colours, modern fittings, tasteful art and a warm welcoming atmosphere. Thikana, which in Hindi means the place to which you belong, is an 8-room property, has very comfortable rooms and a common sitting area with a large-screen TV and a free-to-use computer with Internet. The balconies are inviting if you don't mind the facing traffic. Free wi-fi means guests can use their laptops anywhere at the bed & breakfast. The owners can arrange for daily access to the Gulmohar Club, Niti Bagh Club and Siri Fort Complex, all of which have pools. Massages and yoga instruction can also be scheduled through them. Central Delhi with India Gate, Parliament House and Lodhi Garden can be reached within 20 minutes.

>A-7 Gulmohar Park
Tel: 011 3256 3458; 98181 49019
Rates: Doubles start at Rs 4,500 per night
Web: www.thikandelhi.com

Budget

The **Ginger Rail Yatri Niwas** at the New Delhi Railway Station is a recently renovated property that offers hotel rooms from Rs 999 to Rs 1,999 and rooms of 4 beds for Rs 250 each. The budget hotel has a 24-hour restaurant, TVs in every room, coffee and tea pots, gym, book store and travel desk.

>Ginger Rail Yatri Niwas
New Delhi Railway Station
(Ajmeri Gate side)
Bhav Bhutti Marg
Tel: 011 6663 3333
Rates: From Rs 999
Email: reservations.delhi@gingerhotels.com
Web: www.gingerhotels.com

Vacation packages are a great way to see Delhi and neighbouring cities as they offer attractive discounts for budget-conscious families and the packages eliminate the need to book hotels, cars, flights and excursions separately. Some of the leading hotels offer room, breakfast and transfers to and from the airport and hotel. Beware of bogus agents. It is best to book travel through the Delhi Tourism office. Official guides trained by the Ministry of Tourism usually charge Rs 600 for 1 to 5 hours for a party of 5 and Rs 750 for a full day (4 to 8 hours); Rs 750 for a party of 6 to 14 (half day)/Rs 975 full; Rs 1,050 for a party of 15–35 (half day)/Rs 1,350 for a full day. Fix the price beforehand. Do not pay until the tour is over and feel free to tip for exceptional service. One reliable tour operator, recognized by the Ministry of Tourism is Southern Travels Pvt Ltd. The company specializes in Delhi tours and the Golden Triangle Tour via air-conditioned coaches.

Southern Travels Pvt Ltd
>18/2 Arya Samaj Road, Karol Bagh
Tel: 011 2875 8728; 011 2572 2210; 011 2875 3466; 4353 2805
Web: www.southerntravelsindia.com

Touring

Delhi Tourism and Transport Development Corporation operates sightseeing tours in air-conditioned coaches, covering New and Old Delhi. The New Delhi tour takes in Jantar Mantar, Birla Mandir, Qutab Minar, the Lotus Temple and Safdarjung's Tomb. The Old Delhi tour stops at Red Fort, Jama Masjid, Rajghat and Humayun's Tomb. All tickets must be purchased in advance at the booking office. Most sights have a different admission fee for Indians and foreigners and may also have separate charges for the use of cameras or video cameras.

The easiest way to travel between attractions is by taxi or auto rickshaw.

Delhi Tourism
N-36 Bombay Life Building, Middle Circle, Connaught Place
Tel: 011 2331 5322; 011 2373 0416
Web: http://delhitourism.nic.in

The staff at the government tourist office is very helpful and the office has a lot of free information. Please note that there are various private 'tourist information' offices around Connaught Place claiming to be the official government tourist office. These offices sell their own travel packages and have nothing to do with the government.

The Government of India Tourist Office
>88 Janpath
Tel: 011 2332 0342
Timings: Mon to Fri 9:30 am to 6:00 pm; Sat 9 am to 2 pm
Web: www.incredibleindia.org

Delhi at Night
A unique way to see Delhi is taking a tour by night. The ride is about 5 hours and goes through Akshardam Temple, Lutyen's Delhi, Rashtrapati Bhavan (the presidential palace); the Parliament House, Lodhi Garden and Safdarjung's Tomb. Dinner at Lodhi, the Garden Restaurant, or Parikrama, the revolving restaurant, is included in the price.

>**Tel:** 011 6000 6255
Timings: From 7 pm
Cost: Rs 3,075 for 2 people (Indigo car)
Email: rentacar@sixt.co.in

Transportation

By air

The Indira Gandhi International Airport of Delhi has both domestic as well as international terminals. It is well connected to almost all the cities of the world as well as every city in India. Nearly all the major international airlines operate out of this airport. There is also the Palam Domestic Airport that connects Delhi with almost all major cities in the country. The airport has a free shuttle bus service for passengers every 20 minutes between the domestic terminals and every 30 minutes between domestic and international terminals at IGI Airport. There is a children's play area in the security hold area of Terminal 1A of the airport. Admission to the area is free and the room has swings, climbing structures, soft toys and balls. Airport themes are displayed on the vinyl mats and the walls are decorated with colourful cartoon characters. A changing table and sleeping cot is also available.

There are plenty of food options at the International Airport. The domestic arrival terminal 1A has Café Coffee Day that serves sandwiches, muffins, cookies, shakes, juices and of course, tea and coffee; Hot and Juicy serves hot and juicy corn, hot dogs, momos and soft drinks. At Terminal 1B, about 150 metres away, one can have idlis and vadas at Balaji Express. Both passengers and visitors can dine here. The menu is exhaustive with noodles, full meals, snacks and dessert if you are just craving something sweet. You'll find Nirula's located near the departure gates which serves burgers, snacks, wraps and ice cream; Yo! China serves up decent Chinese food, and you can head to Subway for sandwiches and chips.

The International Airport is undergoing major renovations that have seen terminals upgraded, demolished, expanded and built. The airport will be in flux with the changes for the foreseeable future. Check and double check where the flight is departing from before heading to the airport. Currently, Terminal 1 handles all domestic operations. Terminal 1A caters to all domestic flights operated by Kingfisher Airlines, Air India and its subsidiaries Air India Regional and Indian Airlines. The terminal has undergone significant upgrades including a new modern look and clean Western style toilets. Terminal 1B serves all other domestic carriers including Kingfisher Red, IndiGo Airlines, Jet Airways and JetLite, Jagson Airlines, MDLR Airlines, GoAir and SpiceJet. This terminal added a number of fast food outlets in its upgrade. Terminal 1D is the brand new interim domestic terminal that was inaugurated on February 26, 2009. It can handle 10 million customers a year. All domestic flights operate through this terminal. Plans are afoot for Terminal 3, to be constructed in 2010. This terminal will solely handle low cost carriers. Full fare airlines plan to move to Terminal 3, along with the international flights. Terminal 2 is the current international terminal. Food outlets can be found in the departure area. This terminal is slated for demolition once Terminal 3 is operational.

Flight inquiries

>**Tel:** International 011 2565 2011; Domestic 011 2567 5126

Web: www.delhiairport.com

International and domestic air ticketing

>Delhi Tourism
N-36, Bombay Life Building
Middle Circle, Connaught Place
Timings: Mon to Fri 9.30 am to 6 pm; Sat 9 am to 2 pm

At the airport

>Udaan Bhavan, Terminal 1B, Indira Gandhi International Airport
Tel: 011 2566 1000
Web: www.newdelhiairport.in

Airport telephone numbers

Airport call centre	
	011 2566 1080
Automated inquiry	
	011 2560 2999
	011 2566 2275
Terminal 1 (1A, 1B and domestic arrivals)	
	011 2566 1000
Terminal 2 (International departure and arrivals)	
	011 2560 2000
Cargo Terminal	
	011 2560 1000
Airport Manager	
Terminal 1A	011 2569 6150
Terminal 1B	011 2567 5315
Terminal 2	011 2565 5790
Airport Police	011 2567 5291
Terminal 1	011 2560 2116
Terminal 2	011 2565 4217
Airport Security	
Terminal 1	011 2567 5289
Terminal 2	011 2560 2121
First Aid	
Terminal 1	011 2567 2778
Terminal 2	011 2560 2465

By rail

There are a number of railway stations in Delhi that connect it to almost each and every city in the country, major or minor. The 2 main stations in Delhi are the Old Delhi train station in Old Delhi, and New Delhi train station at Paharganj. Make sure you know which station serves your destination (the New Delhi station is closer to Connaught Place). If you're departing from the Delhi train station you should allow adequate time to make it there, as the traffic becomes a big bottleneck the closer you get to the station.

There's also the Nizamuddin train station, south of Sunder Nagar, where various trains (usually for southbound destinations) start or end. Many trains between Delhi and Jaipur, Jodhpur, Bikaner and Udaipur operate to and from Sarai Rohilla train station, about 4 km northwest of Connaught Place. Railway porters should charge between Rs 20 and Rs 30 per bag. Buy a copy of *Trains at a Glance* (Rs 45), available at most newsstands, or ask tourist office staff for more information on schedules.

The New Delhi Cantonment railway station that caters to luxury trains like the Palace on Wheels,

Fairy Queen and Royal Orient Express. Apart from these, there are a number of other small stations in Delhi for local travel purposes.

Railway Assistance
(For train reservations and Indrail passes)
>International Tourist Bureau, 1st Flr, New Delhi Railway Station, Paharganj side
Tel: 011 2340 5156; 011 2370 1100
Timings: 9:30 am to 6 pm

Inquiry

General Inquiry	131
Reservation Inquiry	
Hindi	1330
Reservation status	
arrivals and departures	1335
Seat availability	125050

Online reservation
Web: www.indianrail.gov.in; www.irctc.co.in

By road

All the main cities of India are linked with Delhi by a network of highways and roads. The main 3 bus terminals in Delhi are the Inter State Bus Terminus (ISBT) at Kashmere Gate, Sarai Kale Khan Bus Terminus and Anand Vihar Bus Terminus. Various state-managed and privately run air-conditioned, deluxe and ordinary coaches operate in and out of Delhi on a daily basis. Taxis are also easily available for long distance travel from Delhi.

>Kashmere Gate
Tel: 011 2386 8836

>Sarai Kale Khan
Tel: 011 2435 8092

>Anand Vihar
Tel: 011 2215 2431

Some important road distances (from Delhi)

Agra	203 kms
Almora	373 kms
Amritsar	447 kms
Bharatpur	190 kms
Chandigarh	238 kms
Jaipur	258 kms

Local buses

One of the cheapest modes of transport in Delhi is the local buses. The city boasts of one of the largest bus transportation systems in India. Almost all the buses in Delhi are owned either by the state-owned Delhi Transport Corporation (DTC) or the private contractors which have over 3,100 buses plying the city. There are different categories of fares ranging in cost from Rs 3 depending on distance and route. Buy a bus pass and save up to Rs 300 on the fare. Passes can be purchased online at www.dtc.nic.in/dt3.htm. DTC also operates daily sight seeing tours from Scindia House.

The fare of Delhi Darshan Service is Rs 100. The fare is half price for children between the ages of 5 to 12. Stops on the tour include Red Fort, Raj Ghat, Indira Gandhi Smriti, Qutab Minar, Lotus Temple, National Rail Museum and Birla Mandir (Shri Laxmi Narayan Temple). Tickets for low-floor red AC buses are between Rs 10 to 25, depending on the distance travelled.

>**Tel:** 011 2435 1763; 97181 90047

Taxis

Taxis are easily available for hire. The taxis are mostly operated by DTC, the Indian Tourism Ministry and various private operators. They are available both for local commuting as well as long-distance purposes. However, one has to go to the taxi stand or telephone a taxi service provider for hiring them. Also, taxis are a slightly expensive mode of transportation in Delhi. Prepaid taxis and autos are available from the airport, both domestic and international (arrivals), all railway stations and bus terminals and other important places. Beware of unlicensed drivers due to safety reasons and monetary reasons, as the price quoted is likely not to be the price you will end up paying by the end of the journey. Go to an official taxi stand. Make sure you get a receipt.

Always take a pre-paid coupon from inside the terminal. IGI Airport has counters for both radio taxis and pre-paid taxis. Pre-paid taxis line up outside the international and domestic terminals. Stand in line and take the taxi allotted to you. Note the license number. Make a point of calling someone once you are on your way to let them know you are on the way, noting the license number to the person on the other end of the phone. Make a pretend phone call for safety sake if no one is at your destination. Never share a taxi with strangers. A number to remember for the police is 100.

>**Tel:** 98114 52220; 011 2301 0101 (Delhi Traffic Police complaint centre)
Web: www.delhitrafficpolice.nic.in/tourist-police.htm

At the airport

Avis
Tel: 011 2390 6259
Web: www.avis.com

Easy Cabs
Tel: 011 4343 4343
Web: www.easycabs.com for reservations online

Independent taxi companies

Carzonrent
A subsidiary of global car rental firm Hertz. Local usage packages are flexible and allow the use of the car for any number of hours or kms. They come in 1hr/10km multiples and 4 hr/40km, 8hr/80 km etc. Renters can choose the self drive or chauffeur driven options, or just an airport transfer.

Cab route: Entire Delhi and NCR; interstate travel available
Tel: 011 4184 1212
Web: www.carzonrent.com
Cost: From about Rs 375

Delhi Cabs
Cab route: Delhi and NCR
Tel: 011 4433 3222
Web: www.radiotaxi.in

Delhi Cab Helpline
Cab route: Delhi and NCR
Tel: 011 4433 3222

Dial-a-Cab
Cab route: Entire Delhi and NCR (commercial vehicle tax extra in Uttar Pradesh)
Tel: 011 2981 3600

Easy Cabs
Radio taxi service operated by Hertz
Cab route: Delhi and NCR
Tel: 011 4343 4343
Web: www.easycabs.com

Mega Cabs
Cab route: Delhi and NCR, including Gurgaon, Faridabad, Noida and Ghaziabad
Tel: 011 4141 4141
Web: www.megacabs.com

Meru Cabs
Cab route: Delhi and NCR
Tel: 011 4422 4422
Web: www.merucabs.com

Orix Cabs aka Delhi Cab
Tel: 011 4562 8200 / 011 2591 7441 for New Delhi; 95124 3014700 for Gurgaon
Web: www.orixindia.com/radiotaxi.aspx

Quick Cabs
Cab route: Delhi and NCR
Tel: 011 4533 3333
Web: www.quickcabs.in

Routes Dial a Cab
Cab route: Delhi and NCR
Tel: 011 4440 4440

Smaart Cab
Mercedes, BMWs, Hondas among fleet of taxis if you want something more upscale.
Cab Route: Delhi, NCR, countrywide
Tel: 011 4647 4647
Web: www.smaartcabs.com

Black and yellow taxis

They are metred. Ensure the metre is turned back before starting the trip. There is a surcharge over the metre and you are advised to check the rate list available from the driver before payment. There are plenty of metred yellow-and-black taxis, but invariably the metres are out of date, not working or the drivers will simply refuse to use them. If this happens, hail another taxi and don't forget to negotiate a fare before the taxi starts moving.

Commuters using the Metro will also be able to use radio taxis that can be hired from kiosks at over 25 Metro stations. These include Rithala, Pitampura, Netaji Subhash Place, Inderlok, Pratap Nagar, Welcome, Shahdara and Dilshad Garden Metro stations on Line 1; Vishwavidyalaya, Kashmere Gate, New Delhi, Rajiv Chowk and Central Secretariat stations on Line 2; Indraprastha, Pragati Maidan, Jhandewalan, Rajendra Place, Moti Nagar, Rajouri Garden, Tilak Nagar, Janakpuri (West), Uttam Nagar (East), Dwarka, Dwarka Sector 10 and Dwarka Sector 9 Metro stations on Line 3. Commuters can book their taxis at the prepaid booths. These taxis will help commuters reach South Delhi, Noida, Gurgaon and the airport.

Auto rickshaws

Auto rickshaws fall in between taxis and buses. They are more expensive than buses but cheaper then taxis. Also, they are easily available as they can be flagged from the road. However, one has to be careful while hiring autos. This is because most of the auto drivers refuse to ply by the metre. If this happens, one should bargain a little and fix fare in advance, before hiring the auto.

Cycle rickshaws

Cheaper than auto rickshaws, these human powered vehicles are great for short trips when you just don't feel like walking. It can comfortably seat 2 adults and 2 small children on a lap, though it won't make the driver happy. A family of 4 with 2 adults and 2 children can take 2 cycle rickshaws. Prices range from Rs 5 or 10 for short hauls. Solar-powered rickshaws, dubbed 'soleckshaws', were introduced in late 2008. Powered by solar energy and pedals, they are designed to take the physical burden off the driver. Soleckshaws can obtain a speed of 15 km per hour and come equipped with FM radios, so you can sing along to your favourite Bollywood song along the way to your destination.

Delhi Metro

The Delhi Metro is convenient and has greatly reduced the number of cars on the roads as more and more commuters have started taking the Metro. The Metro trains run from 6 am until about 11 pm. The Metro still has not reached all over Delhi, but it is under construction and some of the routes have been completed and are already operational. Visit www.delhimetrorail.com for more information. The Metro is operational on 3 lines. Take a look around the stations as some stations have information plaques about nearby monuments. For instance, the Jor Bagh station has information on nearby Safdarjung Tomb and Lodhi Garden. The gold star station is the Kashmere Gate station which is a junction for the Red and Yellow lines. The multi-level station has 65,000 square feet of retail space which boasts restaurants and retail outlets. There's a Dominos, Nirula's, McDonald's and Govardhan, all open from 11 am to 11 pm. Kashmere Gate also serves as the Headquarters for the Delhi Metro.

Line 2 gets you to the Old Delhi (Chandni Chowk, Jama Masjid) and New Delhi railway stations, the ISBT bus terminal and Paharganj. Fares range from Rs 6 to Rs 22. More value for the money if you're planning on being in Delhi for a while is a 'Smart Card'. It can be bought for Rs 100, which is worth Rs 50 and includes a Rs 50 deposit. You can add more to the card as the money is depleted. There is also a 'Tourist Card' allowing unlimited use for Rs 70 a day. This card is good if you plan to stick to one area of the city, dropping off and coming back on the train.

Line 3 takes you to Karol Bagh. The Karol Bagh Metro station is located at the intersection of Pusa Road and Ajmal Khan Road. The RK Ashram Marg station is useful for reaching the western parts of Paharganj. Many stations on Line 3 are not marked on most tourist maps as the line has only recently been opened. It is very important to note that Metro stations all use the new Indian names, so Connaught Place is Rajiv Chowk, Old Delhi Railway Station is Chandni Chowk and ISBT is Kashmere Gate.

Delhi Metro Line One
Shahdara–Rithala

No. of stations: 21
Names of stations: Dilshad Garden, Jhilmil, Mansarovar Park, Shahdara, Welcome,

Seelampur, Shastri Park, Kashmere Gate, Tis Hazari, Pul Bangash, Pratap Nagar, Shastri Nagar, Inderlok, Kanhaiya Nagar, Keshav Puram, Netaji Subhash Place, Kohat Enclave, Pitampura, Rohini East, Rohini West and Rithala.

Delhi Metro Line Two
Vishwa Vidyalaya–Central Secretariat

No. of stations: 10
Names of Stations: Vishwa Vidyalaya, Vidhan Sabha, Civil Lines, Kashmere Gate, Delhi Main, Chawri Bazaar, New Delhi, Rajiv Chowk, Patel Chowk and Central Secretariat.

Delhi Metro Line Three
Yamuna Bank–Barakhamba Road–Dwarka

No. of stations: 32
Names of stations: Yamuna Bank, Indraprastha, Pragati Maidan, Mandi House, Barakhamba Road, Rajiv Chowk, RK Ashram Marg, Jhandewalan, Karol Bagh, Rajendra Place, Patel Nagar, Shadipur, Kirti Nagar, Moti Nagar, Ramesh Nagar, Rajouri Garden, Tagore Garden, Subhash Nagar, Tilak Nagar, Janakpuri East, Janakpuri West, Uttam Nagar East, Uttam Nagar West, Nawada, Dwarka Morh, Dwarka, Dwarka Sector 14, Dwarka Sector 13, Dwarka Sector 12, Dwarka Sector 11, Dwarka Sector 10 and Dwarka Sector 9.

The Metro runs from 6 am and the last train leaves the station at 10 pm. During the rush hours, the frequency of trains is set at 4 minutes. Call 128128 for assistance, queries and complaints. As the system expands, plans are under way for the New Delhi Metro Rail system to cover not only most parts of Delhi, but also cross the borders of Delhi joining Noida, Ghaziabad and Gurgaon.

Airport
Delhi Metro's New Delhi–Indira Gandhi International Airport express link might be the first service to operate round the clock. The high-speed link transports passengers from New Delhi Railway to the airport in just 18 minutes. It is expected to pick up hours after midnight to cater to passengers taking international flights. Passengers would be able to reach Dwarka in 24 minutes. There are 6 stations on the line: New Delhi Railway Station, Shivaji Stadium, Dhaula Kuan, NH 8, IGI Airport and Dwarka Sector 21. Baggage check-in will be available at the New Delhi Railway Station and Shivaji Stadium. The train will stop for 2–4 minutes at each station. Parking will

be available at all of the stations except IGI Airport. The fare is expected to be around Rs 100.

Local trains

Local trains consist of one of the cheapest means and modes of transport in Delhi. Both inter-state as well as intra-state trains ply from various railway stations in Delhi. Commuting by trains is quite time saving. The major railway stations in the capital city are Old Delhi, Hazrat Nizamuddin, New Delhi, Okhla, Pragati Maidan, Shahdara, Shakur Basti and Tilak Bridge. There are numerous other small stations in Delhi for local commuting purposes.

Emergency Care

Indira Gandhi International Airport
The Indira Gandhi International Airport has selected Indraprastha Apollo Hospital to provide medical facilities for its passengers and employees. Apollo provides an emergency ambulance service and runs a 24-hour pharmacy. The hospital runs 2 medical centres with 4 beds each, one at Terminal IC (domestic arrival) and the other at Terminal II. Terminal lA and the cargo terminal has one bed each, with all basic first aid and stabilizing equipment.

All India Institute of Medical Sciences (AIIMS)
>Ansari Nagar (near Safdarjung Hospital)
Tel: 011 2658 8500

Escorts Heart Institute and Research Centre
>Okhla Road
Tel: 011 2682 5000/1/2/3
Emergency: 011 2682 5002/3
Web: www.ehirc.com

Fortis Hospital
>Aruna Asaf Ali Marg, Pocket 1, Vasant Kunj, Sector B (Near GD Goenka School)
Tel: 011 4277 6221/2
Emergency: 011 2692 7000
Web: www.fortishealthcare.com

Ganga Ram Hospital
>Rajinder Nagar
Tel: 011 2573 5205; 011 2586 1463
Web: www.sgrh.com

Holy Family Hospital
>Okhla Road, Jamia Nagar (opposite Escort Heart Hospital)
Tel: 011 2615 5050; 011 2656 6338

Indraprastha Apollo Hospital
>Sarita Vihar, Delhi–Mathura Road
Tel: 011 2692 5858; 011 2692 5801
Emergency: 011 2682 5555

Web: www.apollohospdelhi.com

Max Balaji Hospital
>108-A, Indraprastha Extension, Patparganj
Tel: 011 4303 3333

Max Devi Devki Heart and Vascular Institute
>2 Press Enclave Road, Saket
Tel: 011 2651 5050

Max Hospital
>A-364, Sector 19, Noida
Tel: 0120 254 9999

Max Hospital Gurgaon
>B Block, Sushant Lok I, Gurgaon
Tel: 0124 662 3000

Max Hospital Pitampura
>Near N Tower, Pitampura Wazirpur District Centre
Tel: 011 2735 1844

Max Medicentre
>Chain of hospitals including 3 in South Delhi
Emergency: 011 4055 4055
Web: www.maxhealthcare.in

Max Superspeciality Hospital
>1 Press Enclave Road, Saket
Tel: 011 6611 5050

Other Hospitals

Aashlok Hospital
>25-A, Block AB, Community Centre
Safdarjung Enclave
Tel: 011 2616 5861/2

Batra Hospital And Medical Research Centre
>1 Mehrauli Badarpur Road, Tughlaqabad Institutional Area
Tel: 011 2995 8747

East–West Medical Centre
>The facility is good for arranging unusual emergency services and referrals.
B-28 Greater Kailash I
Tel: 011 2924 3701/2/3
Web: www.eastwestrescue.com

Holy Angels Hospital
>Plot D, Basant Lok Community Centre, Vasant Vihar
Tel: 011 2614 1229

Mohinder Hospital
>C-5 Green Park Extension
Tel: 011 2685 2880

Moolchand Hospital
>Lajpat Nagar III, near Moolchand flyover
Tel: 011 5200 0000

Private Hospital
>DLF Qutab Enclave, Phase II Gurgaon
Tel: 95124 235 2097; 95124 235 1162

Rockland Hospital
>B-33/34 Qutab Institutional Area, Tara Crescent Road
Tel: 011 5122 2222; 011 5168 8752
Web: www.rocklandhospital.com

Safdarjung Hospital
>Safdarjung Enclave
Tel: 011 2616 8336

St Stephen's Hospital
>Tis Hazari
Tel: 011 2396 6024

Vasant Lok Hospital
>Basant Lok Community Centre, Vasant Vihar
Tel: 011 2614 2730; 011 2614 9422

Holy Angels Hospital
>Plot D, Basant Lok Community Centre, Vasant Vihar
Tel: 011 2614 1229

Indraprastha Apollo Hospital
>Sarita Vihar, Delhi Mathura Road
Tel: 011 2692 5858; 011 2692 5801

24-hour Chemist Shops

Apollo Cliniq
>Sector B Pocket 7 Bldg 1, Vasant Kunj
Tel: 011 2613 4810, ext 405

Bharatiya Pharmacy
>8-A Central Market, Lajpat Nagar
Tel: 011 2683 3855

Ellianz Chemist
>Greater Kailash II
Tel: 011 4163 7337

Max Medicentre
>Main Road, Saket
Tel: 011 2615 5050; 011 2656 6338
Web: www.maxhealthcare.in

Mohinder Hospital
>C-5 Green Park Extension
Tel: 011 2685 2880/81

Vasant Lok Hospital
>Basant Lok Community Centre, Vasant Vihar
Tel: 011 2614 2730; 011 2614 9422

INDEX
By 'Useful' Category

INDEX
By Table of Contents

ABOUT THE AUTHOR

Kim Barrington Narisetti is publisher of Urban Crayon Press, an independent publishing house of travel guides geared toward families and children's picture books. She has co-authored the travel guide *Urban Crayon Paris* (2008) besides publishing Pretty *Prickly Patty Porcupine, Find the Colors, Xanthe, I Saw Delhi* and *All of Me.* Trained as a journalist, Kim has worked for many publications including *The Wall Street Journal, The Street.com, Advertising Age,* and *The Source Magazine.* She currently lives in New Delhi with her husband Raju and daughters Leila Isabel, 7, and Zola Isabel, 4.